Understanding Indonesian Grammar

A student's reference and workbook

James Neil Sneddon

ALLEN&UNWIN

First published in 2000 by

Allen & Unwin
83 Alexander Street
Crows Nest NSW 2065
Australia
Phone: (612) 9425 0100
Fax: (612) 9906 2218
Email: info@allenandunwin.com
Web: www.allenandunwin.com

National Library of Australia
Cataloguing-in-Publication entry:

Sneddon, J.N.
   Understanding Indonesian grammar: a student's reference and workbook.

   ISBN J 86448 776 3.

   1. Indonesian language—Study and teaching. 2. Indonesian language—
Grammar. I. Title.

499.221507

Printed by SRM Production Services Sdn. Bhd. Malaysia

10 9 8 7 6 5 4 3 2

CONTENTS

ACKNOWLEDGEMENTS | viii
INTRODUCTION | ix
GLOSSARY | xii

1		**Prefixes**	1
	A	N in prefix **meN-**	1
	B	Prefixes **ber-**, **per-** and **ter-**	3

2		**Noun affixes**	5
	A	Suffix **–an**	5
	B	Circumfix **ke-...-an**	6
	C	Circumfix **peN-...-an**	7
	D	Circumfix **per-...-an**	8
	E	Comparison of noun-forming affixes	8
	F	Prefix **peN-**	11

3		**Transitive and intransitive verbs**	13
	A	Verbs with and without an object	13
	B	Intransitive verb plus preposition	15
	C	Transitive verbs based on intransitives	17

4		**Active and passive**	19
	A	Focusing attention	19
	B	Two types of passive	21
	C	Passives of ditransitive verbs	24

| 5 | | **Intransitive verbs** | 26 |

6		**Verbal suffixes *-kan* and *–i***	29
	A	Verbs with suffix **-kan** based on adjectives	29
	B	Verbs with suffixes **-kan** and **-i** based on nouns	31
	C	Verbs with **-kan** and **-i** based on intransitive verbs	32
	D	Transitive verbs not based on intransitive verbs	34
	E	Optional **-kan** and **-i**	38
	F	Suffix **-kan** indicating an instrument	40
	G	Causative verbs based on transitive verbs	41
	H	Benefactive verbs with **-kan**	42
	I	Suffix **-i** indicating repeated action	45

7		**Verbs with prefix** *per-*	47
	A	Verbs with prefix **per-** alone	47
	B	Verbs with affixation **per-...-kan**	49
	C	Verbs with affixation **per-...-i**	50
8		*Ter-* **verbs**	51
	A	Stative **ter-** verbs	51
	B	Accidental **ter-**verbs	53
	C	Abilitative **ter-** verbs	55
9		*Ke-...-an* **verbs**	58
10		*Ber-...-kan* **verbs**	61
11		*Ber-...-an* **verbs**	63
	A	Reciprocal **ber-...-an** verbs	63
	B	Random action **ber-...an** verbs	64
12		**Base-***meN-* **verbs**	66
	A	Reciprocal base-**meN-** verbs	66
	B	Verbs meaning 'everything to do with'	66
13		**Noun phrases**	68
	A	The head noun	68
	B	Adjectives	68
	C	Possessors	68
	D	Demonstratives	69
	E	Possessor and demonstrative together	69
	F	Modifying nouns	70
	G	Relative clauses	71
	H	Modifying verbs	71
14		**Adjective phrases**	73
	A	Comparative phrases	73
	B	Superlative phrases	74
	C	Equative phrases	75
15		**Predicate phrases**	77
	A	Temporal markers	77
	B	Modals	78
16		**Negatives**	80
	A	**Tidak** and **bukan**	80
	B	Negative answers	80

C	*Belum*	81
D	Negatives occurring with temporals and modals	82
E	*Bukan … melainkan*	83
F	*Bukan untuk … tetapi*	83
17	*Baru*	85
18	**Prepositions**	87
A	Locative prepositions	87
B	*Pada*	88
C	Other prepositions	89
19	*Ada*	91
A	Functions of **ada**	91
B	**Ada yang**	92
20	**Functions of -*nya***	94
A	Possessor	94
B	Third singular: him, her, it	94
C	Linker between noun and possessor	94
D	Definitiser with a noun not previously mentioned	95
21	**Numbers**	97
A	Cardinal numbers	97
B	Ordinals and other numbers	98
C	Marking position in a series	100
D	Fractions	101
22	**Arithmetic**	103
A	Addition	103
B	Subtraction	103
C	Multiplication	103
D	Division	103
23	**Reflexives**	105
A	The reflexive pronoun **diri**	105
B	Expanded reflexive phrases	105
C	**Sendiri**	106
24	**Clause word order**	108
A	Subject-predicate inversion	108
B	Predicate-agent inversion	110

25		**Relative clauses**	113
	A	Defining relative clauses	113
	B	Adjectives in relative clauses	119
	C	Possessive relative clauses	120

26		**Topic-comment clauses**	124
	A	The topic: a way of focusing attention	124
	B	Emphasising the predicate	125

27		**Nominalised relative clauses**	128
	A	Nominalised defining relative clauses	128
	B	Nominalised possessive relative clauses	130

28		*Adalah*	132
	A	The copula	132
	B	**Adalah** before verbal nouns	133
	C	**Adalah** after nominalised relative clauses	134

29		**Nominalised predicate clauses**	136
	A	Nominalising predicates	136
	B	Nominalised predicates with more than one component	137
	C	Nominalised adjectives with and without **-nya**	138
	D	Comparison with **peN-...-an** and **ke-...-an** nouns	140

30		**Identifying clauses**	141
	A	Basic identifying clauses	141
	B	Nominalised relative clauses within identifying clauses	143
	C	Negation in identifying clauses	143

31		**Adjectives with complements**	145
	A	Complements with a passive verb	145
	B	Complements with an active verb	146

32		*Untuk*, *supaya* **and** *bahwa*	148
	A	**Untuk**	148
	B	**Supaya**	148
	C	**Bahwa**	151

33		**Questions**	152
	A	Yes-no questions	152
	B	Specific questions	153
	C	Question words in identifying clauses	155
	D	Questions with **yang mana**	157
	E	**Apa** and **berapa**	159

F   Sentence tags   160
G   Indirect questions   161
H   Questions with **-kah**   162

34   **Indefinite pronouns**   164
A   Question word plus **saja**   164
B   Question word plus **saja** in questions   166
C   **Tidak** plus reduplicated question word   167
D   'No one' and 'nothing' as subject   168

35   **Imperatives**   170
A   Transitive and intransitive imperatives   170
B   Negative imperatives with **jangan**   171
C   Passive imperatives   172
D   Polite imperatives   173

36   **Exclamations**   175

37   **Ellipsis**   177

KEY TO EXERCISES   180

ACKNOWLEDGEMENTS

The suggestion for a workbook to accompany my *Indonesian Reference Grammar* was first put to me by David Reeve when we began work on a graduate certificate in Indonesian for teachers of the language. Some of the units in the book were trialed during the development of the graduate certificate. Malcolm Smith spent much time putting those components into the course materials and recording the responses of participants in the trialing. I am grateful to David and Malcolm and to those Indonesian language teachers who participated in the trialing.

A number of native speakers of Indonesian checked constructions and offered much helpful advice, including Andi Soesmono, Donna Manungkalit, Musnarti Dickinson and Margaret Bocquet-Siek. My thanks to all of them. Needless to say, any errors or deficiencies in the work are solely my responsibility. Malcolm Smith deserves further thanks for advice and much useful assistance. Robyn White generously helped with preparing the manuscript for publication.

Allen & Unwin took a risk with my *Indonesian Reference Grammar*. Had they not done so this follow-up work would never have been conceived. My thanks go to them, especially to John Iremonger for his patience and readiness to go along with my ideas.

INTRODUCTION

Understanding Indonesian Grammar is a reference and practice book designed primarily for intermediate and advanced students, both in senior years of high school and at university. It is not meant for use with any particular language course.

There are 37 units in the book, each containing discussion of a grammar topic with accompanying exercises. Most units are broken up into a number of subsections, each dealing with one or more aspects of the topic for that unit. The book concentrates mainly on morphology (affixes) and syntax (sentence structure). There is very little on 'word usage', apart from consideration of the functions of a small number of syntactically important words. Discussion of grammar topics is far from exhaustive, often being quite brief. More weight is given to constructions likely to be studied at intermediate and higher levels, although some units contain reference to more elementary structures. A more comprehensive coverage of Indonesian grammar is provided in my *Indonesian Reference Grammar* (Allen & Unwin 1996).

To a considerable extent units are self-contained, enabling teachers to select topics in any order, depending on the structure of their course and the needs of their students. Teachers are certainly not expected to work through the book from unit 1 to unit 37. Nevertheless, since the grammar of any language is an interrelated network no unit can be entirely separate from others. Users may find that some exercises contain structures explained elsewhere in the book which they have not yet covered. This cannot be avoided if exercises are to contain more than the most elementary material. When a rule or pattern dealt with in one section needs to be mentioned in another section a cross-reference is given to avoid repetitive description. Grammatical terms are usually explained in the first unit in which they occur. Such terms are also defined in the glossary.

Within a unit users will usually find it practical to work through the subsections from the beginning to the end of the unit. However, in a few units it may not be appropriate to do so. For instance, in dealing with active and passive voice most teachers will find it appropriate to their course to cover some of the earlier discussion and exercises fairly early in their course but to leave the subsection on passives of ditransitive clauses until after the sections on ditransitive *-i* and *-kan* verbs have been covered.

Since the workbook is not intended for use with any particular Indonesian language course the question arises as to what vocabulary is appropriate for use in exercises. It is inevitable that students in any class will be unfamiliar with some of the words occurring in some exercises. Teachers should use their own strategies to deal with this situation; it is important that students not be prevented from completing an exercise because some of the vocabulary is unfamiliar to them. Teachers may wish to provide translations for words which have not yet occurred in their course or allow students to use a dictionary to complete certain exercises.

Scattered through the book are 'note boxes'. These offer useful information which is additional to what is provided in the text but which is not tested in exercises.

One problem facing any work which deals with Indonesian grammar is that there is considerably less agreement on what is 'good standard language' than is the case in English. A construction which is perfectly acceptable to one educated speaker may be rejected by another or at best be regarded as unnatural or clumsy. Indonesian constructions have been checked with native speakers and I have chosen forms which were acceptable to those people.. Nevertheless, teachers and students need to be aware that people from different parts of Indonesia may differ in their attitude to the grammaticality or acceptability of some structures or the appropriateness of some words in certain contexts. They should not be surprised if a native speaker questions some aspects of grammar or vocabulary in this book.

In the discussion of a number of grammatical constructions, particularly verbal suffixes *-kan* and *-i*, mention is made of semantic roles. This is rarely done in teaching texts of Indonesian but is nevertheless very useful for revealing relationships within verbal clauses and thus for allowing a proper understanding of such constructions. The important semantic roles mentioned in this work are defined in the glossary.

To assist in the explanation of some structures 'grammar boxes' are provided. The format of these is as follows:

• A word covers anything directly below it in the box. Thus the following grammar box indicates that *Ali* is the subject and *tidur* is the predicate:

subject	predicate
Ali	**tidur.**
Ali	is sleeping.

• Where a structure contains two or more parts the second line, where those parts are identified, is indented from the label for the structure, given on the first line. Thus the following box indicates that the construction consists of a main clause and an adverb of time. The main clause is a structure containing two parts, a subject and a predicate:

main clause		adverb of time
subject	predicate	
Kami	**baru pulang**	**sore hari.**

For every exercise there are instructions on what the student needs to do. Often an example is included. The example begins with a structure typical of those in the exercise. The next line begins with an arrow (→). What follows, on the same line and any subsequent lines, is an application of the instructions to the example. The student is expected to apply the instructions to the forms in the exercise, as demonstrated in the example.

At the back of the book is an answer key to exercises. Frequently there are several possible translations to a sentence, from either language to the other. In most cases only one possibility is given in the key, on the understanding the teacher will know what alternative translations are possible. Thus if the translation given to 'the book which he read' is *buku yang dia baca*, the teacher should be aware that answers such as *buku yang dibacanya* and *buku yang dibaca oleh dia* are also correct. In such cases the alternative possibilities are described in the appropriate unit in the text. In the case of words, the use of one item does not preclude the possibility that other words may be equally appropriate translations. In such cases also it is assumed the teacher will be aware of the possibilities and that an alternative correct answer will not be ruled incorrect. Sometimes two alternative translations are given in the key if this is thought useful for clarity. In translating 'you' *kamu, saudara* and *Anda* are chosen fairly randomly, unless context indicates that *kamu* is more or less appropriate than the other two words.

GLOSSARY

The following terms are defined as used in this workbook of Indonesian. Some terms may be used in other ways in grammars of either Indonesian or English.

abilitative verb A verb with prefix **ter-** which indicates that the actor has the ability to perform the action.

accidental verb A verb with prefix **ter-** which refers to uncontrolled action. Depending on the particular verb and the context it may refer to action which is unintended, unexpected, agentless, involuntary or sudden.

active voice The form of transitive clause in which the subject refers to the one who performs the action (the actor) and in which the verb is marked by prefix **meN-**.

actor The participant who carries out the action. The actor is expressed by the subject in an active clause, such as **Ali** in **Ali menolong saya** 'Ali helps me'. It occurs as agent in a passive clause, which is optionally marked by **oleh** 'by', such as **Saya ditolong oleh Ali** 'I am helped by Ali'.

adjective A word which refers to a characteristic of a person or thing, such as **besar** 'big', **hijau** 'green'.

adjective clause A clause which has an adjective or adjective phrase as its predicate, such as **rumah itu besar** 'That house is big'.

adjective phrase A phrase which has an adjective as its head word.

adverb A word or phrase which is added to a clause to give information about such matters as manner, time, place and frequency.

adversitive verb A verb with circumfix **ke-...-an** which refers to the adverse effect of the action on the subject.

affix A sound or group of sounds added to a word base to produce a derived word. Depending on where they occur in relation to the base, affixes are called prefixes, suffixes or circumfixes.

agent The phrase in a passive clause which indicates the actor. It sometimes follows the preposition **oleh** 'by'.

base The part of a word which carries the essential meaning and to which affixes are attached, such as **jalan** in **berjalan** 'walk' and **perjalanan** 'journey'. Words are listed under their base in a dictionary.

basic clause A clause which is described without reference to any other clause type and which can occur alone as a sentence.

benefactive verb A verb with suffix **-kan** which indicates that the object is the person, the beneficiary, for whose benefit the action is done.

beneficiary The person for whose benefit an action is performed. It is usually marked by preposition **untuk** 'for'. With benefactive **-kan** verbs it occurs as object, such as **Ali** in **Saya membelikan Ali buku** 'I buy Ali a book'. In passives of such constructions it occurs as subject: **Ali dibelikan buku** 'Ali is bought a book'.

cardinal number a number which precedes a noun in counting, such as **satu** 'one', **dua** 'two', **tiga** 'three'.

causative verb A verb with suffix **-kan** which indicates that the object is caused to perform the action or have the quality mentioned by the verb base.

circumfix An affix which has two parts, one occurring before the base and the other occurring after the base, such as **per-...-an** in **perjalanan** 'journey'.

clause A construction which contains a predicate. Most clauses also contain a subject.

comparative adjective phrase An adjective phrase in which **lebih** 'more' or **kurang** 'less' precedes the adjective, as in **lebih besar** 'bigger'.

complement A component of a clause which resembles an object but which cannot become the subject of a passive clause. Complements include the noun or noun phrase following intransitive verbs, such as **bahasa Perancis** in **Dia belajar bahasa Perancis** 'He is studying French'. Complements can also be clauses, such as **pergi** in **Dia menyuruh saya pergi** 'He ordered me to go'.

copula A word which occurs optionally between the subject and predicate in non-verbal clauses. The copulas are **adalah** and **ialah**.

defining relative clause A relative clause whose subject is omitted because it corresponds to the head noun of the embedding phrase. It is preceded by **yang**, as in **Orang yang duduk di situ** 'The person who is sitting there'.

demonstrative The words **ini** 'this' and **itu** 'that'.

ditransitive verb A verb which has a primary object to indicate the recipient or beneficiary and a secondary object to indicate the patient, such as **memberi** 'give' in **memberi dia uang** 'give him money' and **memilihkan** 'choose' in **memilihkan dia hadiah** 'choose him a present'.

ellipsis The omission of a word because it is clear from context.

equative adjective phrase An adjective phrase which says that one thing is similar to another in the quality indicated by the adjective, such as **sebesar** 'as big as'.

equative clause Another name for a noun clause. Equative constructions state that the person or thing expressed by the predicate is the same as the person or thing expressed by the subject.

exclamation An utterance which expresses the speaker's feelings or attitude, usually in an emphatic way.

first person See **person**.

head word The word around which a phrase is built. A noun phrase always has a noun as its head word. The head word of the noun phrase **mobil besar itu** 'that big car' is **mobil** 'car'. An adjective phrase has an adjective as its head, and so on.

imperative An utterance addressed to someone with the intention that something is done. Imperatives range from strong commands to requests, appeals and suggestions.

indefinite pronoun A pronoun which indicates that a person or thing is being spoken about without a particular person or thing being identified, such as **apa saja** 'anything' and **siapa saja** 'anyone'.

identifying clause A derived clause in which the predicate is placed first for focusing and whose subject is a nominalised relative clause, such as **Orang itulah yang mencuri dompet saya** 'It was that person who stole my wallet'.

indirect question A question which is placed within a statement. Thus the question **Kapan dia akan pindah?** 'When will he move?' becomes an indirect question in **Saya tidak tahu kapan dia akan pindah** 'I don't know when he will move'.

intransitive clause A verbal clause which does not have an object and which contains an intransitive verb.

intransitive verb A verb which occurs in an intransitive clause. It refers to an action which involves only one participant, the actor, such as **tidur** 'sleep', **berjalan** 'walk'.

locative noun A noun which indicates location in relation to the following noun, such as **atas** 'top, above' in **di atas meja** 'on top of the table'.

locative preposition A preposition indicating position or direction. The three locative prepositions are **di** 'at', **ke** 'to' and **dari** 'from'.

locative pronoun A pronoun which indicates position with relation to the speaker. The locative pronouns are **sini** 'here (near speaker)', **situ** 'there (not far off)', and **sana** 'there (far off)'.

main clause A clause in a complex sentence which occurs with a subordinate clause, a complement or other minor sentence component.

main verb The verb in an independent clause which occurs with a subordinate clause or complement. It is called the main verb to distinguish it from the verb in the complement or subordinate clause.

modal A word in the predicate which refers to concepts like possibility, ability and necessity, such as **dapat** 'can' and **harus** 'must'.

modifying noun A noun which follows another noun to give more specific information about it. Thus **buku** 'book' modifies **toko** 'shop' in **toko buku** 'book shop'.

modifying verb A verb which follows a noun to give more specific information about it. It usually indicates what the thing is used for. Thus **tidur** 'sleep' modifies **kamar** 'room' in **kamar tidur** 'bedroom'.

nominalised clause A clause acting as a noun.

nominalised predicate clause A clause acting as a noun by having **-nya** attached to its predicate, such as the first word in **ditutupnya beberapa jalan** 'the closure of several roads'.

nominalised relative clause A relative clause which takes the place of a noun when the noun it would usually follow is omitted. Thus the relative clause **yang biru** in the noun phrase **mobil yang biru itu** 'that blue car' is nominalised when **mobil** 'car' is omitted, as in **Yang biru itu mobil saya** 'That blue one is my car'.

noun A word which refers to a person, such as **guru** 'teacher', thing, such as **pohon** 'tree', or abstract concept, such as **perjalanan** 'journey'.

noun clause A clause whose predicate is a noun, such as **Dia guru** 'He is a teacher'. The negative in a noun clause is **bukan**.

noun phrase A sequence of words which functions in the same way as a noun (for instance, as the subject or object of a clause) and which has a noun as its head word.

object The noun or noun phrase which occurs immediately after an active transitive verb. It usually indicates the patient of the action but with some verbs it identifies the beneficiary or recipient. The object noun phrase becomes the subject when an active clause is changed to a passive clause.

ordinal number A number which indicates where something comes in a sequence and has the prefix **ke-**, such as **kedua** 'second', **kelima** 'fifth'.

participant One of the semantic relationships involved in an event and expressed by a noun phrase standing as subject, object, and so on. Important participants include the actor, which occurs as subject in an active clause and as agent in a passive clause, and the patient, which occurs as object in an active clause.

passive type one A passive clause in which the verb has prefix **di-** and the agent by a follows the verb, sometimes marked by the preposition **oleh** 'by', such as **Surat itu ditulis oleh Ali** 'That letter was written by Ali'. It can only occur if the agent is third person, except with **ter-** and **ke-...-an** verbs, in which a passive construction is always passive type one.

passive type two A passive clause in which the verb has no prefix and the agent precedes the verb, such as **Surat itu saya tulis** 'That letter was written by me'. The agent phrase must be a pronoun.

passive voice The form of transitive clause in which the subject refers to the patient. The actor, if mentioned, is expressed by an agent phrase. The verb is marked by prefix **di-** (passive type one) or has no prefix (passive type two).

patient This participant, sometimes called the *goal*, is the one which is moved or affected by the action. It occurs as object in most active clauses, such as **Ali** in **Mereka menolong Ali** 'They help Ali'. It occurs as subject in passive clauses like **Ali ditolong oleh mereka** 'Ali is helped by them'. With ditransitive verbs the patient can occur as the secondary object. Thus the patient **uang** 'money' occurs as secondary object in **Saya memberi dia uang** 'I give him money'.

person One of three classes of people involved in what is said; first person refers to the person speaking, such as **saya** 'I', second person refers to the person being spoken to, such as **kamu** 'you', and third person refers to the person or thing being spoken about, such as **mereka** 'they' and **orang itu** 'that person'.

phrase A group of words which is grammatically equivalent to a single word, being able to occur in the same places as that word. The phrase is built around a head word, which is a member of the class to which the phrase is equivalent. For instance, a noun phrase is built around a noun. Prepositional phrases have a different structure.

possessive relative clause A relative clause which refers to something possessed, corresponding to a phrase with 'whose' in English, as in **sopir yang namanya Ali** 'the driver whose name is Ali'.

predicate The part of a clause which says something about the subject. The predicate contains a word (verb, noun, and so on) which determines much of the structure of the rest of the clause.

prefix An affix which occurs before a base, such as **ber-** in the word **berjalan** 'walk'.

preposition A word which links a following noun phrase to the rest of a sentence, telling what the relationship of that noun phrase is to the sentence. For instance, the preposition **di** 'in' tells that the following noun **kota** is the location, in **Mereka tinggal di kota** 'They live in the city'.

prepositional phrase A construction consisting of a preposition followed by a noun phrase, such as **untuk orang itu** 'for those people' and **dengan teman saya** 'with my friend'.

primary object The object which immediately follows a ditransitive verb and which becomes the subject when the clause is changed to a passive.

pronoun A word which stands for a noun when it is clear who or what is being spoken about, such as **kita** 'we', **mereka** 'they'.

question word A word occurring in a specific question which corresponds to one of the 'wh-' words in English, such as **siapa** 'who', **kapan** 'when'. Also called an interrogative.

recipient The person at whom an action is directed. It can follow prepositions **kepada** and **pada** 'to'. With some verbs, especially **-i** verbs, it can occur as object, such as **dia** in **Saya memberi dia uang** 'I give him money'. In passives of such constructions it occurs as subject: **Dia diberi uang** 'He is given money'.

reciprocal verb A verb which indicates that two people do the same thing to each other or that two people or things stand in the same relation to each other. Corresponding verbs in English usually have 'each other' as object, as in **Mereka pukul-memukul** 'They hit each other'.

reflexive The word **sendiri** 'self', which occurs with nouns and pronouns to emphasise or make clear who or what is being referred to.

reflexive phrase A phrase which usually occurs as the object of a verb to indicates that the object refers to the same person as the subject. The full phrase is **diri** + pronoun + **sendiri**, as in **Dia meyakinkan dirinya sendiri** 'He convinced himself'.

reflexive pronoun The word **diri** 'self', which can occur alone, as in **menjaga diri** 'look after oneself', or in a reflexive phrase.

relative clause A clause preceded by **yang** and occurring in a noun phrase to give information about the noun. The term usually refers to a defining relative clause, as in **orang yang duduk di situ** 'the person who is sitting there'.

second person See **person**.

secondary object A noun which indicates the patient and which follows the primary object of a ditransitive verb, such as **uang** 'money' in **Dia memberi mereka uang** 'He gave them money'.

semantic role See **participant**.

sentence A construction which can stand alone as a complete utterance. A sentence can be a statement, question, command or exclamation.

sentence tag A word attached to the end of a question for such purposes as seeking confirmation, such as **bukan** in **Saudara mahasiswa, bukan?** 'You are a student, aren't you?'

simple intransitive verb An intransitive verb which has no affixation, such as **tidur** 'sleep', **duduk** 'sit'.

simple transitive verb A transitive verb which consists only of a base and one of the affixes **meN-** or **di-**, such as **menulis** 'write', **ditulis** 'written'.

specific question A question which requires specific information as an answer and which cannot be answered by 'yes' or 'no'. It contains a question word, such as **siapa** 'who', **di mana** 'where'.

stative verb A verb with prefix **ter-** which refers to a state rather than an action and which thus has no actor, such as **terletak** 'located'.

subject The component of a clause which is the thing being discussed, the 'theme' of the utterance. It is frequently something which has been mentioned previously, about which something new (the predicate) is said, as **Ali** in **Ali sudah pulang** 'Ali has gone home'.

subordinate clause A clause which cannot stand alone as a sentence but which occurs with another clause (the main clause) in a complex sentence. It can occur either before or after the main clause to add information to it. The subordinate clause is preceded by a subordinator, such as **sesudah** 'after', in **Mereka berangkat sesudah makan** 'They left after eating'.

suffix An affix which occurs after the base, such as **-an** in **tulisan** 'writing'.

superlative adjective phrase A phrase in which an adjective is preceded by **paling** or **ter-** 'most', as in **paling besar** 'biggest', **tertinggi** 'highest'.

temporal marker A word within the predicate which indicates that the action has occurred, is occurring, or is yet to occur in relation to the moment of utterance or in relation to some other event referred to, such as **masih** 'still', **akan** 'will'.

third person See **person**.

topic The component of a topic-comment clause which occurs first for focusing. It is identified with a component of the basic clause from which the topic-comment clause derives and its place in that clause is marked by **-nya**. Thus, **sopir itu** 'that driver' is the topic in **Sopir itu namanya Ali** '(As for) that driver, his name is Ali'.

topic-comment clause A clause which contains a topic, the rest of the clause, which includes a subject and predicate, forming a comment on the topic.

transitive clause A verbal clause which has an object and which contains a transitive verb.

transitive verb A verb which occurs in a transitive clause. It refers to an action which has two participants, an actor and a patient, such as **membawa** 'carry', **melempar** 'throw'.

verb A word which refers to an action, such as **lari** 'run', **membaca** 'read', or a state, such as **tidur** 'sleep', **terletak** 'located'. It occurs as the predicate of a verbal clause.

yes-no question A question which can be answered by 'yes' or 'no'. It does not contain a question word.

1   PREFIXES

A   *N* in prefix *meN-*

The symbol **N** in the prefix **meN-** stands for a number of different nasal sounds or no sound (zero). What the sound will be in a particular word depends on the first sound of the base following the prefix, as listed below. If the base begins with one of the sounds marked with an asterisk that sound is lost after the nasal.

N → **m** before ***p, b, f, v**
N → **n** before *****t, d, c, j, sy, z**
N → **ny** before *****s**
N → **ng** before *****k, g, h, kh** and vowels
N → zero before **m, n, ny, ng, w, y, l, r**

EXERCISE 1

Below are a number of verb bases.
- Give the correct form of the verbs with the prefix **meN-**.

Example
tulis
→   **menulis**

1.	**ajar**	8.	**garuk**
2.	**beli**	9.	**dengar**
3.	**olah**	10.	**nyanyi**
4.	**lihat**	11.	**serah**
5.	**rasa**	12.	**kirim**
6.	**pakai**	13.	**minta**
7.	**coba**	14.	**jual**

NOTE Initial **p, t, s** and **k** are sometimes retained in words borrowed from other languages. These forms must be learned separately. The first sound becomes less likely to be retained as the word becomes more accepted as an Indonesian word. Sometimes variation occurs before the word becomes fully 'Indonesianised'. Thus you will come across both **menaati** and **mentaati** 'obey' from the base **taat** and both **mengritik** and **mengkritik** 'criticise' from the base **kritik**.

- Sometimes we cannot be certain from the **meN-** form of a verb what the base is. Thus the words **menyewa** 'rent' and **menyanyi** 'sing' begin with the same sequence of sounds. However, the first consists of prefix **meny-** and base **sewa** while the second consists of prefix **me-** and base **nyanyi**. In such cases it may be necessary to look up a number of possibilities in the dictionary to find which the base is.

EXERCISE 2

- Give the meaning, prefix and base of each of the following verbs.
- Note: You will need to use a dictionary.

Example
menulis
→   'write' **men- + tulis**

1.	**menikah**	9.	**menanti**
2.	**menikam**	10.	**menganga**
3.	**mengantar**	11.	**memilih**
4.	**mengecil**	12.	**menyambut**
5.	**memasak**	13.	**menyala**
6.	**mengeja**	14.	**mengisi**
7.	**menganggap**	15.	**mengobrol**
8.	**menyikat**	16.	**menanam**

NOTE   Initial **p** in the prefix **per-** is retained after **mem-**: **meN- + per- + kecil** → **memperkecil**. It is also retained in some words whose base begin with **per** if this 'looks like' a prefix: **meN- + percaya** 'believe' + **-i** → **mempercayai**. Initial **p** is retained in a few other words, the most common being **mempunyai** 'have, own' and **mempengaruhi** 'influence'.

Prefix **peN-** undergoes the same changes as occur to **meN-**. The one exception is that following **peN-** the initial **p** of prefix **per-** is lost: **peN- + per- + satu** → **pemersatu** 'unifier'.

- Verbs with prefix **meN-** can be reduplicated. In this case the prefix is not reduplicated. The reduplicated form of **membagi** 'divide' is **membagi-bagi** 'divide out'. If the sound represented by **N** replaces the first sound of the base then it does occur in the reduplicated part of the base. Thus the reduplicated form of **menunggu** 'wait' – from **meN- + tunggu**, where **n** replaces **t** – is **menunggu-nunggu** 'keep waiting'.

EXERCISE 3

- Give the reduplicated forms of the verbs with prefix **meN-** from the following bases.

Example
tunggu
→   **menunggu-nunggu**

1.	sedot		7.	jadi
2.	ulang		8.	omong
3.	pijat		9.	tulis
4.	garuk		10.	baca
5.	minta		11.	karang
6.	putar		12.	cari

• With single syllable bases, which are all borrowings from other languages, **meN-** optionally becomes **menge-**. The regular form of the prefix can occur instead. In this case initial **p**, **t**, **s**, and **k** are not lost as forms without them would sometimes be difficult to interpret. Thus **meN-** added to base **pel** 'mop' gives **mengepel** or **mempel** 'to mop'.

> **NOTE** Many people regard only the **menge-** forms as acceptable. One-syllable verb bases take the prefix **di-** in the passive: **dipel** 'mopped'.
>
> Prefix **menge-** also occurs with **tahu**: **mengetahui** 'know'. In the passive **ke-** is placed before the base: **diketahui** 'known'.

EXERCISE 4

• Give the two possible **meN-** verbs from the following bases.
• Give the meanings of the verbs.

Example
pel
→   **mengepel, mempel** 'to mop'

1.	cek		4.	rem
2.	tik		5.	lap
3.	bom		6.	dor

B Prefixes *ber-*, *per-* and *ter-*

These prefixes undergo the following changes:

The final **r** is lost if the following base begins with **r**:

ber-	+	**renang**	→	**berenang**
per-	+	**rusak**	→	**perusak**
ter-	+	**rasa**	→	**terasa**

If the base begins with **CerC**, where **C** is any consonant, **r** is lost:

ber-	+	serta		→	beserta
per-	+	kerja	+ -an	→	pekerjaan
ter-	+	pergok		→	tepergok

> **NOTE**   Loss of **r** before a base beginning with **CerC** is not entirely regular; in a few words it does not occur or is optional: **ter- + percaya** → **tepercaya, terpercaya** 'trustworthy'.

With the base **ajar** the **r** of the prefixes is replaced by **l**: **ber- + ajar** → **belajar** 'study'.

EXERCISE 5

In each number below is a prefix (**ber-**, **per-** or **ter-**), base and, sometimes, a suffix.

* Give the correct form of the word when these combinations occur.
* Give the meaning of each word.

Example
ber- + angkat
→   **berangkat** 'depart'

1. **ter-** + **serah**
2. **ber-** + **terbang** + **-an**
3. **per-** + **kerja**
4. **ter-** + **rasa**
5. **ber-** + **kerja**
6. **per-** + **ajar** + **-an**
7. **ber-** + **pergi** + **-an**
8. **ber-** + **keras**

2 NOUN AFFIXES

Many nouns are formed by the addition of an affix to the base. The important noun-forming affixes are discussed in the following sections.

A Suffix *-an*

This suffix derives nouns from a number of word classes but most commonly attaches to verb bases. With many verb bases it produces a noun which stands as object of the related verb. Thus **makanan** 'food' refers to what is eaten (**makan** 'eat'), **pakaian** 'clothes' refers to what is worn (**memakai** 'wear').

Another large group are 'action nouns', which refer to the action of the verb. Thus **serangan** 'attack', as in the noun phrase **serangan terhadap musuh** 'an attack on the enemy', expresses the same action as the verb **menyerang** 'to attack', as in **mereka menyerang musuh** 'they attacked the enemy'. In the same way the noun **ancaman** 'threat' relates to the verb **mengancam** 'threaten'.

EXERCISE 1

In each item below the first sentence contains an underlined verb. The second sentence contains a gap.
* Translate the first sentence.
* Fill in the gap in the second sentence with the **-an** noun corresponding to the underlined verb in the first sentence.
* Translate the second sentence.

Example
Dia <u>menulis</u> surat. _____nya indah sekali.
→   She wrote a letter.
     Tulisannya indah sekali.
     Her writing is very beautiful.

1.   **Dia <u>mengancam</u> pelayan toko. _____nya didengar banyak orang.**
2.   **Dia <u>melukis</u> ayahnya. _____ itu akan digantung di dinding kantor.**
3.   **Sandra <u>memilih</u> gaun merah. Teman-temannya menggemari _____nya.**
4.   **Rusli mencoba <u>menjawab</u> pertanyaan polisi. Sayang, _____nya tidak meyakinkan polisi.**
5.   **Siti selalu <u>mengeluh</u>. _____nya menjengkelkan rekan-rekannya.**

6. **Karena haus dia harus <u>minum</u> banyak. Dia mengambil ____ itu dari kulkas.**
7. **Anak-anak itu <u>dilarang</u> ke luar rumah. ____ itu berlaku sampai besok.**
8. **Mereka <u>mengumpulkan</u> cerita-cerita rakyat di pulau Sulawesi. ____ cerita itu akan diterbitkan di Australia.**
9. **Para seniman <u>memamerkan</u> lukisannya di Taman Ismail Marzuka. ____ itu dikunjungi banyak orang.**
10. **Bambang sudah bertahun-tahun <u>menabung</u> uangnya di bank ini. Sekarang ____nya sudah banyak.**

B   Circumfix *ke-...-an*

The circumfix **ke-...-an** forms abstract nouns. Many such nouns are based on adjectives, such as **kebersihan** 'cleanliness' (from **bersih** 'clean'), **kecantikan** 'beauty' (from **cantik** 'beautiful').

A few are based on intransitive verbs, such as **kedatangan** 'arrival' (from **datang** 'come'), **kehidupan** 'life' (from **hidup** 'live'). The verbal prefixes **ber-** and **ter-** are retained with this affix: **keberangkatan** 'departure' (from **berangkat** 'depart'), **keterbatasan** 'limitation' (from **terbatas** 'limited').

Other **ke-...-an** nouns are based on simple nouns, such as **keanggotaan** 'membership' (from **anggota** 'member'), **kedaerahan** 'regionalism' (from **daerah** 'region'). Many of these forms frequently occur attributive to another noun, such as **kedokteran** 'medical, having to do with doctors' (from **dokter** 'doctor'), as in **fakultas kedokteran** 'faculty of medicine', **keimigrasian** 'having to do with immigration' (from **imigrasi** 'immigration'), as in **undang-undang keimigrasian** 'immigration laws'.

EXERCISE 2

- Translate the following sentences.
- Form sentences with **ke-...-an** nouns according to the pattern in the example.
- Translate your sentences.

  Example
  Banyak orang tahu dia malas.
  →   Many people know he is lazy.
       Banyak orang tahu tentang kemalasannya.
       Many people know about his laziness.

1. **Banyak orang tahu dia berani.**

2. **Banyak orang tahu dia pergi.**
3. **Banyak orang tahu dia berhasil.**
4. **Banyak orang tahu dia gagal.**
5. **Banyak orang tahu dia sehat.**
6. **Banyak orang tahu dia menang.**

C Circumfix *peN-...-an*

The **N-** on prefix **peN-** changes according to the same rules as for **meN-** [see section 1A]. This includes use of **penge-** with one-syllable bases: **peN- + cek + -an → pengecekan** 'checking'. Most **peN-...-an** nouns are based on verbs. They usually refer to the action expressed by the verb and are translatable 'the act of doing what the verb refers to'. Thus **penulisan** means 'the act of writing, the writing': **Penulisan buku ini memerlukan waktu dua tahun** 'The writing of this book required two years'. As in the above example, such nouns can usually occur with an indication of length of time.

EXERCISE 3

In each of the following sentences a verb is underlined.
- Translate the sentences.
- Form sentences containing the **peN-...-an** noun based on the underlined verb, according to the pattern in the example.
- Translate your sentences.

Example
Mereka membuat batik di pabrik ini.
→   They make batik in this factory.
     Pembuatan batik terjadi di pabrik ini.
     The making of batik takes place in this factory.

1. **Perusuh membakar kantornya tahun lalu.**
2. **Panitia mengumumkan keputusannya tadi pagi.**
3. **Bapak menteri membuka acara di ruangan utama.**
4. **Orang miskin menderita di mana-mana.**
5. **Harry mencuri emas itu tahun lalu.**
6. **Polisi memeriksa pencuri itu kemarin.**
7. **Orang yang punya senjata harus mendaftarkan senjatanya di kantor ini.**
8. **Dia menerjemahkan buku saya tahun lalu.**

D   Circumfix *per-...-an*

These nouns often relate to verbs with prefix **ber-**, such as **pertemuan** 'meeting' (**bertemu** 'meet'), **pergerakan** 'movement' (**bergerak** 'move'). Some correspond to transitive verbs, such as **peringatan** 'reminder, warning' (**mengingatkan** 'remind, warn'), **percobaan** 'experiment, attempt' (**mencoba** 'try, attempt'). A few **per-...-an** nouns are based on simple verbs, such as **persetujuan** 'agreement' (**setuju** 'agree'). While many **per-...-an** nouns have an abstract meaning, as in the above examples, others refer to a place where the action occurs, such as **perhentian** 'stopping place' (**berhenti** 'stop'), **percetakan** 'printery' (**mencetak** 'print').

Some **per-...-an** nouns are based on nouns and mean either 'having to do with what the base indicates, affairs dealing with the base', such as **permusuhan** 'enmity' (**musuh** 'enemy'), or 'place where a large number of what is indicated in the base are found', such as **perkebunan** 'plantation' (**kebun** 'garden').

EXERCISE 4

- Translate the following questions.
- Answer the questions with short sentences of your own, using the noun with **per-...-an** related to the underlined verb, as in the example.
- Translate your sentences.

   Example
   Kapan dia akan <u>menolong</u> kami?
   →   When will he help us?
         Pertolongan itu akan diberikan minggu depan.
         The help will be given next week.

   1.   **Jam berapa Anda mulai <u>bekerja</u>?**
   2.   **Tahun berapa mereka <u>bertemu</u>?**
   3.   **Dia <u>bertanya</u> tentang apa?**
   4.   **Kapan dia <u>meminta</u> bantuan kami?**
   5.   **Kapan mereka <u>bercerai</u>?**
   6.   **Di mana mereka <u>melawan</u> musuhnya?**
   7.   **Di mana mereka <u>berkelahi</u>?**
   8.   **Tahun berapa kaum buruh mulai <u>bergerak</u>?**

E   Comparison of noun-forming affixes

The above sections describe some of the major functions of the noun-forming affixes **-an**, **ke-...-an**, **peN-...-an** and **per-...-an**. However, there are numerous other meanings which are found with smaller numbers of words.

Sometimes the choice of affixes is unpredictable, as seen from the following pair:

menolong to help : **pertolongan** help, assistance (with **per- ... -an**)
membantu to help : **bantuan** help, assistance (with **-an**)

While there is some unpredictability in meanings of affixed forms a number of general distinctions can be made, including the following.

- **ke-...-an** and **peN-...-an**

While **ke-...-an** relates directly to the meaning of an adjective base **peN-...-an** relates to the meaning of the transitive verb based on the adjective:

bersih 'clean' : **kebersihan** 'cleanliness'
membersihkan 'make clean' : **pembersihan** '(act of) cleaning'

- **-an** and **peN-...-an**

Affixes **-an** and **peN-...-an** frequently have the same verbal bases. Their respective meanings in such cases are as discussed above. From **menulis** 'write' is derived **tulisan** 'writing', that is 'what has been written'. From the same verb is **penulisan**. This is also translated into English as 'writing' but it means 'the act of writing', not 'the result of writing':

Tulisan Anda sulit dibaca.
Your writing is hard to read.
Penulisan buku ini memerlukan waktu dua tahun.
The writing of this book took two years.

NOTE   While **peN-...-an** and **-an** nouns have distinct meanings in Indonesian the difference is often not reflected in English. Thus **tulisan** and **penulisan** are both translated 'writing', which does not distinguish between the two meanings, except in context. As another example, **terjemahan buku ini** and **penerjemahan buku ini** (from **menerjemahkan** 'translate') would both normally be rendered 'the translation of this book', although the two words have different meanings:

Terjemahan buku ini tepat sekali.
The translation of this book is very accurate.
Penerjemahan buku ini dilakukan di Indonesia.
The translation of this book was done in Indonesia.

The sentence with **penerjemahan** could alternatively be rendered:
The translating of this book was done in Indonesia.

- **per-...-an** and **peN-...-an**

When **per-...-an** and **peN-...-an** nouns have the same base the former usually relates to a **ber-** verb while the latter relates to a transitive verb. Thus **pertemuan** 'meeting' relates to **bertemu** 'meet' while **penemuan** 'discovery' relates to **menemukan** 'discover'.

EXERCISE 5

- Translate the following sentences into Indonesian.
- To translate the underlined word choose a noun with **-an, ke-...-an, peN-...-an** or **per-...-an** as appropriate, based on the word in parentheses.

Examples

The <u>freeing</u> of the prisoners was welcomed by the community. (**bebas**)
→   **Pembebasan orang tahanan disambut baik oleh masyarakat.**

There is no <u>freedom</u> in that country. (**bebas**)
→   **Tidak ada kebebasan di negeri itu.**

1.   The <u>poverty</u> of the people in that region is very saddening. (**miskin**)
2.   Her <u>savings</u> aren't yet enough to buy a house. (**tabung**)
3.   The <u>unifying</u> of the people has been awaited for many years. (**satu**)
4.   What is the <u>difference</u> between these two words? (**beda**)
5.   The general <u>election</u> will be held in March next year. (**pilih**)
6.   The <u>answer</u> we received is not satisfactory. (**jawab**)
7.   The <u>meeting</u> between the two prime ministers will take place in Jakarta. (**temu**)
8.   We experienced <u>difficulty</u> when we applied for visas. (**sulit**)
9.   The <u>building</u> of tall buildings is happening everywhere. (**bangun**)
10.   Mother hasn't yet returned from the <u>shopping</u> centre. (**toko**)
11.   Borobudur is a very old <u>building</u>. (**bangun**)
12.   Before buying a carpet we have to know the <u>measurements</u> of the room. (**ukur**)

EXERCISE 6

- Give the correct noun derived from the word in parentheses in each of the following sentences, together with its translation.
- Translate the sentences.

Example

Amerika Serikat sudah menghentikan (kirim) bahan makanan.
→   **pengiriman** 'the sending'
       The USA has stopped the sending of foodstuffs.

1.   **Semua warga bangga akan (bersih) kota mereka.**
2.   **Tadi saya mendengar (nyanyi) *dangdut* di radio.**
3.   **(periksa) barang-barang itu berlangsung kira-kira tiga jam.**
4.   **(buat)nya memalukan orang tuanya.**
5.   **Dia tinggal di kompleks (rumah) yang tidak jauh dari sini.**
6.   **Dia pulang dari Bali dengan banyak (ukir) dan (lukis).**

7.   (datang) pemimpin disambut oleh rakyat.
8.   (mohon) kita untuk menjadi anggota akan dikabulkan.
9.   Indonesia dan Australia akan mengadakan (janji) baru.
10.   Mobil Holden adalah (buat) Australia.
11.   (buat) jembatan harus dihentikan karena hujan.
12.   Dosen kami tidak dapat menjawab (tanya) yang sulit itu.

F   Prefix *peN-*

This prefix usually attaches to verbs to derive nouns indicating the person who carries out the action. **N-** changes according to the same rules as for **meN-** [see section 1A]:

menulis 'write' : **penulis** 'writer'
menyanyi 'sing' : **penyanyi** 'singer'

PeN- nouns sometimes refer to an instrument for performing the action. Often these modify other nouns:

mencetak 'print' : (**mesin**) **pencetak** 'printer'
menenangkan 'calm (someone)' : (**obat**) **penenang** 'sedative' (= 'calming medicine')

> **NOTE**   There is also a prefix **pe-** which derives a few nouns indicating a person who carries out the action of a verb with prefix **ber-**: **berdagang** 'trade' : **pedagang** 'trader', **bertinju** 'box' : **petinju** 'boxer'.
>
> The verb **belajar** 'study' has the corresponding noun **pelajar** 'student'.

EXERCISE 7

- Translate the following questions.
- Answer the questions, replacing the verbs with **peN-** nouns, as in the example.
- Translate your sentences.

Example
Siapa menulis buku itu?
→   Who wrote that book?
     Penulis buku itu Pak Ali.
     The writer of that book was Mr Ali.

1.   **Siapa menjaga toko itu?**
2.   **Siapa memiliki toko itu?**
3.   **Siapa menyanyikan lagu itu?**
4.   **Siapa memimpin partai itu?**

5.   **Siapa mendirikan partai itu?**
6.   **Siapa menerjemahkan buku itu?**
7.   **Siapa melatih olahragawan itu?**

3 TRANSITIVE AND INTRANSITIVE VERBS

A Verbs with and without an object

Some verbs refer to an action or state which involves only one person or thing. These are *intransitive* verbs; they can occur with a subject and no other noun. **Tidur** 'sleep' is an intransitive verb: **Titik tidur** 'Titik is sleeping'. An intransitive verb occurs in an intransitive clause, which obligatorily contains only a subject and a predicate [see unit 15 for a discussion of predicates].

Transitive verbs refer to actions which involve two people or things. Someone performs the action and it affects someone or something else. These verbs occur with two nouns. One of the nouns indicates the *actor*; this occurs as subject of the verb. The other noun indicates the person or thing affected by the action, called the *patient*; this usually occurs as the object of the verb. The verb **membeli** 'buy' is a transitive verb as it requires a subject (someone who buys) and an object (the thing bought): **Ibu membeli sayur** 'Mother bought vegetables'. A transitive verb occurs in a transitive clause, which obligatorily contains a subject, a predicate and an object.

```
Intransitive clause:
     subject     verb
     Titik       tidur.

Transitive clause:
     subject     verb        object
     actor                   patient
     Ibu         membeli     sayur.
```

The distinction is important in Indonesian because verbs in Indonesian take different forms according to whether they are transitive or intransitive. This is not the case in English. Thus English 'stop' can be either intransitive, translating Indonesian **berhenti**, or transitive, translating Indonesian **menghentikan**:

Bis <u>berhenti</u> di depan gedung sekolah.
The bus <u>stopped</u> in front of the school building.
Sopir <u>menghentikan</u> bis di depan gedung sekolah.
The driver <u>stopped</u> the bus in front of the school building.

Intransitive verbs can be simple (without a prefix), such as **tidur** 'sleep', or have prefix **ber-**, such as **berjalan** 'walk' or **meN-**, such as **menangis** 'cry'. Transitive verbs have prefix **meN-**, such as **membeli** 'buy'. They often have suffix **-i**, such as **mencintai** 'love', or **-kan**, such as **menghentikan** 'stop', and sometimes prefix **per-**, such as **memperpanjang** 'extend'.

Only transitive verbs have a passive form. [Passive forms are discussed in section 4A.]

> **NOTE** Several common transitive verbs beginning with **m** usually occur without prefix **meN-**: **makan** 'eat', **minum** 'drink', **minta** 'request', **mohon** 'request'.
>
> In some forms of colloquial Indonesian the prefix **meN-** is reduced to **N**; that is, the first sound of the base is nasalised. Several common words are also accepted this way in more formal language. Thus both **menonton** and **nonton** 'watch, view' occur, from base **tonton**.
>
> In a very few cases a **ber-** prefix on an intransitive verb is retained on the transitive verb derived from it, giving the affixation **member-....-kan**. The form without **ber-** also occurs. Thus from **berhenti** 'stop' are both **memberhentikan** 'dismiss, sack' and **menghentikan** 'stop (something)'.

EXERCISE 1

Each of the following sentences has a verb with prefix **meN-**.
- Translate the sentences.
- Mark each sentence as either intransitive (I) or transitive (T).

Examples
Anak itu sering menangis kalau ibunya pergi.
→   The child often cries if its mother goes out. (I)

Mereka akan menjemput temannya di stasiun kereta api.
→   They will meet their friend at the railway station. (T)

1.   **Pilot mendaratkan pesawatnya dengan selamat.**
2.   **Kami harus melapor ke kantor imigrasi.**
3.   **Gunung api itu meletus beberapa tahun yang lalu.**
4.   **Kami melaporkan pencurian itu kepada polisi.**
5.   **Saya mau mengecek kebenaran cerita itu.**
6.   **Pesawat mendarat dengan selamat.**
7.   **Sejak kecelakaan itu kesehatannya makin memburuk.**
8.   **Andi menulis surat kepada ibunya setiap minggu.**
9.   **Ayahnya meninggal tahun lalu.**
10.   **Dia memegang tangan saya erat-erat.**

EXERCISE 2

The main verb in each of the following sentences is underlined.
- Give the Indonesian equivalent of each verb, based on the form in parentheses.
- Identify the verb as transitive (T) or intransitive (I).
- Note: You will need to use a good dictionary.

Example
We <u>stayed</u> at that hotel for two nights. (**inap**)
→   **menginap** 'stay, spend the night' (I)

1.   Almost two hundred people <u>attended</u> the meeting. (**hadir**)
2.   The members <u>assembled</u> in the meeting room. (**kumpul**)
3.   They had <u>to surrender</u> their passports at the immigration office. (**serah**)
4.   He <u>hid</u> the toys behind the door. (**sembunyi**)
5.   The enemy <u>surrendered</u> after heavy fighting. (**serah**)
6.   Ali's family <u>moved</u> to Jakarta when his father got work there. (**pindah**)
7.   Almost two hundred people were <u>present</u> at the meeting. (**hadir**)
8.   He <u>waved</u> from the plane window. (**lambai**)
9.   He <u>waved</u> his handkerchief from the plane window. (**lambai**)
10. Very few trees <u>grow</u> in that cold climate. (**tumbuh**)
11. The government <u>raised</u> the price of rice following the drought. (**naik**)
12. His hand <u>moved</u> slowly. (**gerak**)
13. He <u>hid</u> behind the door. (**sembunyi**)
14. The price of rice <u>rose</u> following the drought. (**naik**)

NOTE   Some transitive verbs, in both Indonesian and English, frequently occur without an object being expressed. Thus:
Dia sedang membaca. She is reading.

However, such verbs are not intransitive; the action does carry over to a patient (the object of the verb), which can be expressed if it is important to the context:
Dia sedang membaca buku. She is reading a book.

B   Intransitive verb plus preposition

Some intransitive verbs can be followed by a preposition. Often the verb plus preposition corresponds to a transitive verb in English. Thus **cinta kepada** means 'love':
Pak Basri <u>cinta kepada</u> istrinya.
Mr Basri <u>loves</u> his wife.

In other cases English also has an intransitive verb or adjective with a following preposition. Thus **marah pada** means 'angry at':

Dia <u>marah pada</u> anaknya.
He is <u>angry at</u> his child.

Some combinations of intransitive verb plus preposition can often be replaced by a transitive verb with suffix **-i**. Thus **cinta kepada** can be replaced by **mencintai**:

Pak Basri <u>mencintai</u> istrinya.
Mr Basri <u>loves</u> his wife.

In a number of cases an intransitive verb followed by preposition **tentang** 'about' can be replaced by a transitive verb with **-kan**:

Dia <u>bercerita tentang</u> pengalamannya.
Dia <u>menceritakan</u> pengalamannya.
He <u>talked about/related</u> his experiences.

Sometimes slightly different translations are appropriate for intransitive and transitive verbs. Thus in the above example 'talked about' is a more appropriate translation for **berbicara tentang**, while 'relate' is more appropriate for **membicarakan**.

NOTE In some cases there are other differences in meaning between an intransitive verb + preposition and the corresponding transitive verb. Thus **setuju dengan** means 'agree with (a person or what they say)' while **menyetujui** can only refer to what someone says or does, meaning 'agree with, approve':

Saya setuju dengan dia/usulnya. I agree with him/his suggestion.
Saya menyetujui usulnya. I agree with/approve his suggestion.

The intransitive **marah pada** means 'angry at' while the transitive **memarahi** means 'scold, reprimand'.

EXERCISE 3

- Rewrite the following sentences, replacing the intransitive verb + preposition with the corresponding transitive verb.
- translate your sentences.

Example
Mereka ingin bertemu dengan siapa?
→   **Mereka ingin menemui siapa?**
     Who do they want to meet?

1.   **Andi akan menikah dengan tunangannya bulan depan.**

2.   Mengapa polisi datang ke rumah Anda tadi malam?
3.   Anda ingin bertanya tentang apa?
4.   Banyak turis berkunjung ke pantai ini pada masa liburan.
5.   Kita tidak perlu berpikir tentang hal itu.
6.   Mereka kagum terhadap kepala desa.
7.   Tamu mengadu tentang pelayanan yang kurang baik.
8.   Mereka sadar akan bahaya di tempat itu.
9.   Saya tidak percaya akan cerita itu.
10. Saya tidak mau tidur di atas kasur ini karena kotor.
11. Kami gemar akan makanan Jepang.
12. Jangan duduk di kursi ibu!

> **NOTE**   There are other differences between such transitive and intransitive verbs.
>
> The transitive verbs must be followed by an object, while the intransitive verbs can usually occur at the end of a sentence without a following preposition:
>   **Kami sudah bertemu.** 'We've already met.'
>
> The transitive verbs also have a passive form [see section 4A]:
>   **Siapa yang ditemui mereka?** 'Who was met by them?'

C   Transitive verbs based on intransitives

Some transitive verbs indicate that someone causes someone or something to carry out the action indicated by the corresponding intransitive verb. Thus **bergerak** is an intransitive verb meaning 'move, be in motion'. The corresponding transitive verb is **menggerakkan** 'move (something), cause to move':
    Tangannya bergerak.
    His hand moved.
    Dia menggerakkan tangannya.
    He moved his hand.

Intransitive verbs in this group can be simple or have prefix **ber-** or **meN-**; corresponding transitive verbs usually have suffix **-kan**. [These forms are further discussed in section 6C.]

EXERCISE 4

Below are a number of intransitive verbs in sentences.
- Translate the sentences.
- For each sentence compose another sentence containing the corresponding transitive verb, using the subject of the intransitive verb as the object.
- Use the word in parentheses as the subject of the transitive sentence.
- translate your sentences.

Example

Harga beras turun. (pemerintah)

→   The price of rice fell.

Pemerintah menurunkan harga beras.

The government reduced the price of rice.

1.   **Rapat bubar. (polisi)**
2.   **Anak-anak menjauh dari ular yang masuk rumah. (ibu)**
3.   **Siti bangun jam enam. (ibu)**
4.   **Bis berhenti di depan gedung sekolah. (sopir)**
5.   **Siswa-siswa berkumpul di halaman sekolah. (pak guru)**
6.   **Rakyat bersatu ketika musuh menyerang negerinya. (pemimpin baru)**
7.   **Hubungan telepon dengan kota itu putus. (kaum pemberontak)**
8.   **Lampu menyala. (saya)**
9.   **Kampus Universitas Indonesia sudah pindah ke Depok. (pemerintah)**
10.   **Bom itu meledak di jalan. (teroris)**

4   ACTIVE AND PASSIVE

A   Focusing attention

Active voice is used to focus attention on the person who performs an action - the *actor*. The subject of the sentence refers to the actor and the verb has prefix **meN-**. Transitive verbs also have an object. This follows the verb and indicates the person or thing that undergoes the action - the *patient*. In the following sentence **mereka** is the actor and **Tomo** is the patient:

Active voice:			
subject	active verb	object	location
actor	*meN- verb*	*patient*	
Mereka	**menjemput**	**Tomo**	**di stasiun kereta api.**

Mereka menjemput Tomo di stasiun kereta api.
They met Tomo at the railway station.

In order to focus attention on the patient we can make it the subject in a *passive voice* clause. Only verbs with an object - transitive verbs - can have a passive form. Passive verbs usually have prefix **di-**. The actor is indicated in an *agent* phrase, which follows the verb and usually begins with **oleh** 'by':

Passive voice:			
subject	passive verb	agent	location
patient	*di- verb*	*by + actor*	
Tomo	**dijemput**	**oleh mereka**	**di stasiun kereta api.**

Tomo dijemput oleh mereka di stasiun kereta api.
Tomo was met by them at the railway station.

EXERCISE 1

- Translate the following sentences into English.
- Change the sentences into passive voice.
- Translate your passive constructions.

1. **Ibu saya menasihati Ann.**
2. **Mochtar Lubis menulis buku ini.**
3. **Pelayan akan membawa koper-koper itu ke kamar.**
4. **Ted menelepon Mandy setiap hari.**
5. **Dia menutup jendela.**
6. **Gladys menyambut tamu.**
7. **Halimah membuka semua hadiah.**
8. **Anak itu mengganggu mereka.**

9.   **Mereka akan mengantar kami ke bandar udara.**
10.   **Pak Iwan meletakkan barang itu di dapur.**

•   Passive forms allow us to avoid stating who performs an action; that is, no agent need occur:

Tomo dijemput di stasiun kereta api.
Tomo was met at the railway station.

> **NOTE**   Some intransitive verbs can be followed by a noun phrase. This may appear to be an object and such constructions may be translated by transitive sentences in English. The intransitive verb can be simple or a **ber-** verb:
> **Saya suka nasi goreng.** I like fried rice.
> **Mereka berbicara bahasa Jerman.** They speak German.
>
> However, simple and **ber-** verbs have no passive forms and constructions like those above are therefore not transitive. Thus the noun phrase following the verb is not an object but is called a complement.
>
> A few verbs with prefix **meN-** also have no passive form and are followed by a complement rather than an object. These include **menjadi** 'become', **merupakan** 'be, constitute' and **menyerupai** 'resemble'.

EXERCISE 2

•   Choose the correct prefix for the verb in each of the following sentences (**meN-** if active, **di-** if passive).
•   Translate the sentences into English.

Example
Daging ini ____ beli kemarin.
→   **di-**   This meat was bought yesterday.

1.   **Pekerjaan ini harus ____ selesaikan dengan segera.**
2.   **Ayahnya ____ lahirkan di Yogyakarta 40 tahun yang lalu.**
3.   **Rapat itu ____ batalkan oleh panitia karena hujan.**
4.   **Dia akan pergi ke stasiun kereta api untuk ____ jemput temannya.**
5.   **Mereka ____ tolak usul saya.**
6.   **Saya ____ suruh pergi.**
7.   **Daerah itu ____ hasilkan kayu.**
8.   **Sepedanya ____ curi tadi malam.**
9.   **Mereka masih ____ cari pekerjaan.**
10.   **Kue yang ____ masak oleh ibu selalu enak sekali.**
11.   **Perundingan itu akan ____ lanjutkan pada bulan Mei.**
12.   **Farida sudah ____ undang banyak orang ke pestanya.**

•   Verbs beginning with **m** which usually occur without prefix **meN-**, that is, **makan** 'eat', **minum** 'drink', **minta** 'request', **mohon** 'request', do take prefix **di-** in the passive: **dimakan** 'eaten', etc.

The verb **mengerti** 'understand' retains the active prefix **meN-** in the passive: **dimengerti** 'understood'.

EXERCISE 3

•   Translate the following sentences into English.
•   Change the sentences into passives.

1.   **Tuti sudah membaca surat itu.**
2.   **Mereka tidak mengerti nasihat saya.**
3.   **Utomo melempar batu itu.**
4.   **Mereka akan mendirikan partai baru.**
5.   **Semua orang di desa sudah mendengar cerita itu.**
6.   **Mereka sudah makan nasi itu.**
7.   **Siapa mecuci kemeja ini?**
8.   **Dia harus minum susu ini.**

B   Two types of passive

There are two passive constructions in Indonesian, the choice being determined by the actor. *Passive type one* is the type of passive already mentioned. This occurs when the actor is third person. Third person refers to the person being spoken about and includes pronouns **dia** and **mereka** and nouns. The agent phrase often begins with **oleh** but this can be omitted. Third person singular pronoun **dia** is usually replaced by **-nya**, although **dia** is sometimes used:

    Saya akan dijemputnya/ olehnya.
    Saya akan dijemput (oleh) dia/mereka/teman saya.
    I will be met by her/them/my friend.

Passive type two occurs when the actor is a pronoun. The agent phrase comes before the verb, which has no prefix:

Passive type two:		
subject	agent	passive verb
patient	*actor*	
Pak Ali	**saya/kamu/dia**	**jemput.**

Pak Ali saya/kamu/dia jemput.
Mr Ali was met by me/you/her.

As **dia** and **mereka** are both third person and pronouns, either passive type can be used if they are the agent:

Buku ini belum dia baca. *or* **Buku ini belum dibacanya.**
She hasn't read this book yet.
Buku ini belum mereka baca. *or* **Buku ini belum dibaca (oleh) mereka.**
They haven't read this book yet.

In passive type two nothing can come between the agent and the verb. Negatives, temporal markers (such as **akan** 'will') and modals (such as **dapat** 'can') come before the agent phrase:

Buku ini <u>tidak akan saya baca</u>.
I will not read this book.

> **NOTE**   Passive constructions are used more frequently in Indonesian than in English. Often a passive is the natural construction in Indonesian where a passive translation into English will sound very artificial or clumsy. Indonesian passives should be translated by actives in English where this is the only way to produce a natural English construction. For instance, **Buku ini tidak akan saya baca** is perfectly natural in many contexts in Indonesian, whereas 'This book will not be read by me' is awkward in English.

EXERCISE 4

- Change the following active sentences into passives, choosing the correct passive type (passive type one or passive type two).
- If two passives are possible give both.
- Translate your sentences into English, using an active construction wherever a passive would be clumsy in English.

1.   **Pembantu sudah membersihkan kamar saya.**
2.   **Apa mereka sudah menyelesaikan pekerjaannya?**
3.   **Saya harus memikirkan hal ini.**
4.   **Mengapa Pak Basuki memanggil mereka?**
5.   **Di mana Anda membeli tas ini?**
6.   **Kamu tidak boleh mengambil barang ini.**
7.   **Dia meninggalkan tasnya di mobil.**
8.   **Kita akan mengantar Tomo ke dokter.**
9.   **Pemerintah akan menaikkan harga beras.**
10. **Anak itu memilih kartu yang indah untuk ibunya.**
11. **Saya sudah melihat film itu.**
12. **Mereka mau mengirim surat itu hari ini.**

> **NOTE** Personal names and some common kin terms can be used like pronouns, meaning 'you' or 'I'. In this case they act like first and second person pronouns and so take passive type two:
>
> **Apakah buku ini sudah Bapak/Tomo baca?**
> Have you read this book? (Speaking to an older man or someone named Tomo.)
> **Ibu mau pergi sekarang.**
> I'm going now. (Said by an older woman.)

EXERCISE 5

- Translate the following passive sentences into Indonesian.
- Use verbs built on the bases given in parentheses.

Example
This parcel will be sent to Mr Hasan tomorrow. (**kirim**)
→   **Paket ini akan dikirim kepada Pak Hasan besok.**

1.   I wasn't invited to Farida's party. (**undang**)
2.   Is this room cleaned every day? (**bersih**)
3.   His money was stolen from his room. (**curi**)
4.   The table has been moved to another room. (**pindah**)
5.   Her children were forbidden to leave the house. (**larang**)
6.   These books must be returned to the library. (**kembali**)
7.   Goods like that can be bought in any market. (**beli**)
8.   He was chosen as the party leader (**pilih**)
9.   This problem was discussed last week. (**bicara**)
10.   The meeting was attended by many people. (**hadir**)

EXERCISE 6

- Translate each sentence into Indonesian.
- choose the correct form of the verb given in parentheses, which will be either an intransitive verb or a passive transitive verb.

Example
The demonstrators dispersed (**bubar**)
→   **Para demonstran bubar.**

The demonstrators were dispersed (**bubar**) near the palace.
→   **Para demonstran dibubarkan dekat istana.**

1.   The fertiliser was used (**guna**) in the rice fields.
2.   Why has he moved (**pindah**) to Cairns?
3.   Why isn't tourism being developed (**kembang**) in that country?

4.   Why was the painting moved (**pindah**) from the living room?
5.   The price of petrol was increased (**naik**) last month.
6.   The refugees flew to Pontianak by Cessna. (**terbang**)
7.   The fertiliser was useful for the farmers. (**guna**)
8.   The price of petrol increased (**naik**) last month.
9.   The refugees were flown (**terbang**) to Pontianak by Cessna.
10.   The economy of that country is developing (**kembang**) very fast.

C   Passives of ditransitive verbs

Some transitive verbs can be followed by two nouns. These are called *ditransitive verbs*. They can be either benefactive verbs with suffix **-kan** [see section 6H] or verbs with suffix **-i** [see section 6D]:

Pelayan mengambilkan tamu segelas air.
The waiter fetched the customer a glass of water.
Dosen menyerahi saya tugas ini.
The lecturer gave me this task.

Users should study the sections on ditransitive verbs before continuing with this section.

The first noun after the verb is called the *primary object* and the second noun is called the *secondary object*:

subject	active verb	primary object	secondary object
Pelayan	**mengambilkan**	**tamu**	**segelas air.**
subject	active verb	primary object	secondary object
Dosen	**menyerahi**	**saya**	**tugas ini.**

When such a construction is changed to a passive it is always the first noun after the verb, the primary object, which becomes the subject. The secondary object remains after the verb:

subject	passive verb	agent	secondary object
Tamu	**diambilkan**	**pelayan**	**segelas air.**
subject	passive verb	agent	secondary object
Saya	**diserahi**	**dosen**	**tugas ini.**

Tamu diambilkan pelayan segelas air.
The customer was fetched a glass of water by the waiter.
Saya diserahi dosen tugas ini.
I was given this task by the lecturer.

If the passive is type one the agent (if it occurs) can precede or follow the secondary object. If it follows it must occur with **oleh** 'by':

Saya diserahi tugas ini oleh dosen.
Saya diserahi dosen tugas ini.
I was given this task by the lecturer.

subject	passive verb	agent	secondary object
Saya	**diserahi**	**dosen**	**tugas ini.**

subject	passive verb	secondary object	agent
Saya	**diserahi**	**tugas ini**	**oleh dosen.**

EXERCISE 7

- Translate the following active sentences into English.
- Give the passive equivalent (in Indonesian) of each sentence.
- If two passives are possible give both.

1. **Setiap malam saya membacakan anak saya cerita.**
2. **Dia menamai anaknya Utomo.**
3. **Saya tidak meminjami mereka barang berharga.**
4. **Siapa yang akan memanggilkan saya taksi?**
5. **Sekretaris mengirimi dia surat kemarin.**
6. **Saya akan membuatkan Anda kopi.**
7. **Kami memilihkan Ratna payung untuk perjalanannya.**
8. **Ayah saya akan membayarkan kita ongkos taksi ke sana.**
9. **Supardi memberi Irawati cincin emas.**
10. **Mereka belum menawari kami pekerjaan.**

5   INTRANSITIVE VERBS

Intransitive verbs can be simple, consisting of just the base without any affixes, such as **tidur** 'sleep', or have prefix **ber-**, such as **berjalan** 'walk', or **meN-** such as **menangis** 'cry'.

Verbs with prefix **ber-** or **meN-** can have a verbal base. That is, the base never occurs alone as another word class. They can also have noun bases (that is, the base can occur alone as a noun), such as **berduri** 'thorny' and **mendarat** 'to land'. Some **meN-** verbs also have adjective bases, such as **mengering** 'dry out, become dry'.

If the base is verbal it is not possible to predict whether it will be simple or have prefix **ber-** or **meN-**. Verbs with similar meanings or denoting similar activities may have different affixation, such as **duduk** 'sit' and **berbaring** 'lie'. Sometimes there can be a choice of affixation, although usually one form is more frequent than the other, such as **bernyanyi** and **menyanyi** 'sing', **tumbuh** and **bertumbuh** 'grow'. Note that a verb will have different affixation depending on whether it is transitive or intransitive. Thus **berputar** 'turn, rotate' is intransitive: **roda berputar** 'the wheel turns', while **memutar** 'turn, rotate' is transitive: **memutar roda** 'turn the wheel'.

EXERCISE 1

Below are a number of verb bases.
- Give the correct form of the verb (simple, **ber-** or **meN-**) with its translation.
- If two forms are possible give both.
- Note: If you do not know the words you will need to use a good dictionary. Be sure to identify intransitive meanings of verbs.

1.	**tenggelam**	7.	**batuk**
2.	**lupa**	8.	**pekik**
3.	**ledak**	9.	**jemur**
4.	**doa**	10.	**menang**
5.	**didih**	11.	**ludah**
6.	**diri**	12.	**serah**

- Most verbs with prefix **ber-** have verb bases, such as **berhenti** 'stop', **berenang** 'swim'. There are also **ber-** verbs based on nouns.

The general meaning of such verbs is 'have what the base indicates'. Thus **bernama** 'be named' literally means 'have the name':

Dia bernama John.
He is named John/His name is John.

As in the above example, the literal meaning in Indonesian sometimes does not translate well into English. As another example, **berisi** literally means 'have contents' (**isi** 'contents') but is translated into natural English as 'contains':
Gelas ini berisi air jeruk.
This glass contains orange juice.

EXERCISE 2

The subject in each of the following sentences is a noun, which is underlined.
- Rewrite each sentence so that the subject becomes the base of a **ber-** verb.
- Translate your sentences into natural English.

Example
Warna mobil itu merah.
→   **Mobil itu berwarna merah.**
That car is (coloured) red.

1.   **Rambut gadis itu panjang.**
2.   **Isi koper itu pakaian.**
3.   **Agama mereka Islam.**
4.   **Halaman rumah ini luas.**
5.   **Anak Pak Usman lima orang.**
6.   **Asal Pak Pradeep dari India.**
7.   **Lantai gedung itu sembilan.**
8.   **Bau ikan ini busuk.**

- If the base refers to an article of clothing the verb usually means 'wear what the base refers to': **bertopi** 'wear a hat'. Some other verbs are best translated 'ride, travel by what the base indicates': **bersepeda** 'ride a bike'. Other **ber-** verbs have other translations, depending on the sort of activity they refer to.

EXERCISE 3

- Change the following sentences so that the underlined word is replaced by a **ber-** verb.
- Translate your sentences into natural English.

Example

Dia memakai <u>kemeja</u> batik.

→   **Dia berkemeja batik.**

He's wearing a batik shirt.

1.   **Aminah naik <u>sepeda</u> ke sekolah.**
2.   **Apa dia sudah punya <u>keluarga</u>?**
3.   **Mereka berbicara <u>bahasa Indonesia</u> dengan lancar.**
4.   **<u>Umur</u> Arif 20 tahun.**
5.   **Buku ini tidak ada <u>guna</u>nya.**
6.   **Usahanya tidak membawa <u>hasil</u>.**
7.   **Orang kaya itu punya dua <u>rumah</u>.**
8.   **Tetangga saya selalu memakai <u>topi</u> kalau keluar rumah.**

6   VERBAL SUFFIXES -*KAN* AND -*I*

Transitive verbs have prefix **meN-** in active voice. Many transitive verbs have no other affixes, such as **membuka** 'open' and **menolong** 'help'. These can be called *simple transitive verbs*. There are also transitive verbs which take suffix **-i** or suffix **-kan**. The main functions of these suffixes are considered in the following sections.

A   Verbs with suffix -*kan* based on adjectives

Some **-kan** verbs are based on adjectives. These usually have a causative meaning; the object is caused to have the characteristic indicated by the adjective base. Thus **bersih** 'clean' : **membersihkan** 'to clean, i.e. cause something to be clean, make something clean':

Kamar ini sudah <u>bersih</u>.
This room is clean.
Siti sudah <u>membersihkan</u> kamar ini.
Siti has cleaned this room.

EXERCISE 1

Below are a number of adjectives in sentences.
- Translate the sentences.
- For each sentence compose another sentence containing the **-kan** verb corresponding to the adjective.
- Use the word in parentheses as the subject of the transitive sentence.
- Translate your sentences.

     Example (**jelas** 'clear' : **menjelaskan** 'make clear, i.e. explain')
     Maksudnya jelas. (guru)
→   His purpose is clear.
     Guru menjelaskan maksudnya.
     The teacher explained her purpose.

    1.   **Dia bebas dari penjara. (gubernur)**
    2.   **Daerah itu aman. (tentara)**
    3.   **Air ini sudah panas. (ibu)**
    4.   **Lampu ini harus mati sebelum kita tidur. (kita)**
    5.   **Kalimat ini betul. (guru)**
    6.   **Pekerjaan saya ringan. (bantuannya)**
    7.   **Ibunya marah. (anak nakal itu)**
    8.   **Dasinya lurus. (Pak Yusuf)**

• There is a group of -kan verbs based on adjectives which, while transitive, often occur without an object being expressed. These verbs are based on adjectives which refer to emotions and attitudes and they indicate that the subject causes the object to experience the emotion or attitude expressed by the base. When the object is understood as applying to everyone in general it is typically omitted, as with **membosankan** 'cause (object) to be bored':

Film itu membosankan.
That film is boring.

These verbs can act like ordinary transitive verbs, taking an object if one needs to be expressed. Alternatively they can be followed by a phrase beginning with **bagi** 'for'. Note the different translations for the following examples:

Film itu membosankan saya.
That film bored me.
Film itu membosankan bagi anak kecil.
That film is boring for young children.

As in the above examples, when these verbs have no object or are followed by a phrase with **bagi** they are translated by an adjective; when they have an object they are translated by a verb.

EXERCISE 2

• Translate the following sentences.
• From the adjective in each sentence form a -kan verb.
• Omit any word from the original sentence where necessary, as in the example.
• Translate your sentences.

Example
Apa Anda bingung membaca laporan itu?
→   Are you confused reading that report?
     Ya, laporan itu membingungkan.
     Yes, that report is confusing.

1.   **Apa tamu-tamu puas dengan pelayanan di restoran ini?**
2.   **Apa Tommy sedih karena kematian kucingnya?**
3.   **Apa mereka takut menonton film itu?**
4.   **Apa Ibu Sulastri khawatir dengan penyakit suaminya?**
5.   **Apa Henny kecewa dengan hasil ujiannya?**
6.   **Apa ibu gembira mendengar kabar itu?**
7.   **Apa kamu senang menerima kabar itu?**
8.   **Apa mereka kaget mendengar jawaban itu?**

> **NOTE** The verbs based on emotive adjectives act like adjectives in a number of ways. For instance, they commonly occur with modifiers like **sangat** and **sekali** 'very':
> **Kabar itu sangat menyedihkan.** That news was very saddening.

B Verbs with suffixes *-kan* and *-i* based on nouns

Some transitive verbs are based on nouns. With suffix **-kan** there are several functions. If the base indicates a location the verb means 'put the object in/take the object to the place indicated by the base'. Thus **makam** 'grave' : **memakamkan** 'bury/put in a grave'. Some verbs mean 'cause the object to be/treat the object as/give the object as what is indicated by the base'. Thus **calon** 'candidate' : **mencalonkan** 'nominate (i. e. cause to be a candidate)'.

Many **-i** verbs are also based on nouns. The largest group of these mean 'apply/give what is indicated in the base to the object'. Thus **minyak** 'oil' : **meminyaki** 'to oil (apply oil to)'. Another group mean 'act as/be what the base indicates'. Thus **bintang** 'star' : **membintangi** 'to star in (a movie)'.

> **NOTE** If the base ends in **i** the suffix **-i** merges with it: **memberi** + **-i** → **memberi**, **membenci** + **-i** → **membenci**.

EXERCISE 3

- Add the appropriate suffix to the verb in each of the following sentences.
- Translate the sentences.
- State the meaning of the noun that the verb is based on.

Example
Geoffrey Rush membintangi *Shine*.
→ Geoffrey Rush starred in *Shine*.
The verb **membintangi** 'to star in' is based on **bintang** 'star'.

1. **Mereka menyekolah____ anaknya di Rawamangun.**
2. **Pak Rahman mengetua____ rapat itu.**
3. **Semua mahasiswa baru harus mendaftar____ nama di sini.**
4. **Perjanjian antara kedua universitas itu ditandatangan____ oleh kedua rektor.**
5. **Kompetisi itu disponsor___ oleh Toyota.**
6. **Dokter mengobat____ lukanya dengan antibiotika.**
7. **Orang Toraja mengorban____ banyak kerbau setiap tahun.**
8. **Wartawan itu ingin mewawancara____ menteri.**
9. **Kota diselimut____ asap hitam dari pabrik itu.**

10.   **Para remaja mendewa____ penyanyi baru.**
11.   **Pengacara yang cerdik menyudut____ saksi.**
12.   **Polisi masih belum tahu siapa yang mendalang____ perampokan
      itu.**
13.   **Bom itu meluka____ sepuluh orang.**
14.   **Polisi merahasia____ nama informannya.**
15.   **Grup itu akan mementas____ sandiwara baru bulan depan.**

NOTE   Some verbs with noun bases meaning 'use the base on the object/apply the
base to the object' do not have suffix **-i**. These are often based on nouns referring to
common implements. Thus, from **sapu** 'broom' is the verb **menyapu** (**lantai**) 'sweep
(the floor)'.

EXERCISE 4

- Translate the following sentences into Indonesian.
- Use a verb with the appropriate suffix, based on the noun in parentheses.
- Note: Some verbs are active and others are passive.

Example
He poisoned his wife with cyanide. (**racun**)
→   **Dia meracuni istrinya dengan sianida.**

1.   She is always advised by her parents. (**nasihat**)
2.   Mr Ali represented Indonesia in the discussions. (**wakil**)
3.   He proved that he was not guilty. (**bukti**)
4.   The athletes made the Atlanta Olympics a success. (**sukses**)
5   Ola heads the office in Semarang. (**kepala**)
6.   The farmers market their vegetables in town. (**pasar**)
7.   The thief was jailed for five years. (**penjara**)
8.   The beaches in Bali were flooded with foreign tourists. (**banjir**)
9.   His yard is fenced with bamboo. (**pagar**)
10. Bung Karno inspired the Indonesian people during the revolutionary
     period. (**ilham**)

C   Verbs with *-kan* and *-i* based on intransitive verbs

Many **-kan** verbs based on intransitive verbs are causative [as also discussed in
section 3C]. They indicate that the object is caused to perform the action
described by the corresponding intransitive verb. Thus **bangun** 'wake up' :
membangunkan 'wake (someone) up, i.e. cause someone to wake up':
   Siti bangun. Siti woke up.
   Ibu membangunkan Siti. Mother woke Siti up.

Many **-i** verbs are based on intransitive verbs. The meaning is often the same as or similar to that of the intransitive verb except that the intransitive verb can be followed by a prepositional phrase indicating location while the transitive verb has an object indicating location [as also discussed in section 3B]. Thus **hadir** 'be present' is an intransitive verb which can end a sentence or be followed by a phrase indicating the location, while **menghadiri** 'attend' is a transitive verb which requires an object:

Mereka <u>hadir</u> (di rapat itu). They were present (at the meeting).

Mereka <u>menghadiri</u> rapat itu. They attended the meeting.

With these verbs the suffix **-kan** indicates that the object is caused to perform the action of the base. The suffix **-i** indicates that the object is the place where the action occurs. Sometimes both suffixes can occur with the same base, although they will have different objects. Thus from **masuk** (**ke dalam**) 'enter (into)' can be formed both **memasuki** and **memasukkan**:

Dia memasuki kamar. (cf. **Dia masuk** (**ke dalam kamar**)).

He went into the room.

Dia memasukkan mobil ke dalam garasi.

He put the car in the garage.

NOTE   If an intransitive verb has several meanings the transitive verb based on it may also have the same range of meanings. Thus:

i. **naik**   go up
    menaikkan   raise
    Harga naik : **Pemerintah menaikkan harga.**
    Prices rose : The government raised prices.

ii. **naik**   get aboard (also, travel by: **naik bis** travel on the bus)
    menaikkan   put aboard
    Orang sakit naik pesawat : **Orang sakit dinaikkan ke pesawat.**
    The sick person got on the plane : The sick person was put aboard the
                                                        plane.

EXERCISE 5

* Add the correct suffix (**-kan** or **-i**) to the verb in each of the following sentences.
* Give the intransitive verb on which each transitive verb is based.
* Translate the sentences.

Example

Ibu membangun____ Siti.

→   **Ibu membangunkan Siti.** (based on **bangun** wake up)
     Mother woke Siti up.

1. **Ari menaik____ bis ke kota.**
2. **Toni menjatuh____ batu dari atap.**
3. **Pengimpor itu mendatang____ barang dari Cina.**
4. **Orang sakit diturun____ dari bis.**
5. **Siti menduduk____ kursi ini.**
6. **Saya selalu menjauh____ anak saya dari anjing itu.**
7. **Polisi mendatang____ rumah perjudian.**
8. **Anak itu pandai melompat____ pagar tinggi.**
9. **Ayah memisah____ anak yang berkelahi.**
10. **Pencuri itu dijatuh____ hukuman lima tahun.**
11. **Tuan rumah menduduk____ tamunya di ruang tamu.**
12. **Mereka masih mendiam____ rumah ini.**
13. **Saya selalu menjauh____ anjing itu.**
14. **Susanto memulang____ jenazah ayahnya ke kampung.**

D Transitive verbs not based on intransitive verbs

Many **-kan** and **-i** verbs are not based on intransitive verbs, nor on adjectives or nouns. There is almost always a difference in meaning between the two suffixes with the same base, although a verb is often translated the same way into English, whichever suffix it has. There are two groups of these verbs.

• Suffix **-kan** marks the object as the *patient*, the participant handled or manipulated in some way. With **-i** the object is the *recipient*, the person at or to whom the action is directed.

In the following example the base **tawar** 'offer' occurs with **-kan**, as **menawarkan** 'offer (something)', and the object **makanan** 'food' (which has the role of patient). It occurs with **-i**, as **menawari** 'offer (someone something)', and the object **tamu** 'guest' (which has the role of recipient):

Ibu menawarkan makanan kepada tamu.
Mother offered food to the guest.
Ibu menawari tamu makanan.
Mother offered the guest food.

As in the example above, if the object identifies the patient then the recipient is identified in a phrase beginning with **kepada**. If the object identifies the recipient the verb is *ditransitive*. The first noun after the verb is called the *primary object* and the second noun is called the *secondary object*. The primary object identifies the recipient and the secondary object identifies the patient:

subject	active verb	primary object	secondary object
actor		*recipient*	*patient*
Ibu	**menawari**	**tamu**	**makanan.**
Mother	offered	the guest	food.

EXERCISE 6

- Add the correct suffix to the verb in each of the following sentences.
- Translate the sentences into English.

Example

Siapa mengirim____ surat itu kepada kamu?

→   **mengirimkan** - Who sent that letter to you?

1.   **Saya tidak mau meminjam____ nya mobil saya.**
2.   **Tolong beri____ buku ini kepadanya.**
3.   **Jangan menyerah____ saya tugas yang berat!**
4.   **Siapa yang mengirim____mu foto-foto ini?**
5.   **Pak Sutrisno selalu menyerah____ tugas yang berat kepada orang lain.**
6.   **Kepala sekolah menghadiah____ kamus bahasa Inggris kepada siswa yang paling pandai.**
7.   **Pers Inggris menjuluk____ Margaret Thatcher 'Wanita Besi'.**
8.   **Mengapa Anda mau memberi____nya buku ini?**
9.   **Minah, suguh____ tamu kopi!**
10. **Saya tidak mau meminjam____ mobil saya kepadanya.**
11. **Bank menyodor____ kontrak baru kepada nasabahnya.**
12. **Kepala sekolah menghadiah____ siswa itu kamus bahasa Inggris.**

EXERCISE 7

- Translate the following sentences.
- Restructure the sentences by placing the underlined word or phrase directly after the verb.
- Change the form of the verb and make any other necessary changes.
- Translate your sentences.

Example

Maaf, saya tidak dapat meminjami Anda <u>buku ini.</u>

→   Sorry, I can't lend you this book.

   Maaf, saya tidak dapat meminjamkan buku ini kepada Anda.

   Sorry, I can't lend this book to you.

1.   **Hakim menjatuhkan hukuman berat kepada <u>penjahat.</u>**

2.   **Kapan dia menawarkan bantuan itu kepada <u>kamu</u>?**
3.   **Warung ini menyuguhkan kopi manis kepada <u>tamunya</u>.**
4.   **Ia menyodori tamunya <u>kopi dan biskuit</u>.**
5.   **Tuhan menganugerahi suami-istri itu <u>seorang anak</u>.**
6.   **Dia menitipi Ibu Suparno <u>anaknya</u>.**

• Many verbs which take both **-kan** and **-i** do not occur in ditransitive constructions. If the verb has **-i** the object refers to the recipient or the location of the action. The patient, if it is expressed, is preceded by **dengan**. The verb **tanam** is translated as 'to plant' in both the following sentences, although it has a patient object with **-kan** and location object with **-i**:

Petani menanamkan padi di sawahnya.
The farmer planted rice in his field.
Petani menanami sawahnya dengan padi.
The farmer planted his field with rice.

> **NOTE**   For some Indonesian ditransitive verbs with **-i** a word-for-word translation into English is clumsy and a paraphrase is preferable, because the corresponding verb in English won't allow a recipient object. Thus it would be awkward to translate the following sentence while retaining 'letter' as the object of **melampiri** 'attach, enclose':
>   **Ayah melampiri surat dengan kwitansi.**
>
> The least awkward way of translating this is to make 'receipt' the object in English, thus translating the sentence in the same way as:
>   **Ayah melampirkan kwitansi dalam surat.** Father enclosed a receipt in the letter.
>
> Sometimes different translations allow us to retain the Indonesian structure. Thus, while **menghujankan** can be translated 'to rain', **menghujani** can only be translated 'to shower':
>   **Mereka menghujankan bom ke atas kota itu.** They rained bombs on that city.
>   **Mereka menghujani kota itu dengan bom.** They showered that city with bombs.

EXERCISE 8

• Add the correct suffix to the verb in each of the following sentences.
• Translate the sentences into English.

1.   **Jalan baru ini akan menghubung____ kota dengan pelabuhan.**
2.   **Buruh memuat____ beras ke atas truk.**
3.   **Petani ini menyemprot____ pestisida dua kali seminggu.**
4.   **Gadis-gadis itu menabur____ bunga di sepanjang jalan.**
5.   **Para demonstran mencoba menghindar____ polisi.**
6.   **Buruh memuat____ truk itu dengan beras.**
7.   **Dia selalu menabur____ makanannya dengan garam.**
8.   **Dia melumur____ badannya dengan minyak.**

9. **Petani ini menyemprot____ sayur-sayurannya dua kali seminggu.**
10. **Dia berhasil menghindar____ anak-anaknya dari bahaya.**
11. **Saya akan menghubung____ mereka besok.**
12. **Dia melumur____ minyak pada badannya.**

NOTE   The expression *salah kaprah* means something is grammatically incorrect but is widely accepted as correct. For instance, many people use **memberikan** with a recipient object. Purists regard this as especially unacceptable in the passive, as in: ***Dia diberikan informasi** 'He was given information'. You should use **diberi** here, as it is acceptable to everyone: **Dia diberi informasi.** (The form **memberi/diberi** is actually the '-i form', with -i lost after the final i of the base.)

Other common *salah kaprah* verbs which are frequently used with **-kan** if there is a recipient object are **mengenakan** 'impose on, subject to' and **menugaskan** 'assign':
   Dia dikenakan denda. Preferable: **Dia dikenai denda.**
   He was fined (literally: subjected to a fine).
   (cf. **Denda dikenakan padanya.** 'A fine was imposed on him.'

   Dia ditugaskan menjaga rumah. Preferable: **Dia ditugasi menjaga rumah.**
   He was assigned to guard the housed.

A few **-i** and **-kan** verbs with the same base do have the same meaning, acceptable to all. Among the most common are **menamai**, **menamakan** 'name' and **mengingini**, **menginginkan** 'desire'.

EXERCISE 9

Below are a number of verbs with two possible objects.
* Give each verb in a short sentence with each of the objects in turn.
* Choose the verbal suffix appropriate for each object.
* Use a subject of your own choice.
* Note: With some **-i** verbs a word-for-word translation is clumsy in English, in which case the two sentences can be translated identically, as in the example. Alternatively, different verbs in English may allow both sentences to be translated word-for-word.

Example
melampir____ (surat, kwitansi)
→   **Dia melampirkan kwitansi dalam surat.**
     Dia melampiri surat dengan kwitansi.
     (both:) He enclosed a receipt in the letter.

1. **menuang____ (cangkir, kopi)**
2. **menetes____ (mata, obat)**
3. **menyiram____ (bunga, air)**

4.   **menyorot_____** (lampu santer, gang)
5.   **membeban_____** (saya, banyak tugas baru)
6.   **menanam_____** (lereng ini, pohon mangga)
7.   **mengoles_____** (luka, salep)

E   Optional -*kan* and -*i*

With most verbs with which they occur, as discussed in sections A to D above, **-kan** and **-i** cannot be omitted (at least without changing the meaning). However, there are some verbs with which they occur optionally. With these verbs the meaning is the same whether or not the suffix occurs.

One example is **mengirim/mengirimkan**, both forms meaning 'send (something)':
Saya mengirim uang kepadanya.
Saya mengirimkan uang kepadanya.
I sent money to him.

Likewise, both **menghias** and **menghiasi** mean 'decorate':
Kamarnya dihias dengan foto-foto bintang film.
Kamarnya dihiasi dengan foto-foto bintang film.
Her room is decorated with photos of film stars.

When the suffix is optional it can be indicated in parentheses: **mengirim(kan)**, **menghias(i)**. (In previous exercises on suffixes **-kan** and **-i** they have been treated as if they are obligatory on every verb with which they occur.)

EXERCISE 10

- Translate each sentence into Indonesian, using the base in parentheses for the verb.
- Choose the correct suffix for the verb.
- Place the suffix in parentheses if it is optional.
- Note: You will need to use a good dictionary for this exercise.

Example:
She decorated her room with photos of film stars. (**hias**)
→   **Dia menghias(i) kamarnya dengan foto-foto bintang film.**

He cleans his room every week. (**bersih**)
→   **Dia membersihkan kamarnya setiap minggu.**

1.   Mr Warouw planted this tree three years ago. (**tanam**)
2.   He sprays these flowers every day. (**siram**)
3.   We will have to discuss this matter tomorrow. (**bicara**)

4.   He didn't want to give his school report to his father. (**beri**)
5.   We will contribute one hundred dollars to the victims of the flood.
      (**sumbang**)
6.   Mr Ahmed was arrested for poisoning his wife. (**racun**)
7.   I write to my mother every week. (**surat**)
8.   People entering this library must leave their bags at the counter.
      (**titip**)
9.   I lent my pen to Titik two weeks ago. (**pinjam**)
10.   I don't want to cross this road because the traffic is too heavy.
      (**seberang**)
11.   The host served the guests after they sat down. (**layan**)
12.   You will have to repeat this exercise. (**ulang**)
13.   The flood last month damaged many villages. (**rusak**)
14.   The police followed the thief to his house. (**ikut**)
15.   This radio station often broadcasts Indonesian music. (**siar**)
16.   I'm going to accompany Sally to her house. (**antar**)

NOTE   No general rules can be given for how frequently an optional suffix is likely to occur. A suffix may be very infrequent with one verb but be rarely omitted with another verb. Usage may vary between Indonesians of different regional background. Moreover, for some verbs people differ as to whether they regard a suffix as optional or obligatory. Thus some people allow **mengirim dia surat** 'send him a letter', while others treat the suffix **-i** as obligatory and only allow **mengirimi dia surat**.

Learners need to be aware that, as with many aspects of Indonesian grammar, there are no hard and fast rules which cover all cases. They should not be surprised to find there are Indonesians who disagree with some of the decisions given here on whether a suffix is optional or obligatory with a particular verb base.

With a few verbs the optionality of a suffix differs between active and passive forms. Thus **-kan** is optional in active **memberi(kan)** 'give (something)' but obligatory in passive **diberikan** 'given':
   Ibu memberi/memberikan koran kepada ayah.
   Mother gave the newspaper to father.
   Koran diberikan kepada ayah. The newspaper was given to father.

Another verb like this is active **mengajar(kan)** 'teach (something)' but passive **mengajarkan** 'taught':
   Mereka mengajar/mengajarkan bahasa Jepang. They teach Japanese.
   Bahasa Jepang diajarkan di sekolah itu. Japanese is taught at that school.

F   Suffix -*kan* indicating an instrument

Some simple transitive verbs, which do not have a suffix, can indicate an action performed with an instrument which, if it occurs, is expressed in a phrase beginning with **dengan**:

> **Dia mengikat anjing dengan tali.**
> He tied the dog with a rope.

Many of these verbs can also take suffix **-kan** to indicate that the object is the instrument. The object of the verb without **-kan** must now be expressed by a locative phrase:

> **Dia mengikatkan tali ke anjing.**
> He tied a rope to the dog.

Frequently there is no direct translation into English of **-kan** instrumental forms and they must be expressed in another way, as in the following example:

> **Dia memukul anjing dengan tongkat.**
> He hit the dog with a stick.
> **Dia memukulkan tongkat pada anjing.**
> He used the stick to hit the dog with/He hit the dog with a stick.

NOTE   While the two sentences are sometimes best translated into English in the same way they have different focuses, just as active and passive sentences do. Thus in the above example **memukul anjing** tells what he did to the dog, while **memukulkan tongkat** tells what he did with the stick. In the first sentence **dengan tongkat** can be omitted. In the second sentence pada anjing can be omitted if it is clear from context or not specifically important information.

Although **-kan** verbs in this group usually have an object which can be regarded as an instrument, this is not always the case. Thus **kaki** 'foot' cannot be regarded as an instrument with which to **menginjak rumput** 'step on the grass' in **Dia menginjakkan kakinya di atas rumput** 'He set his foot on the grass'.

EXERCISE 11

In the following exercise are a number of sentences with simple transitive
    verbs and an instrument indicated in a prepositional phrase. In each case:

- Translate the sentence.
- Add **-kan** to the verb to make it an instrumental verb.
- Rearrange the sentence as necessary.
- Translate the new sentence, using paraphrase where necessary.

Example

Perawat membalut luka pasien dengan kain.

→   The nurse bound the patient's wound with a cloth.
    Perawat membalutkan kain ke luka pasien.
    The nurse bound a cloth on the patient's wound.

1.   **Dul menikam tangan musuhnya dengan pisau.**
2.   **Tomo menutup mukanya dengan topinya.**
3.   **Burung elang mencengkeram ikan dengan cakarnya.**
4.   **Dia menggosok kulitnya dengan sabun.**
5.   **Dia mengetok meja dengan sendoknya.**
6.   **Amie menggaruk kepalanya dengan pensil.**
7.   **Dia mengiris roti dengan pisau panjang.**
8.   **Pembantu menyeka meja dengan lap yang kotor.**
9.   **Perajin memotong kayu itu dengan parangnya.**
10.   **Dokter menyuntik paha pasien dengan obat baru.**

G   Causative verbs based on transitive verbs

Some **-kan** verbs are based on simple transitive verbs and have in general a causative meaning, as in the following example. Simple transitive verbs are transitive verbs without any affix other than **meN-** (or **di-** in the passive), such as **meminjam**.

> **Ali meminjam buku saya.**
> Ali borrowed my book.
> **Saya meminjamkan buku saya kepada Ali.**
> I lent my book to Ali.

In both sentences Ali is the one who borrows my book. In the second sentence I am the one whose action results in Ali borrowing the book; I am the one who causes the action. Very often word-for-word translations of such sentences are not possible, although in the above example the occurrence of two different words in English ('borrow' and 'lend') makes it simpler. Often a paraphrase is necessary in English, stating 'Subject has something done (by someone)', as in the following example:

> **Dokter Utomo memeriksa mata saya.**
> Dr Utomo examined my eyes.
> **Saya memeriksakan mata pada/ke dokter Utomo.**
> I had my eyes checked by Dr Utomo.

In the second sentence above I 'cause' the doctor to check my eyes; that is, I get him to perform the action. The sentence could alternatively be translated: 'I got the doctor to check my eyes'. The one who does the action is indicated in a phrase beginning with **ke** or **pada**.

NOTE   Some verbs in this group can also occur as benefactive verbs [see section 6H], depending on the context. Thus:

> **Saya mencucikan jas ke wanita itu.** (Causative)
> I had my jacket washed by that woman.
> **Wanita itu mencucikan saya jas.** (Benefactive)
> That woman washed my jacket for me.

EXERCISE 12

In each of the sentences below there is a simple transitive verb and a possessor within the object. In each case:

- Translate the sentence.
- Make a sentence with a **-kan** verb, following the model of the example.
- Translate your sentence, using a word-for-word translation if possible (using a different verb), otherwise using a paraphrase.

Example

Wanita itu mencuci pakaian saya.

$\rightarrow$ That woman washes my clothes.

Saya mencucikan pakaian pada wanita itu.

I have my clothes washed by that woman.

1.   **Tukang jahit itu menjahit kemeja saya.**
2.   **Bengkel ini mereparasi mobil saya.**
3.   **Percetakan baru itu mencetak kartu undangan saya.**
4.   **Keluarga ini menyewa rumah saya.**
5.   **Penggiling itu menimbang beras para petani.**
6.   **Siapa memeriksa matamu?**
7.   **Pelelang itu akan melelang rumah saya besok.**
8.   **Dokter itu mengoperasi mata Ibu Yusup.**

> **NOTE**   The person who carries out the action indicated by the verb is often not mentioned:
> **Saya harus mereparasikan atap rumah.** I must get my roof fixed.
> **Di mana saya dapat mencucikan pakaian ini?** Where can I have these clothes washed?

H Benefactive verbs with *-kan*

Many transitive verbs which have no suffix can add **-kan** to indicate that the object is the person for whose benefit the action is performed, called the *beneficiary*. The patient is then indicated by the secondary object. One of the verbs which can function like this is **mengambil** 'get, fetch':

Pelayan mengambil segelas air.

The waiter got a glass of water.

Pelayan mengambilkan Edi segelas air.

The waiter got Edi a glass of water.

subject	benefactive verb	object	secondary object
actor		*beneficiary*	*patient*
Pelayan	**mengambilkan**	**Edi**	**segelas air.**

Many benefactive verbs have counterparts in English which also allow a benefactive object, as in the above example. Sometimes, however, the corresponding English verb requires the beneficiary to be expressed by a phrase beginning with 'for'. For instance, in English it is not possible to say 'carry me the case' whereas in Indonesian it is possible to say **membawakan saya koper**:

Sopir membawakan saya koper yang berat.
The driver carried the heavy suitcase for me.

> **NOTE**   The verb **menuliskan** is a benefactive verb meaning 'write for':
> **Dia menuliskan ayahnya surat.** He wrote a letter *for* his father.
>
> The sentence 'He wrote his father a letter', meaning 'He wrote a letter *to* his father' has to be expressed: **Dia menulis surat kepada ayahnya.**

The object can be omitted; the suffix still indicates that the action is done for someone else's benefit, although it is not indicated who this is (context usually makes it clear):

Pelayan mengambilkan segelas air.
The waiter got (someone) a glass of water.

Benefactives can always be replaced by constructions in which the beneficiary is expressed by an **untuk** phrase:

Pelayan mengambil segelas air untuk Edi.
The waiter got a glass of water for Edi.

For most transitive verbs, including all verbs with suffix **-kan** where this has another function, the beneficiary can only be indicated by an **untuk** phrase.

EXERCISE 13

- Change the following sentences into benefactive constructions.
- Translate your sentences.

Example
Ibu membeli sepatu baru untuk saya.
→   **Ibu membelikan saya sepatu baru.**
    Mother bought me new shoes.

1.   **Bu Slamet memasak nasi goreng untuk keluarganya.**

2. **Pak Hartono mencari sekolah untuk anaknya.**
3. **Pak Budi membuat main-mainan untuk anaknya.**
4. **Tono mengambil koran untuk ayahnya.**
5. **Dia memanggil dokter untuk temannya.**
6. **Tuti mengiris roti untuk ayah.**

NOTE   Many people use benefactive **-kan** even though the beneficiary is expressed in a phrase with **untuk**:
Pelayan mengambilkan segelas air untuk Edi.
The waiter got a glass of water for Edi.

However, this construction is regarded as incorrect by some people and so is best avoided.

EXERCISE 14

The sentences in this exercise indicate either (a) an action done for the benefit of someone not mentioned, in which case **-kan** has a benefactive function, or (b) an action directed at someone not mentioned, in which case **-kan** does not have a benefactive function.

With (a) type sentences the beneficiary can be indicated after the verb, as can occur with the verb **membelikan** 'buy (for someone)':
Dia membelikan kado yang mahal.
He bought (someone) an expensive present.
→   **Dia membelikan saya kado yang mahal.**
He bought me an expensive present.

With these verbs, alternatively, **-kan** can be omitted, to form a non-benefactive transitive verb, such as **Dia membeli kado** 'He bought a present'.

With (b) type sentences the person to whom the action is directed cannot be mentioned after the verb. For most of these verbs a form without a suffix does not occur.

- Translate the following sentences.
- Mark each verb as benefactive (B) or not (N).

   Example
   Siti membelikan kado yang mahal.
   →   Siti bought (someone) an expensive present. (B)

1. **Siti membereskan kamar.**
2. **Siti membersihkan kamar.**

3.   **Siti mencucikan pakaian.**
4.   **Siti mengirimkan pakaian.**
5.   **Siti memintakan uang.**
6.   **Siti menjahitkan baju.**
7.   **Siti memilihkan baju.**
8.   **Siti menawarkan pekerjaan.**
9.   **Siti membukakan pintu.**
10.   **Siti mencurikan pakaian.**

I   Suffix *-i* indicating repeated action

Some transitive verbs which have no suffix can add **-i** to indicate that the action is performed more than once. This is usually called the *repetitive* function of **-i**. The precise meaning of repetitive **-i** depends on the particular verb base and the context. It usually indicates either repeated action on a single object or action done separately to a number of objects:

> **mencium** 'to kiss' : **menciumi** 'kiss one person repeatedly or kiss many
> people'
> **Dia menciumi pacarnya.**
> He kissed his girlfriend a number of times/repeatedly.
> **menjemput** 'pick up, meet' : **menjemputi** 'pick up, meet one person
> repeatedly or many people separately'
> **Kita akan menjemputi mereka di stasiun kereta api.**
> We will pick them up at the railway station (making more than one trip).

Repetitive **-i** is optional to the construction; it can always be omitted. If it does not occur the verb does not refer to repeated action. Thus **-i** can be omitted in the above example, giving: **Kita akan menjemput mereka** 'We will collect them', which has the same meaning except that repeated action is not indicated. In its other functions **-i** is usually obligatory [but see section 6E]. For instance, in the word **menasihati** 'advise (someone)', **-i** cannot be omitted as there is no word *menasihat.

> **NOTE**   With some verbs **-i** indicates intensity or thoroughness of action rather than repetition. Thus **memandang** 'look at' : **memandangi** 'look at intensely, gaze at', **memeriksa** 'inspect' : **memeriksai** 'inspect carefully'.

EXERCISE 15

Each of the following sentences contains a verb with suffix **-i**.
*   Translate the sentences.
*   Mark each verb as repetitive (R) or not (N).

Example

Dia menciumi pacarnya.

→   He kissed his girlfriend repeatedly. (R)

Mereka tidak menghadiri rapat tadi malam.

→   They didn't attend the meeting last night. (N)

1.   **Semua saran Pak Sarif disetujui.**
2.   **Maling yang masuk rumah Ibu Suparno dipukuli oleh orang kampung.**
3.   **Para demonstran melempari wartawan dengan batu dan sampah.**
4.   **Dia mengangkati koper-koper itu satu per satu.**
5.   **Anak yang nakal tidak berani menghadapi kepala sekolah.**
6.   **Siapa yang meminjami Anda kamus ini?**
7.   **Dia menderita luka parah karena ditikami perampok.**
8.   **Siapa yang menulisi kertas ini?**
9.   **Ibu marah karena Siti menggigiti kukunya.**
10.   **Mereka mengambili batu dari sungai.**
11.   **Manajer ingin mengurangi jumlah pekerja di pabriknya.**
12.   **Sekretaris membukai surat-surat sebelum memberikannya kepada Pak Hadi.**

7   VERBS WITH PREFIX *PER-*

Prefix **per-** has a number of functions with transitive verbs. In some functions it co-occurs with a suffix . When prefix **meN-** occurs the initial **p** of **per-** is not lost; in the passive **per-** follows **di-**

    meN- + per- + luas → memperluas
    di- + per + luas → diperluas

A   Verbs with prefix *per-* alone

Many verbs with prefix **per-** are based on adjectives. They indicate that the subject causes the object to have the characteristic indicated by the base. Thus **memperluas** 'widen, increase the size of, expand', literally: 'cause (object) to be wider/extensive' (**luas** 'wide, extensive'):

    Kami harus memperluas kebun ini sebelum musim hujan.
    We have to expand this garden before the rainy season.

EXERCISE 1

Below are a number of adjectives in sentences. In each case:
* Translate the sentence.
* Compose another sentence containing the **per-** verb based on the adjective.
* Use the word in parentheses as the subject of your sentence (with the original subject becoming the object).
* translate your sentence.

    Example
    Kebun ini luas. (Kami)
    →   This garden is extensive.
        Kami sudah memperluas kebun ini.
        We have extended this garden.

    1.   **Penjagaan di bandar udara ketat. (polisi)**
    2.   **Rumahnya besar. (Kardi).**
    3.   **Liburannya panjang. (keluarga itu)**
    4.   **Rapat itu singkat. (ketua)**
    5.   **Pisau ini tajam. (bapak)**
    6.   **Taman itu indah. (tukang kebun)**
    7.   **Bahasa Indonesianya lancar. (mahasiswa itu)**
    8.   **Kesembuhannya cepat. (obat baru itu)**

• Sometimes a verb with prefix **per-** based on an adjective has the same meaning as a **-kan** verb built on the same base. Thus **memperluas** and **meluaskan** both mean 'to widen, expand'. Sometimes both forms occur but with somewhat different meanings. This can happen when the **per-** form has a figurative meaning, such as **memperdalam pengetahuan** 'deepen one's knowledge', while the **-kan** form is only used in a literal sense, such as **mendalamkan lubang** 'deepen a hole'. Sometimes only one of the two possible forms actually occurs, such as **memperindah** 'beautify'. (There is a word **mengindahkan** but it has an unrelated meaning.) There are a lot more **-kan** verbs based on adjectives than **per-** verbs; for instance, there is no **per-** verb corresponding to **membersihkan** 'to clean'.

Causative verbs with **per-** are based on adjectives. Causative verbs based on intransitive verbs all have **-kan**. Thus there is no **per-** verb corresponding to **membangunkan** 'wake (someone) up', which is based on the intransitive verb **bangun** 'wake up'.

> **NOTE** Existing dictionaries rarely indicate clearly if there is a difference in usage between **-kan** and **per-** forms, such as that between **memperdalam** and **mendalamkan**. It is thus important to observe how Indonesians use the words. Some teaching texts claim there is a difference in meaning when the two forms both occur, **-kan** meaning 'give (object) a characteristic it does not have' and **per-** indicating 'give (object) more of a characteristic it already has'. Thus **membesarkan** 'make big (something that is small)', **memperbesar** 'make bigger (something that is already big)'. However, it is doubtful if many people actually make this distinction in their natural speech.

EXERCISE 2

Each of the following sentences contains a base in parentheses, which is either an adjective or a verb.
• Indicate whether the base can take both **-kan** and **per-** or only **-kan**.
• Translate the sentences.
• Use a passive verb if the form in parentheses is preceded by **di-**.
• Note: You will need a good dictionary to do this exercise. Some adjectives only allow a causative verb with **-kan**.

Example
Kapan mereka akan (keras) permukaan jalan ini?
→   **Kapan mereka akan mengeraskan/memperkeras permukaan jalan ini?**
     When will they harden the surface of this road?

1.   **Saya mau (besar) foto-foto ini.**
2.   **Sandiwara itu (sedih) semua penonton.**

3. **Lampu lalu lintas akan dipasang di perempatan ini untuk (lancar) lalu lintas.**
4. **Jalan ini akan di-(lebar).**
5. **sopir (henti) bis di luar gedung sekolah.**
6. **Anak-anak itu (jatuh) batu ke dalam sungai.**
7. **Bendera harus di-(turun) setiap malam.**
8. **Bank ini bersedia (lunak) syarat-syaratnya untuk nasabah baru.**
9. **Tentara (bebas) kota itu dari kaum pemberontak.**
10. **Pedagang itu (datang) barang dari luar negeri.**

> **NOTE** Some people use a few verbs based on adjectives with affixation **per-...-kan**. The verb **mempermalukan** 'embarrass' is widely accepted but some others, like **memperbesarkan** 'enlarge', are regarded as incorrect by many people and usually do not occur in dictionaries.

B Verbs with affixation *per-...-kan*

Some verbs occur with prefix **per-** and suffix **-kan** together. The largest group of these have verb bases. With some bases **per-...-kan** occurs instead of **-kan** alone, for instance **memperlihatkan** 'to show' (literally: 'cause (someone) to see'). With some bases **per-...-kan** and **-kan** both occur with the same meaning, **per-** thus being optional, such as **mempergunakan**, **menggunakan** 'to use'. Sometimes the **per-...-kan** verb has a different meaning from the **-kan** verb built on the same base, such as **mempekerjakan** 'to employ' and **mengerjakan** 'to perform, do'. No clear rules can be given and forms must be learned individually.

EXERCISE 3

- Translate the following sentences.
- Translate the underlined verb with a verb based on the form given in parentheses, choosing affixation **per-...-kan** or **-kan**, as required.
- If both **per-...-kan** and **-kan** verbs can occur, give both.
- Note: You will need to use a good dictionary for this exercise.

Examples
I used a very sharp knife. (**guna**)
→ **Saya menggunakan/mempergunakan pisau yang tajam sekali.**

I showed the photos to the visitors. (**lihat**)
→ **Saya memperlihatkan foto-foto itu kepada para tamu.**

1. Tomo warned his younger brother not to play near the road. (**ingat**)
2. She is listening to dangdut music. (**dengar**)
3. They presented new dances last night. (**tunjuk**)

4.   Why did you <u>treat</u> her like that? (**laku**)
5.   I haven't yet <u>introduced</u> Titik to my parents. (**kenal**)
6.   I want to <u>compare</u> all the cars before choosing one. (**banding**)
7.   This map <u>indicates</u> the road to Salatiga. (**tunjuk**)
8.   She <u>played</u> dangdut music at her party. (**dengar**)
9.   I will <u>consider</u> your request. (**timbang**)
10.   Arif <u>questioned</u> the referee's decision. (**tanya**)
11.   He <u>asked about</u> the cost of the journey to Bali. (**tanya**)
12.   Dewi <u>carried out</u> her duties well. (**laku**)
13.   Maria <u>prepared</u> the report for the school principal. (**siap**)
14.   The university must <u>calculate</u> the cost of the new building. (**hitung**)

C   Verbs with affixation *per-...-i*

A very limited number of verbs have the affixation **per-...-i**. A few are based on adjectives and the others on verbs. With some **per-** is optional, while with others it is obligatory.

EXERCISE 4

* Translate the following sentences.
* Translate each underlined verb with a verb based on the form given in parentheses, choosing affixation **per-...-kan**, or **per-...-i**, as required.
* If verbs with and without **per-** can occur with the same meaning, give both.
* Note: You will need to use a good dictionary for this exercise.

Example
We have to <u>repair</u> the damaged bridge. (**baik**)
→   **Kita harus memperbaiki jembatan yang rusak.**

1.   They are <u>renovating</u> their house. (**baru**)
2.   The government is <u>studying</u> their proposal. (**ajar**)
3.   They have <u>equipped</u> their house with new furniture. (**lengkap**)
4.   The old people want to <u>defend/maintain</u> the old traditions. (**tahan**)
5.   The government does not want to <u>arm</u> the people. (**senjata**)
6.   Mrs Hamam <u>invited</u> the guests to sit down. (**sila**)
7.   The Indonesian people <u>commemorate/celebrate</u> Independence Day on 17 August. (**ingat**)
8.   The general suceeded in <u>uniting</u> the army. (**satu**)

8   *TER-* VERBS

Prefix **ter-** occurs with verbs and adjectives and with some other word classes. With adjectives it forms superlative phrases [see section 14B].

> **NOTE** At the beginning of a word **ter-** is not always a prefix; sometimes it is just part of the word base. For example, **terbang** is a simple verb meaning 'to fly'; **teriak** is a base which occurs with a number of affixes, such as **berteriak** 'to shout', **teriakan** '(a) shout'; **terjemah** is a verb base occurring in **menerjemahkan** 'to translate', **terjemahan** 'translation'.

Most verbs with prefix **ter-** can be placed in one of three categories: stative, accidental and abilitative.

A Stative *ter-* verbs

Stative verbs refer to a state rather than an action; they are the most frequent of the **ter-** verbs. Stative verbs cannot occur with an agent. Often they contrast with **di-** verbs, which indicate an action. Thus **diletakkan** 'put (by someone)' refers to an action, while **terletak** 'located', refers to the state resulting from that action:

Koran siapa yang diletakkan di atas meja?
Whose newspaper has been put on the table?
Koran siapa yang <u>terletak</u> di atas meja?
Whose newspaper <u>is (located)</u> on the table?

As in the above example, a suffix on the **di-** or **meN-** verb is dropped with the corresponding stative **ter-** verb. Another example of this is the following, with both **meN-** verb (**membatasi** 'restrict') and **di-** verb (**dibatasi** 'restricted') shown, along with the corresponding **ter-** verb (**terbatas** 'restricted, limited'):

Pemerintah membatasi jumlah mobil yang boleh diimpor.
The government has restricted the number of cars which may be imported.
Jumlah mobil yang boleh diimpor dibatasi oleh pemerintah.
The number of cars which may be imported has been restricted by the
     government.
Jumlah mobil yang boleh diimpor <u>terbatas.</u>
The number of cars which may be imported is <u>limited</u>.

EXERCISE 1

- Complete the second sentence in each of the following.
- Translate each sentence.

Example

Tadi pagi saya meletakkan koran di atas meja.
Sekarang ...

→   This morning I put the newspaper on the table.
  Sekarang koran terletak di atas meja.
  Now the newspaper is on the table.

1.   **Tadi pagi saya mengunci pintu.**
  Sekarang ...
2.   **Tadi pagi saya membuka jendela.**
  Sekarang ...
3.   **Tadi pagi limbah dari pabrik itu mencemari sungai.**
  Sekarang ...
4.   **Tadi pagi semua pengunjung mencatat namanya dalam buku tamu.**
  Sekarang ...
5.   **Tadi pagi mahasiswa baru mendaftarkan namanya untuk kursus ini.**
  Sekarang ...
6.   **Tadi pagi pemberontak memutuskan hubungan dengan ibu kota.**
  Sekarang ...

EXERCISE 2

In each sentences below a passive verb with **di-** or a stative verb with **ter-** is appropriate.
- Choose the correct form for the verb.
- Translate the sentences.

Examples

Tas yang cokelat itu lebih murah karena ____buat dari plastik.
→   **Tas yang cokelat itu lebih murah karena terbuat dari plastik.**
  That brown bag is cheaper because it is made of plastic.

Kursi ini ____buat oleh ayah saya.
→   **Kursi ini dibuat oleh ayah saya.**
  This chair was made by my father.

1.   **Jangan naik mobil ke kota. Lalu-lintas di sana tidak ____atur.**
2.   **Saya minta pintu kantor ini ____kunci sebelum Anda pulang.**
3.   **Mengapa pintu toko itu ____buka lebar?**
4.   **Meja ini harus ____atur sebelum tamu-tamu tiba.**
5.   **Obat ini mengandung zat yang ____larang.**
6.   **Nama kepala sekolah ____tulis di pintu kantornya.**

7. **Meskipun dia sudah pulang pintu kantornya tidak ____kunci.**
8. **Jangan lupa! Pintu toko harus ____buka sebelum jam delapan pagi.**
9. **Kata-kata yang kasar itu dengan sengaja ____muatnya dalam pidatonya.**
10. **Pestisida itu ____larang oleh Departemen Kesehatan.**
11. **Dalam harian *Kompas* tadi pagi ____muat foto rombongan dari Hong Kong.**
12. **Surat ini ____tulis kemarin.**

B Accidental *ter-* verbs

The word *accidental* is a cover term for a variety of situations where the action is uncontrolled. Depending on the particular verb and the situation it may refer to action which is sudden, unexpected, unintended, undesirable or beyond the control of the actor. The term 'accidental' then is not always an accurate description of the meaning conveyed by **ter-**.

Accidental verbs can be intransitive:
   Latif <u>tertidur</u> di kelas.
   Latif <u>fell asleep</u> in class.

They can also be transitive. In this case the verb is passive. Even if a first or second person agent occurs the construction is passive type one [see section 4B]:
   Maaf, kopi saudara <u>terminum</u> oleh saya.
   Sorry, I <u>drank</u> your coffee <u>by mistake</u>.

Frequently an actor is not relevant to the situation. In the following there is no mention of who forced the government:
   Pemerintah <u>terpaksa</u> menurunkan harga beras.
   The government <u>was forced</u> to lower the price of rice.

> **NOTE**   In English verbs do not distinguish between accidental and deliberate action. The statement 'I drank your coffee' does not out of context indicate whether I intended to drink it or whether I drank it by mistake, thinking it was mine. Indonesian, however, makes the distinction:
> **Saya minum kopi Anda.** I (deliberately) drank your coffee.
> **Kopi Anda terminum oleh saya.** I drank your coffee (in error).

As with stative **ter-** verbs, accidental verbs usually lose a suffix if there is one on the corresponding **meN-** verb. Thus **menghapuskan** 'wipe out', **terhapus** 'accidentally wiped out':

Semua data di komputer terhapus ketika listrik mati secara tiba-tiba.
All the data on the computer was wiped out when power was suddenly lost.

NOTE   Although suffixes **-kan** and **-i** are usually lost with accidental **ter-** verbs this is not always the case and, especially in journalistic style, there is a great deal of inconsistency in usage. However, they are always lost on stative **ter-** verbs and never lost on abilitative verbs [as discussed in section 8C].

EXERCISE 3

Each of the following sentences contains a **ter-** verb.
- State for each verb its meaning and whether it is stative or accidental.
- Translate each sentence.

Examples
Keluarga Pak Denny tersebar di seluruh Indonesia.
→   **tersebar** 'scattered' - stative
Mr Denny's family is scattered throughout Indonesia.

Dia terbangun karena ribut di luar rumahnya.
→   **terbangun** 'wake suddenly' - accidental
He woke suddenly because of the noise outside his house. (or more natural in English: He was woken by the noise outside his house.)

1.   **Kebebasan pers terjamin di negeri itu.**
2.   **Sopir mobil terlempar ke jalan ketika mobilnya menabrak pohon.**
3.   **Kita mudah terpesona oleh barang-barang mahal.**
4.   **Pengetahuannya sangat terbatas.**
5.   **Tuti harus dibawa ke dokter sesudah dia tergelincir di tangga.**
6.   **Anak itu menangis ketika kakinya tersepak temannya.**
7.   **Bukunya tertinggal di kantin.**
8.   **Namanya tidak tercantum dalam daftar orang yang lulus ujian.**

NOTE   The verb **teringat** 'recall, suddenly think of, come to mind' is used either as an active verb or a passive verb:
    Saya teringat akan keluarga itu.
    Keluarga itu teringat oleh saya.
    I suddenly thought of that family.

C Abilitative *ter-* verbs

Abilitative verbs indicate that the actor is able to perform the action. These verbs are always transitive and passive. As with accidental **ter-** verbs, passive type one always occurs, even if the actor is first or second person.

Usually inability is referred to, with **tidak** or, more rarely, **belum**:

Mobil semahal itu tidak terbeli oleh kami.

We can't afford to buy a car as expensive as that.

Soal kemacetan lalu-lintas belum terpecahkan.

The problem of traffic congestion can't yet be solved.

They can occur in the positive, although this is less common:

Kesebelasan Ajax akhirnya terkalahkan juga.

Finally the Ajax (soccer) eleven was able to be beaten. (That is, another
team managed to beat Ajax.)

If suffix **-kan** or **-i** occurs with a **meN-** verb it is usually retained on the corresponding abilitative **ter-** verb. The verb **terkalahkan** 'beatable' in the above example relates to **mengalahkan** 'to defeat'.

> **NOTE** Instead of a **ter-** verb to indicate ability, a **di-** verb preceded by **bisa** or **dapat** 'can' is very frequently used:
>
> **Soal kemacetan lalu-lintas belum dapat dipecahkan.**
> The problem of traffic congestion can't yet be solved.
>
> Sometimes context is very important in indicating if a **ter-** verb is stative, accidental or abilitative. In the first sentence below **terbawa** means 'able to carry', while in the second sentence it means 'accidentally carried':
>
> **Apa paket-paket itu terbawa oleh kamu sendiri?**
> Were you able to carry those parcels by yourself?
> **Maaf, paket saudara terbawa oleh saya.**
> Sorry, I took your parcel by mistake.

EXERCISE 4

Each of the following sentences contains a **ter-** verb.
- Translate the sentences.
- State for each verb its meaning and whether it is accidental or abilitative.

Examples

Waktu gunung api meletus orang desa terpaksa mengungsi.

→   **terpaksa** 'forced' : accidental
     When the volcano erupted the village people were forced to
     evacuate.

Suara dosen tidak terdengar dari sini.

→   (**tidak**) **terdengar** 'can(not) be heard, (in)audible' : abilitative
The lecturer can't be heard from here.

Remember: *Accidental* is a cover term. Depending on the particular verb and the context it may mean there is no actor, or that the event is involuntary (outside the control of the actor), or is sudden, unexpected, or undesired.

1.   **Ali terjatuh dari pohon.**
2.   **Meja itu tidak terangkat oleh mereka.**
3   **Rumah siapa yang terbakar kemarin?**
4.   **Regu penyelamat membagikan obat-obatan kepada orang desa yang terkena banjir.**
5.   **Penduduk setempat mencoba menyelamatkan ikan paus yang terdampar di pantai.**
6.   **Penduduk setempat tidak akan terpengaruh oleh rencana pemerintah.**
7.   **Kemarahan para demonstran tidak terkendalikan.**
8.   **Tablet itu termakan anak saya.**
9.   **Dia meninggal sesudah tertabrak mobil.**
10.   **Tulisan di buku ini begitu kecil sehingga tidak terbaca.**
11.   **Dia berteriak waktu lukanya tersentuh perawat.**
12.   **Jumlah bintang di langit tidak terhitung.**

EXERCISE 5

- Translate each of the following sentences.
- State whether the **ter-** verb is stative, accidental, or abilitative.

Example
Batu seberat itu terangkat juga oleh Hasan.
→   Hasan did manage to lift such a heavy rock. : abilitative

1.   **Maaf, nasimu termakan oleh saya.**
2.   **Apa termakan olehmu nasi sebanyak itu?**
3.   **Mereka terkejut mendengar kabar itu.**
4.   **Makan siang tersedia di kamar makan.**
5.   **Dia meninggal dunia akibat terlindas truk.**
6.   **Amarah mereka tidak terkendalikan.**
7.   **Bus yang jatuh ke dalam jurang sekarang terbalik.**
8.   **Kabar itu termuat dalam semua koran.**
9.   **Kaki siapa yang terinjak olehnya?**
10.   **Apakah rumahnya terlihat dari sini?**

11. **Pekerjaan itu tidak terselesaikan oleh kami.**
12. **Saya terbangun jam empat tadi pagi.**

NOTE Many verbs with **ter-** do not fit easily into any of the three categories mentioned above. Some verbs like **tertawa** 'laugh' and **tersenyum** 'smile' can be placed with accidentals, indicating action which is considered beyond the control of the actor. Some words with **ter-** are not verbs and with some **ter-** no longer functions as a prefix in the modern language. Such words include **terlalu** 'too', **terhadap** 'towards', **terutama** 'especially' and numerous others.

---

9   *KE-...-AN* VERBS

Most verbs with circumfix **ke-...-an** indicate that the subject undergoes an undesired or unpleasant experience. They focus attention on the adverse effect of the event on the subject and because of this they are sometimes called *adversitive verbs*. The difference between **ke-...-an** verbs and **di-** passive verbs is shown by the following:

Mobil Tomo dicuri.
Tomo kecurian mobil.
Tomo's car was stolen.

The first sentence merely states what happened to Tomo's car, while the second specifically states that Tomo suffers something unpleasant. A more literal translation would be: 'Tomo had his car stolen' or 'Tomo was robbed of his car'. The focus is on Tomo and the undesirable thing that happened to him, rather than on what happened to his car.

There are only a limited number of **ke-...-an** verbs. Some, like **kecurian,** take a following noun phrase. This is called a complement, and is something possessed by the subject. Some others have the same meaning as **di-...-i** verbs except that they explicitly indicate that the event is something unfortunate for the subject. The difference is shown by the following pair:

Bu Hartini didatangi wartawan.
Mrs Hartini was visited by a journalist.
Bu Hartini kedatangan wartawan.
Mrs Hartini was visited by a journalist (and this was unexpected and
        unwelcome).

• Some **ke-...-an** verbs have no complement. Among these are verbs based on nouns, such as **kemalaman** 'be overtaken by night':

Mereka kemalaman di hutan.
They were overtaken by night in the forest.

• Another subgroup are based on adjectives; they indicate that the subject suffers to a severe degree what the base indicates. Thus while **takut** means 'afraid', **ketakutan** means 'terrified':

Kami ketakutan ketika semua lampu mati.
We were terrified when all the lights went out.

EXERCISE 1

• Translate the following sentences into English.

1. **Didi harus pindah ke kota lain sesudah kehilangan pekerjaan.**
2. **Sayang, kami kehujanan waktu berpiknik kemarin.**
3. **Di daerah itu banyak orang kekurangan makanan.**
4. **Dia kedatangan tamu ketika sedang mandi.**
5. **Orang yang digigit nyamuk di daerah itu kadang-kadang ketularan penyakit malaria.**
6. **Kasihan wanita itu; ia kecopetan di bus.**
7. **Ali kedapatan merokok oleh ibunya.**
8. **Banyak petani kelaparan karena panen gagal.**
9. **Kami kedinginan tadi malam karena lupa membawa pakaian tebal.**
10. **Maaf, saya terlambat karena ketinggalan bus.**

NOTE ke-...-an verbs should not be confused with **ke-...-an** nouns [see section 2B]. Sometimes these have similar meanings, though they occur in different positions in a sentence. Thus **ketakutan** can be a verb meaning 'terrified' or a noun meaning 'fear':
 Dia ketakutan. He is terrified. (Here it is a verb)
 Dia hidup dalam ketakutan. He lives in fear. (Here it is a noun)

When the form is a verb it is negated by **tidak**:
 Dia tidak ketakutan. He isn't terrified.

EXERCISE 2

- Use the correct form of the verb in parentheses in each of the following sentences.
- Use a **ke-...-an** verb wherever possible.
- Translate the sentences.

 Examples:
 Turis-turis asing (banjir) pulau Bali.
 → **Turis-turis asing membanjiri pulau Bali.**
  Foreign tourists are flooding Bali.

 Pulau Bali (banjir) turis-turis asing.
 → **Pulau Bali kebanjiran turis-turis asing.**
  Bali is being flooded by foreign tourists.

1. **Karena gula (habis) saya harus pergi ke toko.**
2. **Jam tangan saya (hilang) waktu saya bermain di pantai.**
3. **Tadi malam ada pencuri (masuk) rumah kami.**
4. **Karena kami (habis) gula saya harus pergi ke toko.**
5. **Dompet Ani (curi) sementara dia makan di restoran.**
6. **Saya (hilang) jam tangan waktu saya bermain di pantai.**

7.   **Polisi (tahu) Hamzah mencuri mobil itu.**

8.   **Ani (curi) dompet sementara dia makan di restoran.**

9.   **Kakinya patah karena dia (jatuh) dari pohon.**

10.   **Kakinya patah karena dia (jatuh) pohon.**

11.   **Kadang-kadang petani (racun) karena menggunakan terlalu banyak pestisida.**

12.   **Petani itu (racun) oleh istrinya.**

13.   **Dia (mati) ayah tahun lalu.**

14.   **Hamzah (tahu) mencuri mobil itu oleh polisi.**

NOTE   Two common **ke-...-an** verbs are not adversitive. These are:
kelihatan 'visible, can be seen':
Rumahnya kelihatan dari sini. Her house can be seen from here.
It can also mean 'looks':
Dia kelihatan sakit. She looks sick.

kedengaran 'audible, can be heard':
Suara guru tidak kedengaran di belakang kelas.
The teacher's voice can't be heard from the back of the classroom.
It can also mean 'sounds':
Suaranya kedengaran parau. He sounds hoarse.

10   *BER-....-KAN* VERBS

Most verbs with the circumfix **ber-....-kan** are based on nouns. They are followed by a noun phrase, called the complement. The verb indicates that the subject has the complement as the thing indicated in the verb base. Thus **berdasarkan** 'be based on' literally means 'have the complement as a **dasar** (base, basis)':

> **Filsafat Indonesia berdasarkan Pancasila.**
> The philosophy of Indonesia is based on Pancasila. (literally: The
>   philosophy of Indonesia has Pancasila as a basis.)

NOTE   Some **ber-....-kan** verbs can be replaced simply by **ber-**. Thus **berisikan** 'contain, have as contents' frequently occurs as **berisi**:
> **Gelas ini berisi air putih.** 'This glass contain drinking water'.

Some of these verbs can occur without a complement. In this case **-kan** cannot occur:
> **Tuduhannya tidak berdasar.** 'His charges have no basis.'

EXERCISE 1

- Translate each of the following sentences into Indonesian.
- Use a **ber-....-kan** verb based on the noun given in parentheses.
- For each English sentence a literal translation of the required Indonesian sentence is given, according to the model: '(Subject) has (complement) as (verb base)'.

Example:
This glass contain drinking water. (**isi**)
(This glass has drinking water as contents.)
> →   **Gelas ini berisikan air putih.**

1. He was armed with a sword. (**senjata**)
   (He had a sword as a weapon.)
2. That association has more than a hundred members. (**anggota**)
   (That association has more than a hundred people as members.)
3. The houses in that village have bamboo walls. (**dinding**)
   (Houses in that village have bamboo as walls.)
4. He is married to a Javanese woman (**isteri**)
   (He has a Javanese woman as a wife.)
5. His garden is fenced in by tall trees. (**pagar**)
   (His garden has tall trees as a fence.)
6. The floor in their house is covered with mats. (**alas**)
   (The floor in their house has mats as a covering.)

7.   That political party is symbolised by a star. (**lambang**)
      (That political party has a star as a symbol.)
8.   Indonesian originates from Malay dialects. (**asal**)
      (Indonesian has Malay dialects as an origin.)

11   *BER-...-AN* VERBS

Verbs with the circumfix **ber-...-an** have one of two meanings.

A   Reciprocal *ber-...-an* verbs

Some of these verbs indicate *reciprocal relationship*. There are two types of reciprocal verbs. Some indicate that two people do the same thing to each other. These are based on transitive verbs, such as **bersalaman** 'greet each other by shaking hands' from **menyalami** 'greet (by shaking hands)':

Mereka bersalaman ketika bertemu.
They shook hands when they met.

Other verbs indicate that two people or things stand in the same relationship to each other. These verbs either have a base which indicates a location, such as **berdekatan** 'near each other' from **dekat** 'close, near', or are based on nouns, such as **berpacaran** 'be boyfriend and girlfriend' from **pacar** 'boy/girl friend':

Rumah kami berdekatan.
Our houses are near each other.
Tom dan Mary berpacaran.
Tom and Mary are boyfriend and girlfriend (to each other).

The two people or things involved in the action or relationship can be expressed in the same phrase:

Kapal tangki dan kapal barang bertabrakan.
The tanker and the cargo ship collided (with each other).

Alternatively, one can be expressed in a phrase with **dengan** 'with':

Kapal tangki bertabrakan dengan kapal barang.
The tanker collided with the cargo ship.

Verbs indicating an action frequently have a reduplicated base:

Mereka berpukul-pukulan.
They were hitting each other.

> **NOTE**   Some verbs which might appear to be **ber-...-an** verbs are actually not. These are verbs with prefix **ber-** based on nouns which have suffix **-an**. Thus in the sentence **Kapal ini bermuatan beras** 'This ship is loaded with rice', the verb **bermuatan** 'have a load, contain' consists of **ber-** and base **muatan** 'load, contents', which itself is based on **muat** 'to contain, hold'. Likewise, **berpakaian** 'be dressed' consists of **ber-** and base **pakaian** 'clothes'.

EXERCISE 1

- Translate the following sentences into Indonesian.
- Use **ber-...-an** verbs based on the words given in parentheses.

Example
Irian Jaya borders on (shares a border with) Papua New Guinea. (**batas**)
→   **Irian Jaya berbatasan dengan Papua Nugini.**

1.   The children were pushing and shoving in the school grounds.
      (**desak**)
2.   We don't yet know each other. (**kenal**)
3.   We often send letters to each other. (**kirim**)
4.   My house faces the church. (**hadap**)
5.   The two houses are next to each other (side by side). (**sebelah**)
6.   The two leaders embraced each other when they met. (**peluk**)
7.   The children were chasing each other in the yard. (**kejar**)
8.   His arrival coincided with the holiday. (**tepat**)
9.   They kissed each other under the tree. (**cium**)
10.   They have been enemies for a long time. (**musuh**)

B   Random action *ber-...-an* verbs

Some **ber-...-an** verbs do not indicate reciprocal relationship. These indicate *random action* carried out by a number of participants. That is, the action is performed by more than one person or thing, but in an uncoordinated way, each person or thing performing the action independently. These verbs are all based on intransitive verbs. Thus **berdesingan** means 'whizzing in all directions' (**desing** 'whizz, buzz'), **beterjunan** means 'jump down (of many people acting in an uncoordinated manner)' (**terjun** 'jump down'):

Peluru berdesingan.
Bullets were whizzing in all directions.
Ketika kapal terbakar penumpang beterjunan ke laut.
When the ship caught fire the passengers jumped into the sea.

Because the actor has to be plural there is no need to indicate plurality on the noun:

Burung beterbangan.
Birds are flying about.

EXERCISE 2

- Translate the **ber-...-an** verb in each of the sentences below and mark it as reciprocal or random action.
- Translate the sentences into English.

Examples

Mereka duduk berdampingan di kereta api.

→   **berdampingan** 'be side by side' : Reciprocal.
They sat side-by-side in the train.

Di Jakarta gedung-gedung baru bermunculan dimana-mana.

→   **bermunculan** 'appear all over the place, spring up' : Random
In Jakarta new buildings are springing up everywhere.

1.   **Ruangan ini semrawut; kertas-kertas berserakan.**
2.   **Murid-murid berlarian di halaman sekolah.**
3.   **Kedua restoran itu bersaingan.**
4.   **Kalong bergantungan di pohon-pohon itu.**
5.   **Karena sudah lama hujan kodok berloncatan di rumput.**
6.   **Kedua remaja itu berkasih-kasihan.**
7.   **Mereka berpegangan tangan.**
8.   **Tamu mulai berdatangan.**
9.   **Bintang-bintang bertaburan di langit.**
10.   **Bob dan Mary duduk berpandang-pandangan.**

NOTE   A few **ber-...-an** verbs do not fit into the above categories. They indicate action which is neither reciprocal nor random, and which can have a single actor. These include **bepergian** 'go on a voyage, travel' and **berjualan** 'sell things for a living'.

Some verbs consist of a base followed by the **meN-** form of the verb, such as **pukul-memukul** and **jahit-menjahit**. There are two meanings.

A   Reciprocal base-*meN*- verbs

Some base-**meN** verbs indicate that two people do the same thing to each other, such as **pukul-memukul** 'hit each other':

Kedua anak itu selalu pukul-memukul.

Those two children are always hitting each other.

Reciprocal base-**meN-** verbs always derive from transitive verbs which normally have a person as their object.

> **NOTE**   Some reciprocal verbs have affixation **ber-...-an** [see section 11A]. A few verbs can take either form to indicate reciprocal action, such as **memukul** 'hit': **berpukul-pukulan**, **pukul-memukul** 'hit each other'. However, many verbs have only one reciprocal form. These forms are not predictable and are best learned as they occur.
>
> Many verbs have no reciprocal form. With these verbs reciprocity is indicated by placing **saling** before the verb. This can occur with any verb which allows a human object, including those which can also have **ber-...-an** or base-**meN-**. Thus, in addition to the two forms above, 'hit each other' can also be **saling memukul**.
>
> A number of **-i** verbs take the base-**meN-** reciprocal form: **cinta-mencintai** 'love each other', **jauh-menjauhi** 'avoid each other'. A few optionally drop the **-i**: **kunjung-mengunjung/kunjung-mengunjungi** 'visit each other' (**mengunjungi** 'visit').
>
> One of the few **-kan** verbs which can take the reciprocal form is **maaf-memaafkan** 'forgive each other'. With others **saling** should be used.

B   Verbs meaning 'everything to do with'

Some base-**meN-** verbs mean 'everything to do with, affairs relating to what the base indicates', thus **jahit-menjahit** 'anything to do with sewing':

Kalau soal jahit-menjahit, jangan berikan kepada saya.

If it's anything to do with sewing don't give it to me.

The **jahit-menjahit** type verbs are based on transitive verbs. They refer to actions which do not have a person as object and so cannot be reciprocal. The verbs often refer to creative activities and can also be translated 'the art of what the verb indicates', such as **pahat-memahat** 'the art of carving, everything about carving'. They are never based on verbs with a suffix **-kan** or **-i**.

EXERCISE 1

Each of the following sentences contains a base-**meN**- verb.
*   Mark the verb as (R) if it is reciprocal or (E) if it means 'everything to do with'.
*   Translate the sentences.

Example
Karena kedua mahasiswa itu tidak mampu membeli semua buku yang mereka perlukan mereka selalu pinjam-meminjam.
→   (R)   Because those two students can't afford all the books they need they are always borrowing from each other.

1.   **Andi dan Mina sering telepon-menelepon.**
2.   **Urusan angkat-mengangkat saya serahkan kepada mereka yang lebih kuat.**
3.   **Semua orang harus harga-menghargai.**
4.   **Arif dan tetangganya suka tolong-menolong.**
5.   **Kalau saudara mau tahu tentang tari-menari hubungi Pak Nyoman.**
6.   **Kedua anak itu nakal sekali. Mereka sering berkelahi dan gigit-menggigit.**
7.   **Mereka sudah lama berteman dan sering kunjung-mengunjung.**
8.   **Julia mau membuka restoran karena dia ahli dalam hal masak-memasak.**
9.   **Adik saya akan ikut kursus tentang lukis-melukis.**
10   **Di Indonesia orang biasa tawar-menawar di pasar.**
11.   **Kalau mau menjadi petani kamu harus tahu tentang tanam-menanam.**
12.   **Kami tidak surat-menyurat lagi.**
13.   **Dosen itu mengajar tentang karang-mengarang.**
14.   **Tentara dan kaum pemberontak tembak-menembak di pegunungan.**

13 NOUN PHRASES

A The head noun

A *noun phrase* is a sequence of words which functions in the same ways as a noun, that is it can occur in the same positions in a sentence as a single noun. In the first sentence below there is a single noun, **mobil**, standing alone. In the second sentence a whole phrase stands in that position, which includes **mobil**:

> **Dia punya <u>mobil</u>.**
> He owns a car.
> **Dia punya <u>dua mobil besar yang dia beli di Singapura</u>.**
> He owns <u>two big cars which he bought in Singapore</u>.

As in the above example, the noun phrase is built around a single noun, which is called the *head noun*. In the above example the head noun is **mobil** 'car'.

Some of the important constituents of noun phrases are discussed below, although there are a number of other components of noun phrases.

B Adjectives

Adjectives refer to characteristics of people or things, such as **besar** 'big', **hijau** 'green'. The adjective follows the noun:

> **rumah besar** a big house
> **daun hijau** a green leaf

An adjective can be preceded by **yang**. In this case it is actually a kind of relative clause [see section 25B]:

> **rumah yang besar** a big house

C Possessors

A *possessor* follows the head noun. It may be a noun or pronoun:

> **mobil Tomo** Tomo's car
> **rumah saya** my house

A possessor can itself have a possessor:

> **kantor ayah saya** my father's office

A possessor follows an adjective unless the adjective is preceded by **yang**, in which case the possessor precedes it:

> **rumah besar saya** my big house
> **rumah saya yang besar** my big house

Possessive 'its' is always **-nya**: **namanya** 'its name', while 'his' and 'her' are either **-nya** or **dia**: **namanya**, **nama dia** 'his/her name'.

D   Demonstratives

The main *demonstratives* are **ini** 'this' and **itu** 'that'. These always occur at the end of the noun phrase. A word or phrase following **ini** or **itu** cannot be in the same noun phrase; the demonstrative thus always marks the end of the phrase if it occurs. In the following examples the symbol # marks the end of the noun phrase:

gunung tinggi itu # that tall mountain (one noun phrase ending with **itu**)

Gunung itu # tinggi. That mountain is tall. (a clause with **itu** marking the end of the subject noun phrase)

Itu # gunung tinggi. That is a tall mountain. (a clause with **itu** standing alone as the subject noun phrase)

EXERCISE 1

Some of the following constructions are noun phrases, others are clauses standing alone as sentences, without punctuation given.

- Translate the constructions.
- Indicate whether each is a sentence (S) or a noun phrase (N).

Examples
rumah besar ini

→   this big house (N)

rumah ini besar

→   This house is big. (S)

1.	**ini rumah besar**	9.	**saya guru pandai**
2.	**kota itu besar**	10.	**gedung tinggi itu jelek**
3.	**guru pandai saya**	11.	**teman baik Siti**
4.	**kamar Tomo bersih**	12.	**mobilnya tua**
5.	**mobil tuanya**	13.	**guru saya pandai**
6.	**Siti teman baik**	14.	**kamar bersih Tomo**
7.	**gedung jelek itu tinggi**	15.	**teman Siti baik**
8.	**itu kota besar**	16.	**kota besar itu**

E   Possessor and demonstrative together

When a possessor and demonstrative occur together in English the possessor has to be expressed in a different way. Instead of 'my' we say 'of mine', and so on. There is no similar change in Indonesian:

rumah saya <u>my</u> house
but   **rumah saya ini** this house <u>of mine</u>

When possessive pronouns like 'mine, yours, ours, her' occur in English as separate phrases there is no equivalent in Indonesian. In Indonesian the pronoun must come after a noun to indicate that it is possessive. Thus 'This car is <u>mine</u>' must be expressed: **Mobil ini mobil saya**, which literally means 'This car is my car'. However, Indonesians are much more likely to omit the first mention of the thing and say: **Ini mobil saya** 'This is my car'. In some contexts the noun cannot be omitted so has to be repeated:

Rumah saya dekat rumah Kardi. My house is near Kardi's.

EXERCISE 2

Some of the following constructions are noun phrases, others are clauses
standing alone as sentences, without punctuation given.

• Translate the constructions into English.

1.	**perawat ini Detty**	10	**sekretaris pandai kita ini**
2.	**dosen Budi itu**	11.	**Detty perawat ini**
3.	**dokter itu ayah saya**	12.	**anak itu dia**
4.	**dia anak itu**	13.	**itu dokter ayah saya**
5.	**ini perawat Detty**	14.	**ini sekretaris pandai kita**
6.	**tas Anda ini**	15.	**anak dia itu**
7.	**dokter ayah saya itu**	16.	**sekretaris kita ini pandai**
8.	**anak mereka itu**	17.	**Budi dosen itu**
9.	**dosen itu Budi**	18.	**ini tas Anda**

EXERCISE 3

• Translate the following into Indonesian.

1.	That is a big house.	8.	that expensive car
2.	That house is big.	9.	That is his expensive car.
3.	that big house	10.	That is an expensive car.
4.	My house is big.	11.	That car of his is expensive.
5.	That is my big house.	12.	that expensive car of his
6.	That house of mine is big.	13.	That car is expensive.
7.	that big house of mine	14.	His car is expensive.

F   Modifying nouns

A *modifying noun* follows the head noun to give information about it. There is a wide range of relationships between the two nouns; for instance, the modifying noun may indicate what the head noun does (**pemain tenis** tennis player), is made of (**sate ayam** chicken *sate*), what it does (**mesin pendingin** cooling machine), and so on.

A modifying noun comes directly after the head noun and nothing can come between them.

> **NOTE** If a demonstrative follows a possessive noun, a modifying noun or a noun at the end of a relative clause there may be ambiguity; the demonstrative may refer to the head noun or to the other noun. Thus the phrase **keputusan menteri itu** could be interpreted as meaning 'that decision of the minister' or 'the decision of that minister':
>
> In practice the context in which the phrase is used usually makes clear what is meant.

G Relative clauses

Relative clauses are discussed in more detail in section 25A. They are preceded by **yang**. Relative clauses follow all components of the phrase except **itu** and **ini**:

rumah <u>yang dijualnya</u> itu
that house <u>which he sold</u>

H Modifying verbs

These immediately follow the head noun and describe what the noun is used for. The verb usually has no affixes: **kamar mandi** 'bathroom'.

EXERCISE 4

Below are lists of words in random order.
- Reorder the words in each list to make a noun phrase.
- Note: Some orders will give sentences but only one sensible noun phrase can be obtained from each list.
- Translate the correctly ordered lists.

Example
itu -nya mahal mobil
→   **mobil mahalnya itu**
        that expensive car of his

1.   **mereka buku toko itu**
2.   **bapak besar kantor yang itu**
3.   **itu papan kotor tulis**
4.   **saya ini merah kemeja**
5.   **pandai saya yang anak**

6. itu -nya buku yang ditulis
7. dicuri yang mobil kemarin Alex
8. yang cantik anak perempuan
9. kotor yang -nya celana
10. yang kapal nelayan tenggelam
11. yang dari dikirim paket berat Inggris
12. kamar ini duduk sempit yang
13. kotor -nya celana
14. itu kayu sepeda tukang motor

14   ADJECTIVE PHRASES

Adjectives refer to characteristics of people or things, such as **besar** 'big', **hijau** 'green'. Adjectives act as heads of a number of phrases including *comparative*, *superlative* and *equative* phrases.

A   Comparative phrases

If we want to indicate that someone or something has more of a quality than someone or something else we place **lebih** 'more' before the adjective: **lebih besar** 'bigger', **lebih cantik** 'more beautiful'. The person or thing being compared is indicated in a phrase beginning with **dari** or **daripada**:

> **Dia <u>lebih tinggi dari/daripada</u> saya.**
> She is <u>taller than</u> me.

If we want to indicate that something has less of a quality than something else we use **kurang** 'less':

> **Mobil saya <u>kurang mahal daripada</u> mobil Kardi.**
> My car is <u>less expensive than</u> Kardi's.

The word **lebih** can be preceded by a number of modifiers , which state in what way something has more of a quality than something else. These include **jauh** 'far', **sedikit** 'a little' and indicators of distance, weight and measure:

> **Rumah saya <u>jauh/sedikit lebih besar</u>.**
> My house is <u>far/a little bigger</u>.
> **Rumah saya <u>dua kali lebih besar</u>.**
> My house is <u>two times bigger</u>.

Phrases like 'as big as' are expressed by equative constructions, mentioned below. However, the expression 'twice as big as', which means the same as 'two times bigger than', is a comparative phrase:

> **Rumah saya <u>dua kali lebih besar</u> daripada rumah Kardi.**
> My house is <u>twice as big as</u> Kardi's house.

EXERCISE 1

- Translate each of the following sentences into Indonesian.

    1.   Jakarta is bigger than Solo.
    2.   Solo is smaller than Jakarta.
    3.   Simon is less clever than Alice.
    4.   Melbourne is far colder than Brisbane.

5. Houses in Sydney are three times more expensive than houses in Brisbane.
6. Ali is five centimetres taller than Tom.
7. This book is two hundred pages longer than that book.
8. This road is two metres wider than the road to Bogor.
9. Your work is no more heavy than mine.
10. My work is no less heavy than yours.
11. Bob's Indonesian is a little more fluent than Jane's.
12. Ratna can run twice as fast as her younger sister.

> **NOTE** While **lebih** comes directly before an adjective it cannot come directly before a noun. If we want to say that someone has more of something than someone else we put **lebih banyak** before the noun. So 'more rice' is **lebih banyak nasi**:
> **Ali makan lebih banyak nasi dari saya.**
> Ali eats more rice than I do.

B   Superlative phrases

If we want to say that someone or something has more of a quality than any other we put **paling** or prefix **ter-**, both meaning 'most', before the adjective: **paling besar** 'biggest', **terbaik** 'best'.

The superlative phrase can be followed by a number of phrases which give information limiting the phrase, including phrases beginning with **di** and **dari**:

Ini restoran yang terbaik di kota.

This is the best restaurant in the town.

Parman orang yang paling kaya dari semua teman saya.

Parman is the richest of all my friends.

The prefix **ter-** does not usually occur with adjectives of more than two syllables, with which usually only **paling** occurs: **paling berani** 'bravest'. The superlative phrase often contains a verb acting like an adjective. In this case also only **paling** can be used: **paling berguna** 'most useful', **paling menyenangkan** 'most pleasing'. When a superlative phrase occurs within a noun phrase it is often preceded by **yang** [see also section 25B].

EXERCISE 2

- Translate the following sentences into Indonesian.
- Choose **ter-** wherever it can occur, otherwise use **paling.**

1. Amir is the cleverest student in this class.
2. Which movie is the most frightening?
3. Tokyo is the most expensive city in the world.

4.   Which movie is the best this week?
5.   This cake is the sweetest of all the food on the table.
6.   The crocodile is the most dangerous animal in Indonesia.
7.   Bill Gates is the richest person in the world.
8.   This is the most interesting book.

C   Equative phrases

If we want to say something is similar to another in a particular characteristic we can use one of two constructions.

We can attach **se-** to the adjective:
   Gedung ini <u>setinggi</u> gedung itu.
   This building is <u>as tall as</u> that building.

We can use a phrase with **sama** adjective-**nya dengan**:
   Gedung ini <u>sama tingginya dengan</u> gedung itu.
   This building is <u>as tall as</u> that building.

The two constructions cannot always substitute for each other. Only the one with **se-** can follow **tidak**. Only the **sama …-nya** construction can be used if the two things being compared are both expressed in the subject:
   John <u>tidak setinggi</u> saya.
   John <u>isn't as tall as</u> me.
   John dan Mary <u>sama pandainya</u>.
   John and Mary are as clever as each other/John and Mary are equally
       clever.

Hampir 'almost' can precede the **se-** phrase:
   Dia hampir setinggi saya.
   He is almost as tall as me.

EXERCISE 3

- Translate the following sentences.
- Give both equative constructions if they can both occur.

1.   My room is as clean as Henry's.
2.   Is Jakarta as big as London?
3.   He isn't as old as me.
4.   Bananas and papaws are equally tasty.
5.   Melbourne is almost as big as Sydney.
6.   Henry isn't as polite as his younger sister.
7.   Those two boys are just as naughty as each other.

8.   Goods in Jakarta now are as cheap as goods in Singapore.
9.   Yogyakarta is as busy Semarang.
10.   These meetings are equally important/just as important as each other.

15 PREDICATE PHRASES

A *predicate* is the part of the clause which says something about the subject. A predicate has an obligatory centre. This can be a noun, as in **Dia guru** 'She is a teacher', an adjective, as in **Dia cantik** 'She is pretty', a verb, as in **Dia tidur** 'She is sleeping', or one of a number of other word classes. A predicate phrase optionally contains some other components, the more important ones being discussed below. The temporals and modals convey concepts such as tense and aspect, which are in part marked on the verb in English.

A Temporal markers

Temporal markers or *temporals* indicate that an action or state has occurred, is occurring or is yet to occur. The main temporal markers are:

sudah This indicates that an action has occurred or that a state has been achieved:

> **Saya sudah makan.** I've eaten.
> **Dia sudah duduk.** She has sat down.

telah This means the same as **sudah** but is more formal.
sedang This indicates action in progress.
pernah This indicates action which had happened in the past or used to happen.
akan This indicates action in the future.
masih This indicates an action which is still occurring.
baru This indicates an action which has just occurred. [**Baru** is further discussed in unit 17.]

These indicate time in relation to the present or in relation to some other event. Thus:

> **Dia sedang makan.**
> She is eating at present.
> **Ketika saya datang di rumahnya tadi pagi dia sedang makan.**
> When I went to her house this morning she was eating.

Referring to the past **akan** indicates something was going to happen or that someone intended to do something:

> **Kemarin dia akan makan di restoran tapi uangnya habis.**
> Yesterday she was going to eat at a restaurant but she had no money left.

Some temporal markers can combine; the only common combination being **akan** and another:

> **Kami akan sudah selesai kalau Anda kembali jam lima.**
> We will already be finished if you come back at five o'clock.

Temporals can occur with nouns and adjectives, although some combinations are uncommon:

Ratna sudah guru. Ratna is (already) a teacher.

Ratna masih cantik. Ratna is still pretty.

EXERCISE 1

- Translate the following sentences into English.
- Underline the word or words which translate the part underlined in Indonesian.

Example

Ketika saya sampai di rumahnya Tom sudah bangun.

→   When I got to his house Tom had already got up.

1.   **Saya baru bangun.**
2.   **Apakah Anda pernah pergi ke Eropah?**
3.   **Ketika kami tiba semua tamu lain sudah duduk.**
4.   **Adrian selalu menyanyi waktu sedang mandi.**
5.   **Ketika saya sampai di rumahnya Tom masih makan.**
6.   **Kuliah sudah mulai ketika Paul sampai di kelas.**
7.   **Alex baru bangun waktu istrinya berangkat kerja tadi pagi.**
8.   **Saya akan menemui mereka besok.**
9.   **Ketika saya datang di rumahnya Tom sedang makan.**
10.   **Apa teman Anda sudah pulang?**
11.   **Nasi ini akan dimakan nanti.**
12.   **Daerah itu pernah dihuni orang tetapi sekarang sudah kosong.**
13.   **Setiap hari Alex baru bangun waktu istrinya berangkat kerja.**
14.   **Saya pernah mendengar dia berpidato.**
15.   **Sekarang sudah jam sembilan tapi dia masih mandi.**

B   Modals

Modals refer to such concepts as possibility, ability and necessity. The most frequent modals are **dapat**, **bisa** 'can, be able', **boleh** 'may, be allowed', **harus** 'must, have to'.

These are translated differently depending on whether past, present or future action is referred to:

Saya harus pergi. I have to go.

Kemarin saya harus pergi. Yesterday I had to go.

Besok saya harus pergi. Tomorrow I will have to go.

A number of combinations of temporal markers and modals occur, such as the following:

Saya <u>akan harus</u> menemui dia.

I <u>will have to</u> meet him.

EXERCISE 2

- Translate the following sentences into English.
- Underline the word or words which translate the part underlined in Indonesian.

Example

Martina masih muda tetapi <u>sudah dapat</u> berenang.

→   Martina is still young but she <u>can already</u> swim.

1.   **Dia <u>boleh</u> masuk sekarang.**
2.   **Dia <u>harus boleh</u> masuk sekarang.**
3.   **Dia <u>sudah boleh</u> masuk.**
4.   **Kalau dia datang besok dia <u>akan boleh</u> masuk.**
5.   **Martina <u>sudah bisa</u> berenang sebelum berumur lima tahun.**
6.   **Martina <u>akan dapat</u> berenang sebelum berumur lima tahun.**
7.   **Martina sudah berumur sepuluh tahun tetapi <u>baru bisa</u> berenang.**
8.   **Anda <u>harus bisa</u> berenang kalau mau menjadi polisi.**
9.   **Kalau kamu singgah di rumah terlalu malam saya <u>akan sudah</u> tidur.**
10. **Kalau kamu singgah di rumah sesudah jam delapan saya <u>akan sudah</u> makan.**
11. **Kalau kamu singgah di rumah pada jam tujuh saya <u>akan sedang</u> makan.**
12. **Para penonton <u>sudah harus/harus sudah</u> duduk di teater sebelum jam delapan.**
13. **Dapur ini <u>masih harus</u> dibersihkan.**

> **NOTE**   The sequence **akan baru** means 'will just (happen)', while the sequence **baru akan** means 'will not (happen) until (something else happens)'. Note the following constructions:
>
> **Pada jam lima saya <u>akan baru</u> mulai.** At five I <u>will have just</u> begun.
>
> **Saya <u>baru akan</u> mulai pada jam lima.** I'<u>m not going to</u> begin <u>until</u> five.
>
> The second sentence above can also be expressed:
>
> **Baru jam lima saya akan mulai.** Not until five o'clock will I begin.
>
> Constructions like the last one are discussed in unit 17.

16   NEGATIVES

A   *Tidak* and *bukan*

These words come before the predicate to indicate 'not'. If the predicate contains a noun **bukan** is used; if it contains a word of another class, such as a verb or adjective, **tidak** is used:

Dia bukan teman saya.
She isn't my friend.
Dia tidak sakit/bekerja.
She isn't sick/working.

EXERCISE 1

- Fill in the gaps in the following sentences by choosing **tidak** or **bukan**.
- Translate the sentences into English.

1. **Saya _____ malas.**
2. **Kota Jakarta _____ kecil.**
3. **Ayah saya _____ polisi.**
4. **Bahasa Indonesia _____ sukar.**
5. **Ini _____ pena saya.**
6. **Ali _____ sopir.**
7. **Anak itu _____ mandi.**
8. **Kamar tidur saya _____ kotor.**
9. **Ani _____ tidur.**
10. **Tom _____ sekretaris.**

> **NOTE**   Either **bukan** or **tidak** can be used before some prepositions, such as **untuk** 'for':
> **Ini bukan/tidak untuk Anda.** This isn't for you.
>
> **Tidak** occurs before indefinite numbers:
> **tidak banyak orang** not many people

B   Negative answers

The negative words **tidak** and **bukan** are used in answer to questions where 'no' is used in English. The choice depends on whether the word negated is a noun or not:

Apa kamu sakit?   **Tidak.**
Are you sick?   No.

Apa Anda dokter? Bukan.
Are you a doctor?   No.

C *Belum*

This word, meaning 'not yet', is used to negate a sentence with **sudah**:
Ibu belum pulang.
Mother hasn't come home yet.

This is the negative of:
Ibu sudah pulang.
Mother has come home.

It is also used for 'no' in answer to a question containing **sudah**:
Apa kamu sudah makan? Belum.
Have you eaten yet?   No (not yet).

NOTE **Belum** is almost always used to negate a question which implies that something may happen, even though it may never happen. So in answer to the question 'Have you seen the movie *Star Wars*?' the normal answer is **Belum** 'Not yet', even if you may never see it:
Apa kamu sudah melihat *Star Wars*?   Belum.
Have you seen *Star Wars*?   No.

EXERCISE 2

- Translate the following questions.
- Answer the questions in the negative, using **tidak**, **bukan** or **belum** as appropriate.

Example
Apa dia guru?
→   Is she a teacher?
     Bukan.

1. **Apa guru mereka sudah tiba?**
2. **Apa guru mereka malas?**
3. **Apa guru mereka orang Inggris?**
4. **Apa Anda capek?**
5. **Apa Anda petani?**
6. **Apa Anda sudah pergi ke Amerika?**
7. **Apa orang itu ayahmu?**
8. **Apa orang itu menunggu bis?**
9. **Apa dia sudah menunggu lama?**

D   Negatives occurring with temporals and modals

The negative words can occur together with other words in the predicate. The negative usually comes first:

Saya <u>tidak akan</u> pergi dengan mereka.
I <u>will not</u> go with them.

In some cases reverse ordering of words is possible, usually with a change in meaning. The first word modifies the meaning of everything that follows in the predicate. In the first example below **tidak** modifies **boleh hadir** 'may be present', giving 'not the case that (you) may be present'. In the second example **boleh** indicates the possibility of **tidak hadir** 'not present', giving 'permissible (for you) not to be present':

Kamu tidak boleh hadir.
You are not allowed to be present.
Kamu boleh tidak hadir.
You are allowed to be absent.

The combination of negative and **sudah** gives **belum** 'not yet'. The combinations **sudah tidak** and **sudah bukan** can also occur, indicating that what follows is no longer the case. The word **lagi** 'any more' can also occur and if it does **sudah** is optional:

Dia (sudah) tidak tinggal di sini lagi.
He no longer lives here.

EXERCISE 3

- Translate the following sentences into English.

1.   **Pelamar tidak harus kawin.**
2.   **Pramugari harus belum kawin.**
3.   **Kami tidak pernah pergi ke sana.**
4.   **Saya tidak akan mengantar kamu ke bioskop.**
5.   **Dia masih tidak mau menolong kita.**
6.   **Dia masih tidak bisa dipercaya.**
7.   **Dia tidak sedang tidur.**
8.   **Saya belum makan.**
9.   **Kami belum pernah pergi ke sana.**
10.   **Mereka belum akan berangkat.**
11.   **Mereka belum harus berangkat.**
12.   **Martina belum bisa berenang.**
13.   **Kami tidak boleh masuk teater tadi malam karena tiba terlambat.**
14.   **Dia tidak dapat berbicara bahasa Jepang.**

15. **Saya tidak akan pernah pergi ke sana.**
16. **Kota sudah tidak kelihatan lagi dari sini karena terlalu banyak polusi.**
17. **Pak Soenjono sudah bukan guru lagi.**
18. **Kamu tidak boleh duduk sebelum guru duduk.**
19. **Kamu belum boleh masuk.**
20. **Kamu masih tidak boleh masuk.**

E *Bukan ... melainkan*

Two clauses can occur in a sentence where the first, beginning with **bukan**, states what is incorrect and the second, beginning with **melainkan** or **tetapi**, states what is correct:

Bukan dia bodoh, malainkan/tetapi malas.

It's not that he's stupid, but rather that he's lazy.

In such constructions **-nya** can optionally be attached to **bukan**. **Bukan** can follow the subject of the first clause if the second clause has the same subject:

Bukannya dia bodoh, tetapi malas.
Dia bukan(nya) bodoh, tetapi malas.

It's not that he's stupid, but rather that he's lazy.

The clause following **bukan** can contain a negative:

Bukannya saya tidak percaya kepadanya …

It's not that I don't believe him…

The two clauses are usually separated by a comma in writing. While **tetapi** can always occur in the second clause, **melainkan** only occurs if the two clauses have the same subject.

> **NOTE**   A number of variants of this construction occur. **Melainkan** can also follow a clause containing **tidak**:
> **Kami tidak pergi ke Solo, melainkan ke Yogya.**
> We didn't go to Solo but to Yogya.
>
> **Tetapi/tapi** occurs in other constructions; **melainkan**, however, can only follow a clause with **bukan** or **tidak**.

F *Bukan untuk ... tetapi*

There are sentences which state that an action is performed not for one purpose but for another. In English we usually use constructions such as: 'I didn't come here to play but to study', where 'not' comes before the first verb. In formal language we can say 'I came here not to play but to study'. In Indonesian it is this second structure which is used, with **bukan** placed before the second verb:

Saya datang ke sini bukan untuk bermain, tetapi untuk belajar.
I didn't come here to play but to study.

EXERCISE 4

- Translate the following sentences into Indonesian.
- Use the **bukan ... melainkan** construction (or any of its variants) or the **bukan untuk ... tetapi** construction, as required.

1. I didn't come here to stay in a tourist hotel but to mix with the local people.
2. It wasn't the price of rice that rose but the price of goods from overseas.
3. It's not that I don't want to buy a new house but I don't have enough money.
4. I didn't go to town to shop but to meet a friend.
5. When arrested they didn't surrender but attacked the police with stones.
6. He didn't fall down because he was drunk but because the road was slippery.
7. It isn't he who is wrong but me.
8. It isn't that I don't want to talk with you but I am very busy now.
9. It's not that I can't swim but the water was too cold.
10. I didn't sit down to rest but to read a book.

The word **baru** occurs within the predicate to indicate that an action has just begun:

Kami baru pulang. We've just come home.

In the sentence above **baru** is a temporal marker within the predicate [see section 15A]. As well as coming before the verb **baru** can also precede the subject of the main clause in a sentence which also contains an adverb of time or a subordinate clause indicating time. It then indicates that the action of the main verb does not occur until the time mentioned:

Sore hari baru kami pulang.
Not until evening did we go home/We didn't go home until evening.

Instead of coming before the main clause **baru** can come before the time indicator:

Baru sore hari kami pulang.
Not until evening did we go home.

	adverb of time		main clause
	Sore hari	**baru**	**kami pulang.**
or		adverb of time	main clause
	Baru	**sore hari**	**kami pulang.**

The word **baru** can only precede the whole main clause if this follows the part of the sentence indicating the time. If the main clause comes first **baru** must come after the subject, becoming a temporal within the predicate phrase:

Kami baru pulang sore hari.
We didn't go home until evening.

main clause		adverb of time
subject	predicate	
Kami	**baru pulang**	**sore hari.**

EXERCISE 1

- Translate the following sentences into English.
- Rewrite the sentences, placing **baru** in the other position in which it can occur.

Example

Setelah keluar dari rumah baru ia mulai merasa sakit.

→   Only after leaving the house did he begin to feel sick/He didn't
begin to feel sick until he left the house.
Baru setelah keluar dari rumah ia mulai merasa sakit.

1.   **Malam harinya baru aku pergi ke kantor.**
2.   **Berita itu baru terdengar pukul tiga.**
3.   **Krisis ini baru akan berlalu setelah bulan Juli.**
4.   **Sesudah menerima janji pegawai itu baru dia membayar gaji.**
5.   **Baru hari berikutnya pekerjaan itu dimulai.**
6.   **Tony baru tidur sesudah orang tuanya pulang.**
7.   **Saya akan mulai bekerja baru jam lima.**
8.   **Baru pada akhir tahun kedua petani itu pulang ke desa.**

NOTE   Ambiguity may sometimes occur in writing as to whether **baru** links with a
preceding noun or following verb. Thus out of context the example to the exercise -
Setelah keluar dari rumah baru ia mulai merasa sakit - could alternatively mean
'After coming out of the new house he began to feel sick'. Some people therefore place
a comma: **Setelah keluar dari rumah, baru ia mulai merasa sakit.**

In speech intonation and the positioning of a pause make the meaning clear.

18   PREPOSITIONS

A *preposition* is a word which links a following noun to the rest of the sentence. It shows what relationship the noun has to the sentence. Thus **di** 'in' shows that **kota** 'city' is the location in **Dia tinggal di kota** 'He lives <u>in the city</u>'.

A   Locative prepositions

The most important group of prepositions are the *locative prepositions*. These are **di** 'in, at, on', which indicates action at the place mentioned by the following noun, **ke** 'to', which indicates movement towards, and **dari** 'from', which indicates movement away. These can combine with a set of three *locative pronouns* which indicate position in relation to the speaker. These are **sini** 'here', **situ** 'there (not far off)', and **sana** 'there (far off)'. These combinations produce a nine-way distinction of location and direction, such as **di sini** '(at) here', **ke situ** 'to there (close)', **dari sana** 'from there (far)'.

The three locative prepositions also combine with *locative nouns*, such as **atas** 'top, above', **depan** 'front', **dalam** 'inside', to indicate place and direction in relation to the following noun, as in **ke dalam laci** 'into the drawer (literally: to the inside of the drawer)'.

EXERCISE 1

- Translate the following sentences into Indonesian.
- Use combinations of locative prepositions with locative pronouns and nouns.

   Example
   She put her money into the drawer.
   →   **Dia memasukkan uangnya ke dalam laci.**

   1.   They came here from Japan.
   2.   The children were playing at the side of the house.
   3.   She came from behind the house.
   4.   The children ran across the road (to the other side of the road).
   5.   He threw the ball from the top of the building.
   6.   We stored the old suitcases under the house.
   7.   She chased the dog out of the house.
   8.   Can our house be seen from there?
   9.   You can sit there.
   10.   She placed the food on (top of) the table.

11.   She took the pen from inside her handbag.
12.   Charlie fetched the ball from under the table.

> **NOTE**   The preposition 'to' is sometimes omitted in English even though direction towards something is meant. In Indonesian **ke** must be used:
> **Dia melempar pakaiannya <u>ke atas</u> tempat tidur.** He threw his clothes <u>on</u> the bed.
>
> When the following noun is a person **kepada** is used instead of **ke**:
> **Saya memberikan buku itu <u>kepada</u> John.** I gave the book <u>to</u> John.
>
> The phrase **ke dokter** is used for 'to the doctor' in the expression **pergi ke dokter** 'go to the doctor'.
>
> The preposition 'for' indicating direction is **ke** in Indonesian:
> **Dia sudah berangkat <u>ke</u> Jepang.** She's left <u>for</u> Japan.

B   *Pada*

In both Indonesian and English there are many other prepositions besides the locative prepositions. One frequently occurring preposition is **pada**. This is similar in meaning to **di** and they can sometimes replace each other in the meaning 'in, at, on'. However, while **di** usually indicates location in physical space, **pada** often refers to time. It therefore occurs before words referring to times and dates:
Saya tidak bisa datang <u>pada Hari Senin</u>.
I can't come <u>on Monday</u>.

Pada also indicates figurative location:
pada hemat saya in my opinion
tergantung pada cuaca it depends on the weather

EXERCISE 2

* Translate the following sentences into Indonesian.
* Use **di** or **pada** for the underlined preposition according to which is more appropriate.

1.   The train leaves <u>at</u> three o'clock.
2.   They live <u>in</u> Bandung.
3.   My grandmother died <u>in</u> 1981.
4.   That word also occurs <u>in</u> French.
5.   There are three secretaries <u>in</u> my father's office.
6.   She sat <u>in</u> this chair.
7.   <u>At</u> night time he always returns home.
8.   Her mother died <u>at</u> the end of October.

9.   The cat is lying <u>on</u> the kitchen floor.
10.   Ratna is <u>at</u> her friend's house now.

C   Other prepositions

Some Indonesian prepositions have a variety of equivalents in English, depending on the context. Among these are **dengan**, **terhadap** and **atas**.

EXERCISE 3

- Translate the following sentences into English.
- Translate each underlined preposition with the word most appropriate to the context.

1.   **Malcolm mencuci tangannya <u>dengan</u> sabun.**
2.   **Pemerintah menyatakan perang <u>dengan</u> musuh.**
3.   **Mereka bepergian <u>dengan</u> kapal laut.**
4.   **Iklim di Hobart sangat berbeda <u>dengan</u> iklim di Jakarta.**
5.   **Saya agak khawatir <u>dengan</u> bahaya terhadap tradisi kita.**
6.   **Kami berterima kasih <u>atas</u> kebaikan Anda.**
7.   **Pulau Jawa dibagi <u>atas</u> tiga provinsi.**
8.   **Mereka berhak <u>atas</u> rumah itu.**
9.   **Kemenangan tim Australia <u>atas</u> Korea sangat mengherankan.**
10.   **Pemerintah menyatakan perang <u>terhadap</u> musuh.**
11.   **Susan jengkel <u>terhadap</u> adiknya.**
12.   **Kebaikan mereka <u>terhadap</u> keluarga saya sangat menyenangkan.**
13.   **Cinta ibu <u>terhadap</u> anaknya kuat sekali.**
14.   **Prasangka orang itu <u>terhadap</u> orang asing luar biasa.**

- Learners of Indonesian need to be aware that there is not always a one-to-one correspondence between a particular Indonesian preposition and a particular English preposition, as the above exercise shows.

In some contexts two or three different prepositions may be possible in Indonesian. In such cases English may allow only one preposition. Prepositions can follow intransitive verbs, adjectives and some nouns. If an intransitive verb and preposition in Indonesian correspond to a transitive verb in English then no preposition occurs in English [see section 3B].

Adverbs in Indonesian are formed from adjectives in a number of ways, including placing preposition **dengan** before the adjective. No preposition occurs in English:

Dia lari <u>dengan cepat</u>. She ran <u>quickly</u>.

NOTE   Some words function as a preposition in one context but not in other contexts. Thus **akan** means 'will' and **atas** means 'top, above' but both also function as prepositions in some situations:

Saya sadar <u>akan</u> bahaya itu. I'm aware <u>of</u> that danger.

Buku ini terdiri <u>atas</u> delapan bab. This book consists <u>of</u> eight chapters.

EXERCISE 4

- Translate the following sentences into English.
- Note: If two or more prepositions are given, separated by a slash, they are all rendered in English by the one preposition. In some cases there is no preposition in English.

1.   **Bantuan itu sangat penting <u>bagi/untuk/buat</u> kami.**
2.   **Saya tidak kenal <u>dengan/akan</u> mereka.**
3.   **Indonesia kaya <u>akan</u> minyak bumi.**
4.   **Ratna rindu sekali <u>pada/kepada</u> ayahnya.**
5.   **Saya marah <u>pada/kepada/terhadap</u> Allan.**
6.   **Saya tidak percaya <u>dengan/kepada</u> dia.**
7.   **Mereka bernyanyi <u>dengan</u> senang.**
8.   **Mengapa saudara curiga <u>pada/terhadap/kepada</u> mereka?**
9.   **Indonesia terdiri <u>dari/atas</u> beribu-ribu pulau.**
10.   **Kami sudah tahu <u>tentang/akan</u> hal itu.**
11.   **Tulisannya berbeda <u>dengan/dari</u> tulisan saya.**

NOTE   In some cases English has a phrasal verb, consisting of a verb + preposition, where Indonesian has a transitive verb followed by an object:

Dia <u>melamar</u> pekerjaan di pabrik itu. He <u>applied for</u> work at that factory.

Dia <u>mencari</u> jamnya. She's <u>looking for</u> her watch.

Dia <u>melihat</u> foto-foto saya. She's <u>looking at</u> my photos.

19 ADA

A Functions of *ada*

Ada is an intransitive verb which differs in the way it functions from other verbs. The major functions are listed below.

- It is commonly translated 'there is, there are' or, in the past, 'there was, there were':
  Ada dua mobil di jalan.
  There are two cars on the road.

In questions there is no change in word order:
  Ada dokter di sini?
  Is there a doctor here?

Ada is usually omitted before **banyak** 'many':
  Di Yogya banyak tempat yang menarik.
  In Yogya there are many interesting places.

- It is used to state or ask if someone is present or in (at home, at the office etc):
  Joko ada?
  Is Joko in/there?

Note the difference in meaning with the difference in word order:
  Ada dokter (di sini). *and* **Dokter ada.**
  There is a doctor (here).   The doctor is in.

- It is usually used when asking for something, where in English we would ask 'Do you have any…?', for instance in a shop:
  Ada sepatu tenis?
  Do you have any tennis shoes?

- In informal speech **ada** frequently means 'have, possess':
  Saya ada dua mobil.
  I have two cars.

- Before a phrase beginning with **di** the word **ada** simply means 'is, are' and is optional:
  Kapal itu sudah ada di pelabuhan *or* **Kapal itu sudah di pelabuhan.**
  The ship is already in the harbour.

- **Tidak** comes before **ada** to negate it:

Tidak ada mobil di jalan.

There are no cars on the road.

EXERCISE 1

- Translate the following sentences into Indonesian using **ada**.
- Place **ada** in parentheses if it is optional.

1. Tomo has a new girl friend.
2. Is there a good market in Cikini?
3. Where is there a cheap hotel in this town?
4. There are four people in that taxi.
5. Are there many students at that university?
6. I don't have any money.
7. There was a meeting here last night.
8. Do you have any fresh fish today?
9. Are there any *becaks* in Australia?
10. Is your mother in?
11. Mother's in the kitchen.
12. There aren't any restaurants in this street.
13. What is there in this bag?
14. There aren't many shops here.
15. The teacher isn't in yet.

B *Ada yang*

In English there is a variety of expressions with 'some', such as 'some are big, some are little' and expressions with 'someone' and 'something'. These frequently correspond to Indonesian expressions with **ada yang**:

Ada yang besar, ada yang kecil.

Some are big, some are little.

Ada yang lulus ujian, ada yang tidak (lulus).

Some passed the exam, some didn't (pass).

Ada yang menggigitnya.

Something bit him.

Expressions with **tidak ada yang** sometimes correspond to English expressions with 'no one' or 'nothing':

Banyak orang masuk kamar tapi tidak ada yang mau duduk.

Lots of people came into the room but no one wanted to sit down.

EXERCISE 2

- Translate the following sentences using **ada yang**.

1. There are lots of goods at the market today; some are cheap, some are expensive.
2. No one helped him when he left.
3. I don't know why he's angry; perhaps something annoyed him.
4. I asked them to go to the movies with me but no one wanted to come along.
5. Many tourists arrived in Bali that day; some stopped in Denpasar, some continued on to Ubud.
6. Some believe him, some don't.
7. Something smells bad in the fridge.
8. No one met Tomo at the airport.
9. I don't like this food; none of it can be eaten.
10. After the party some of the children went home, some played in the back yard.

Suffix **-nya** has a number of functions, some of the most important being the following. Some other functions are dealt with in other sections of this book.

A   Possessor

It indicates a third person possessor 'his, her, its'. While basically indicating singular it is sometimes also used for plural, instead of **mereka**:

> **Siti pulang ke rumah<u>nya</u>.**
> Siti returned to <u>her</u> house.
> **Mahasiswa-mahasiswa itu melanjutkan pendidikan<u>nya</u> di luar negeri.**
> Those students continued <u>their</u> education overseas.

B   Third singular: 'him, her, it'

Following an active verb it indicates 'him, her, it' as object. Following a passive verb it indicates the agent:

> **Saya melihatnya.** I saw him/her/it.
> **Saya dilihatnya.** I was seen by him/her/it.

It also indicates third person singular after a number of other words, including some prepositions, such as **kepada**:

> **Saya memberi buku saya kepadanya.**
> I gave my book to him/her.

C   Linker between noun and possessor

It can link a possessive noun to the preceding possessed noun:

> **Rumahnya guru saya di jalan ini.**
> My teacher's house is in this street.

In this function **-nya** is optional; its absence makes no difference to the meaning:

> **Rumah guru saya di jalan ini.**
> My teacher's house is in this street.

In some contexts it helps make the meaning clear. Thus **Ibu Suparjo** can mean 'Mrs Suparjo' or 'Suparjo's mother'; **Ibunya Suparjo** can only be possessive and so means only 'Suparjo's mother'.

> **NOTE**   Suffix **-nya** is not used as a linker by all speakers of Indonesian; it is most common in the usage of people whose regional language has a similar form.

D   Definitiser with a noun not previously mentioned

Once we have used a noun to identify something we can mention it again using the definite marker **itu**:

Ibu sudah memasak nasi. Nasi itu di lemari.

Mother has cooked rice. It is in the cupboard. (literally: That rice is in the cupboard.)

If the noun has not been used before we cannot use **itu** after it. However, if the noun has not been used before but the thing referred to is clear from context then -**nya** can be attached to the noun. For instance, when eating is mentioned in Indonesia it is assumed that rice is involved; the context of eating entails rice and so -**nya** can be attached to the word **nasi**:

Kalau mau makan, nasinya di lemari.

If you want to eat the rice is in the cupboard.

Thus -**nya** makes a noun definite if it is clear in the context of the conversation but has not previously been mentioned. In this function -**nya** can be called a definitiser.

As another example, the following question might be asked in a house to which a newspaper is delivered. The question presupposes or entails that the daily paper is present in the house:

Di mana korannya?

Where's the newspaper?

NOTE   While this use of -**nya** is common it is not used by all Indonesians. In some contexts -**nya** can be left out, while in other situations some people may use a different construction. Thus the following may be used instead of the above sentence:

Kalau mau makan ada nasi di lemari.

If you want to eat there is rice in the cupboard.

EXERCISE 1

Each sentence below contains -**nya**.
*   Indicate the function of -**nya**: possessor, object, agent, linker, definitiser.
*   Translate the sentences into English.

Example

Sepedanya Ali dicuri tadi malam.

→   Linker

Ali's bike was stolen last night.

1.   **Pengemis itu diberinya uang.**

2.   **Saya membelinya kemarin.**

3.   **Istrinya lahir di Solo.**

4.   **Kami pergi ke bioskop tadi malam. Filmnya bagus sekali.**

5.   **Kamu belum membersihkan rumah baik-baik. Kamar mandinya masih kotor.**

6.   **Ibunya teman saya bekerja di Sarinah.**

7.   **Karena Tom tidak mau bekerja kami menyuruhnya pergi.**

8.   **Kami diserahinya tugas ini.**

9.   **Kakaknya Tuti mengajar di sekolah ini.**

10   **Sardi ingin menjual mobilnya.**

11   **Kami harus naik taksi karena busnya terlambat.**

12.   **Saya mau mandi tapi airnya terlalu dingin.**

21   NUMBERS

A   Cardinal numbers

Cardinal numbers are the numbers we use when stating how many things we are referring to: **tiga orang** 'three people', **lima rumah** 'five houses', **tiga ratus pulau** 'three hundred islands'.

Cardinal numbers can act as predicates:
   Rumahnya lima.
   He has five houses.

The Indonesian sentence literally means 'His houses are five'. It is also possible to use a construction similar to the English, using **punya** 'have, possess':
   Dia punya lima rumah.
   He has five houses.

The indefinite numbers **banyak** 'many' and **sedikit** 'few, a little' can also occur in such constructions.

> **NOTE**   Numbers in the predicate can optionally be followed by the appropriate classifier:
> **Anak perempuan saya dua.** *or* **Anak perempuan saya dua orang.**
> I have two daughters. (cf. **dua anak perempuan** *or* **dua orang anak perempuan** 'two daughters')
> **Anjing saya tiga.** *or* **Anjing saya tiga ekor.**
> I have three dogs. (cf. **tiga anjing** *or* **tiga ekor anjing** 'three dogs'.)

EXERCISE 1

- Translate the following sentences into Indonesian.
- give constructions both with number predicates and with **punya**.

   Example
   I have two daughters.
   →   **Saya punya dua anak perempuan.**
       Anak perempuan saya dua.

   1.   Ronny has two cars.
   2.   My uncle has a lot of friends.
   3.   Mr. Ali has fifteen buffalos.
   4.   He has almost a hundred chickens.
   5.   I have more than fifty books.

6.   Joe has two younger brothers.
7.   We have only a little money.
8.   That rich man has three farms.

B   Ordinals and other numbers

•   *Ordinal numbers* are the numbers used when stating where something comes in a series or sequence. In Indonesian **ke-** is prefixed to the cardinal number to form an ordinal. Ordinals follow the noun, optionally preceded by **yang**: **orang yang kedua** 'the second person', **rumah kelima** 'the fifth house', **anggota yang ketiga ratus** 'the three hundredth member'. The common word for 'first' is **pertama**, although **kesatu** also occurs.

•   Numbers with prefix **ke-** can also precede the noun to indicate a specific group of that many. The noun is always definite. In English cardinal numbers are used in this case:
    Saya sudah membaca <u>keempat buku itu</u>.
    I've read <u>those four books</u>.

Kedua before the noun translates '(the) two' or 'both':
    <u>Kedua</u> anaknya pergi ke sekolah ini.
    Her <u>two</u> children/<u>both</u> her children go to this school.

When a specific number is not referred to a cardinal number is used:
    Saya sudah membaca <u>empat buku</u> minggu ini.
    I've read <u>four books</u> this week.

•   A cardinal number followed by **dari** is used to indicate a certain number out of a larger group:
    <u>Tiga dari temannya</u> masih di sekolah.
    <u>Three of his friends</u> are still at school.

A phrase like 'three of' refers to a non-specific three out of a larger group. However, 'all three of' does not refer to a larger group; the whole group is three. Therefore the people referred to are specific and **ketiga** is used:
    <u>Ketiga temannya</u> pergi ke sekolah ini.
    <u>All three of his friends</u> go to this school. *or* <u>His three friends</u> go to this
        school.

EXERCISE 2

•   Translate the following sentences into Indonesian.
•   Choose a cardinal number or an ordinal number following the noun or a number with **ke-** preceding the noun as appropriate.

1.   He sent both his children to school in Australia.
2.   Two children are playing on the road.
3.   Her five children are sick.
4.   Five of her children are sick.
5.   Seven friends visited Allan in hospital.
6.   His second child is attending school in Australia.
7.   Allan's seven friends visited him in hospital.
8.   Her fifth child is sick.
9.   John was the seventh friend to visit Allan in hospital.
10.   Martin is their first child.
11.   Four of those people helped me.
12.   All four of those people helped me.
13.   Four people helped me.
14.   The fourth house is mine.

•   Ordinal numbers can occur in superlative phrases [see section 14B] to indicate ranking. The ordinal can precede or follow the superlative adjective. If it precedes the adjective **yang** optionally comes between them:
    Dia petinju terbaik kedua/Dia petinju kedua (yang) terbaik.
    He is the second best boxer.

•   While numbers with **ke-** precede nouns to indicate a specific group, forms with **ber-** follow pronouns:
    ketiga orang itu those three people
    mereka bertiga those three

Pronouns followed by the **ber-** form only refer to humans.

•   Numbers indicating a specific group can occur with suffix **-nya** if there is no following noun, such as **keduanya** 'both of them', **ketiganya** 'all three of them', and so on. (The number can be reduplicated and **ke-** can be dropped. So 'both of them' can also be **kedua-duanya** or **dua-duanya**.)

There is a difference in meaning between the **keduanya** type and the **mereka berdua** type when referring to third person human. In a first mention, such as when pointing, **mereka berdua** is used, meaning 'those two'. Subsequently **keduanya** is used, meaning 'both of them':
    Mereka berdua teman saya. Keduanya tinggal di Kebayoran.
    Those two are my friends. Both of them live in Kebayoran.

•   Expressions such as 'the first three pages' and 'the last three pages' are expressed as follows:
    ketiga halaman yang pertama the first three pages
    ketiga halaman yang terakhir the last three pages

EXERCISE 3

- Translate the following sentences into Indonesian.

1. Surabaya is the second biggest city in Indonesia.
2. Both of us work in the city.
3. He has four dogs. All four of them are big.
4. I will be very busy for the last three weeks of this year.
5. I bought three books this morning. All three of them were expensive.
6. You must read the first ten pages of this book.
7. Those four work in the city. All four of them get this train.
8. Willy is the third best player in his team.
9. There are two roads to that village. Both of them are good.
10. You three can go now.
11. My uncle is the fifth richest man in this town.
12. Her first three children are very pretty.

C   Marking position in a series

Things which are typically distinguished by their position in a series are identified by using a cardinal number after the noun, rather than using an ordinal number. This is also common in English with such words. Thus: **halaman tiga** 'page three'. Compare this with **halaman ketiga** 'the third page' and **tiga halaman** 'three pages'. (When we ask questions about such things we use **berapa** rather than **apa** - see section 33E.)

This system is also used with dates. The cardinal number follows **tanggal** 'date': **tanggal lima Maret** '5th of March/March 5th'. It is also used with hours: **jam lima** 'five o'clock'. Compare this with **lima jam** 'five hours'.

To state a year the word **tahun** 'year' is placed before the number: **tahun sembilan belas sembilan puluh delapan** or **tahun seribu sembilan ratus sembilan puluh delapan** '(the year) 1998'. If the number comes before **tahun** it refers to the number of years: **sembilan puluh delapan tahun** '98 years'.

EXERCISE 4

- Translate the following sentences into English.

1. **Pak Hasan mengajar kelas empat.**
2. **Kami harus bekerja enam jam kemarin.**
3. **Hari ini kami mulai dengan pelajaran dua puluh.**
4. **Dia tinggal di lantai tujuh.**
5. **Umurnya delapan puluh tahun.**

6. Kami akan pindah ke sana pada tanggal lima belas.
7. Dia sudah tinggal di sini delapan tahun.
8. Kami sudah menyelesaikan dua puluh pelajaran dalam buku ini.
9. Saya sudah membaca halaman sepuluh.
10. Kami mulai bekerja jam enam kemarin.
11. Kami akan berangkat pada tanggal enam belas April.
12. Kamus Oxford terdiri dari dua belas jilid.
13. Saya mau meminjam jilid dua belas.
14. Pak Hasan mengajar empat kelas.
15. Dia lahir pada tahun sembilan belas delapan puluh.
16. Saya sudah membaca sepuluh halaman.

D   Fractions

Fractions are formed by attaching **per-** to the larger number and placing the smaller number before it:

> **dua pertiga** two thirds

If the smaller number is 'one' **se-** is used:

> **sepertiga** one third

Fractions follow full numbers:

> **Dua dua pertiga** Two and two thirds

The special term **setengah** is used for 'half':

> **Dua setengah** two and a half

EXERCISE 5

•   Write out the following numbers in Indonesian.

Examples
¼ (one quarter)
→   **seperempat**

2¼ (two and a quarter)
→   **dua seperempat**

1.	$^3/_4$		7.	$^1/_8$
2.	$^2/_5$		8.	$^1/_{100}$
3.	$^3/_7$		9.	$2^1/_4$
4.	$^6/_{10}$		10.	$3^1/_2$
5.	$^4/_5$		11.	$5^3/_{10}$
6.	$^2/_{100}$		12.	$6^1/_3$

- Fractions precede the noun they refer to:

Dua pertiga penduduk Indonesia tinggal di pulau Jawa.
Two thirds of the population of Indonesia live on the island of Java.

EXERCISE 6

- Translate the following sentences into Indonesian.

1. Two thirds of the students in the class are female.
2. Three quarters of the teachers at this school have cars.
3. He drank a quarter of a glass of water.
4. Tomo only worked for two and a half hours.
5. He lived in Bandung for four and a quarter years.
6. He ran one and three quarter kilometres.
7. Alice is one and a half years old. (literally: Alice's age is one and a half years.)
8. I've read one and a half pages.
9. It costs just four and a half dollars. (literally: Its price is just…)
10. I've been waiting for half an hour.

> **NOTE**   In decimal numbers in Indonesian **koma** 'comma' is used, equivalent to English 'point', represented by a comma in writing:
> **dua koma tiga (2,3)** two point three (2.3)
> **satu koma satu juta (1,1 juta)** one point one million (1.1 million)
>
> When writing numbers a point is used instead of a comma to mark off thousands:
> **1.000 (seribu)** 1,000
> **2.300.000 (dua juta tiga ratus ribu)** 2,300,000

22　ARITHMETIC

Simple arithmetic operations are described in the following sections.

A　Addition

The formula used is:
> (number) **tambah** (number) **sama dengan** (total)
> **Dua tambah dua sama dengan empat.**
> Two plus two equals four.

The word **tambah** here means 'plus' or 'add'; **sama dengan** means 'the same as' or 'equals'. Some people use **ditambah** (from **menambah** 'to add') instead of **tambah**: **dua ditambah tiga** 'two plus three'.

B　Subtraction

The formula used is:
> (number) **kurang** (number) **sama dengan** (total)
> **Sepuluh kurang tiga sama dengan tujuh.**
> Ten minus three equals seven.

The word **kurang** means 'less' or 'minus'. Some people use **dikurangi** (from **mengurangi** 'to reduce, subtract') instead of **kurang**: **tiga dikurangi dua** 'three take away two'.

C　Multiplication

The formula used is:
> (number) **kali** (number) **sama dengan** (total)
> **Dua kali tiga sama dengan enam.**
> Two times three is six.

The word **kali** means 'times'.

D　Division

The formula used is:
> (number) **dibagi** (number) **sama dengan** (total)
> **Sepuluh dibagi dua sama dengan lima.**
> Ten divided by two equals five.

The word **dibagi** is the passive of **membagi** 'to divide'. The symbol used for division in Indonesia is (:); thus **10 : 5 = 2** means the same as '10 ÷ 2 = 5'.

EXERCISE 1

- Write the following symbols out in full in Indonesian.

    Example
    5 x 3 = 15
    →   **Lima kali tiga sama dengan lima belas.**

1.	3 + 4 = 7	9.	6 − 1 = 5
2.	5 + 4 = 9	10.	12 − 3 = 9
3.	25 + 17 = 42	11.	20 − 3 = 17
4.	50 + 23= 73	12.	105 − 12 = 93
5.	3 x 3 = 9	13.	8 : 2 = 4
6.	6 x 4 = 24	14.	9 : 3 = 3
7.	7 x 5 = 35	15.	100 : 5 = 20
8.	10 x 8 = 80	16.	200 : 4 = 50

23   REFLEXIVES

A   The reflexive pronoun *diri*

A transitive verb can be followed by a reflexive pronoun to indicate that the object is the same as the subject. In Indonesian **diri** is used:

Dia membela <u>diri</u>.
He defended <u>himself</u>.
Kami mempersiapkan <u>diri</u>.
We prepared <u>ourselves</u>.

EXERCISE 1

- Translate the following sentences into Indonesian.
- Use the word in parentheses for the Indonesian verb.

  Example:
  You must guard (**menjaga**) yourself well.
  →   **Anda harus menjaga diri baik-baik.**

1.   The guest introduced (**memperkenalkan**) himself.
2.   You must adjust (**menyesuaikan**) yourself to the new situation.
3.   I tried to calm (**menenangkan**) myself.
4.   Sutan released (**melepaskan**) himself from the rope.
5.   They armed (**mempersenjatai**) themselves with knives.
6.   Irawati had to look after (**mengurusi**) herself after her husband died.

> **NOTE** Sometimes Indonesian has a transitive verb followed by **diri** where an intransitive verb occurs in English:
> **Dia menceburkan diri ke laut.**
> He plunged into the sea. (literally: He plunged himself into the sea.)
> **Pencuri itu melarikan diri.** The thief fled.

B   Reflexive phrases

For emphasis **diri** can be followed by a possessive pronoun, which must correspond in person and number to the subject:

Kita harus meyakinkan <u>diri kita</u>.
We must convince <u>ourselves</u>.

It can also be followed by **sendiri**, which emphasises a contrast with someone else:

Kita harus meyakinkan <u>diri sendiri</u>.
We must convince <u>ourselves</u> (not someone else)

The possessive pronoun and **sendiri** can occur together for extra emphasis:
> **Kita harus meyakinkan <u>diri kita sendiri</u>.**
> We must convince <u>ourselves</u>.

A reflexive phrase can also follow a preposition to refer back to the subject; in this case **diri** cannot occur alone:
> **Anita marah terhadap <u>dirinya sendiri</u>.**
> Anita was angry at <u>herself</u>.

EXERCISE 2

- Translate the following sentences into Indonesian.
- Translate a pronoun by the word in parentheses after it (if there is one).
- Use the word in parentheses after the verb for the Indonesian verb.
- Use a full reflexive phrase, making sure to choose the pronoun which corresponds with the person and number of the subject.

Example
He stabbed (**menikam**) himself.
→   **Dia menikam dirinya sendiri.**

1.   I (**aku**) didn't defend (**membela**) him; I defended myself.
2.   She blamed (**menyalahkan**) herself.
3.   He wrote (**menulis**) about himself.
4.   How can they govern (**memerintah**) others? They can't govern themselves yet.
5.   You (**kamu**) always think about (**memikirkan**) yourself.
6.   Before we (**kita**) understand (**mengerti**) other people we must understand ourselves.
7.   I (**saya**) directed (**menujukan**) those words at myself.
8.   Joko bought (**membeli**) the cigarettes not only for his friends but also for himself.

> **NOTE**   As in other constructions, in reflexive phrases **-nya** may refer to third person plural instead of **mereka**:
> **Mereka harus meyakinkan dirinya sendiri.** They must convince themselves.
>
> In an impersonal construction with no subject only **diri sendiri** 'oneself' is used:
> **Mengerti diri sendiri penting.** Understanding oneself is important.

C *Sendiri*

The reflexive **sendiri** 'self' follows nouns and pronouns to emphasise or make clear who is being referred to:

Ibu <u>sendiri</u> memasak kue ini.
Mother <u>herself</u> baked these cakes.

Referring to the subject **sendiri** can optionally be placed at the end of the clause:
Ibu memasak kue ini <u>sendiri</u>.
Mother baked these cakes <u>herself</u>.

Following a possessor **sendiri** is translated 'own':
Ini buku saya <u>sendiri</u>.
This is my <u>own</u> book.

NOTE   When **sendiri** immediately follows the subject many speakers prefer to use
yang:
Ibu sendiri yang memasak kue ini.

This literally means 'It is mother herself who baked these cakes' or 'Mother herself is
the one who baked these cakes' and is actually an identifying clause [see section 30A].

EXERCISE 3

* Translate the following sentences into Indonesian.

1.   That person is Arjuna's own father.
2.   Mr Umar built this house himself.
3.   We'll have to clean the house ourselves.
4.   Detty returned to her own village.
5.   You three will have to do the shopping yourselves.
6.   I was bitten by my own dog.
7.   Is this Tomo's own car?
8.   This is your own house, isn't it?
9.   Why ask me? You know yourself what happened.
10.   I myself often go there.

NOTE   When we say in English 'by herself', 'by themselves' etc. we mean 'alone,
not with others'. In Indonesian this is **sendirian** or, more formally, **seorang diri**:
Pak Kardi tinggal sendirian/seorang diri. Mr Kardi lives by himself/alone.

It is common in everyday speech for people to use **sendiri** instead of **sendirian**:
Pak Kardi tinggal sendiri. Mr Kardi lives by himself/alone.

Out of context this use of **sendiri** can be ambiguous. Thus **Saya pergi sendiri** could
mean the same as **Saya sendiri pergi**, meaning 'I went myself (and not someone else)'
or it could mean the same as **Saya pergi sendirian** 'I went alone (without anyone else)'.

A *clause* is a construction which contains a subject and a predicate. A basic clause can occur by itself as a sentence, although sentences can be complex and contain more than one clause. A transitive clause also contains an object and all clause types can contain other components, such as phrases indicating time and place.

The normal word order in an intransitive clause in Indonesian is:

Subject + Predicate

subject	predicate
Ali	**sedang tidur.**
Ali	is sleeping.

In a transitive clause the normal order is:

Subject + Predicate + Object

subject	predicate	object
Ali	**melihat**	**Mary.**
Ali	sees	Mary.

In a passive clause the normal word order is:

Subject + Predicate + Agent

subject	predicate	agent
Mary	**dilihat**	**(oleh) Ali.**
Mary	is seen	by Ali.

Sometimes the normal word order is changed. This usually occurs when the speaker wants to focus on something in particular; when a constituent of a clause is out of its normal place it usually receives greater attention.

A Subject-predicate inversion

One common change of word order is when the subject and predicate change places. This is called *subject-predicate inversion*. It is most frequent if the verb is intransitive or passive transitive.

The following sentence has normal word order:

Dia sudah pulang. She's gone home.

The inverted form of this, which puts emphasis on what she has done by placing the predicate first, is:

Sudah pulang dia. She's gone home.

The following sentence has normal word order:

Rumah-rumah yang modern didirikan di daerah ini.

Modern houses have been built in this region.

This can have the inverted form:

Di daerah ini didirikan rumah-rumah yang modern.

In this region have been built modern houses.

---

normal word order:

subject	predicate	adverb of place
Rumah-rumah yang modern	**didirikan**	**di daerah ini.**

inverted word order:

adverb of place	predicate	subject
Di daerah ini	**didirikan**	**rumah-rumah yang modern.**

In the above example the subject, which is new information, gets highlighting or focus by being put last; the inversion brings to it the listener's attention.

Note that the adverb of place has also changed places. In Indonesian, as in English, if subject-predicate inversion occurs then something which would usually go after the predicate is usually placed before it. This gives the sentence balance, allowing the predicate to retain its place in the 'middle' of the clause.

EXERCISE 1

- Invert the subject and predicate of the following clauses.
- Make any other changes of word order to retain balance in the clause.
- Translate your constructions. Do not invert subject and predicate in the English translation if it would sound unnatural.

Example

Warung kecil akan dibukanya tahun depan.

→   **Tahun depan akan dibukanya warung kecil.**

Next year he will open a small stall.

1.   **Sebuah menara tinggi didirikan di atas gunung.**
2.   **Seorang tetangga datang sekitar pukul tiga.**
3.   **Lampu lalu lintas dipasang untuk melancarkan lalu lintas.**
4.   **Sepatu khusus dibuat bagi dia.**
5.   **Tarian klasik Jawa dipergelarkan tiap malam.**
6.   **Alat-alat modern tersedia di tokonya.**
7.   **Enam pengusaha yang melakukan kejahatan meringkuk di penjara itu.**
8.   **Suara harimau terdengar dari hutan.**

• A long subject is often placed after the predicate to avoid a stylistically clumsy construction.. In general, the longer a subject the more likely it is to follow the predicate. In the following example the subject is underlined:

Sekarang di toko Tuan Ong tersedia <u>alat-alat yang menarik perhatian orang desa yang berkunjung ke kota</u>.

Now in Mr Ong's store are available <u>implements which attracts the interest of villagers visiting the town</u>.

• Frequently, especially in writing, **-lah** is attached to the predicate when subject-predicate inversion occurs. It thus marks the predicate when it is out of its normal order in the clause and, since the predicate is usually placed before the subject for emphasis or highlighting, **-lah** is often regarded as emphasising the predicate. In some cases it is possible to catch the emphasis in English by using 'there':

Lalu <u>datanglah</u> seorang musyafir ke desa itu.

Then <u>there came</u> a traveller to that village.

EXERCISE 2

• Invert the subject and predicate of the following clauses.
• Place **-lah** in the appropriate place.
• Make any other changes of word order to retain balance in the clause.
• Translate your constructions. Do not invert subject and predicate in the English translation if it would sound unnatural.

1. **Lalu dia menyeberang.**
2. **Suatu rapat besar yang dinamakan Kongres Pemuda diadakan pada tahun 1928.**
3. **Pengaruh Islam masuk di Indonesia kira-kira tahun 1400.**
4. **Suatu Indonesia merdeka tercipta pada hari itu.**
5. **Pasukan menghadang massa dan suara tembakan terdengar.**
6. **Surat dari isteri saya datang ketika saya di Bandung.**
7. **Kami berangkat setelah hujan berhenti.**
8. **Kamu tertipu!**

B   Predicate-agent inversion

Sometimes the speaker wants to treat the agent of a passive verb as important information; in this case it can be placed before the verb. This is called *predicate-agent inversion*. The preposition **oleh** must occur and the phrase can go before or after the subject. From the clause:

Sayur-mayur masih kurang dihargai oleh banyak orang.

Vegetables are still not appreciated by many people.

can be derived the following structures:

Sayur-mayur oleh banyak orang masih kurang dihargai.
Vegetables by many people are still not appreciated.
Oleh banyak orang sayur-mayur masih kurang dihargai.
By many people vegetables are still not appreciated.

subject	agent	predicate
Sayur-mayur	**oleh banyak orang**	**masih kurang dihargai.**

agent	subject	predicate
Oleh banyak orang	**sayur-mayur**	**masih kurang dihargai.**

NOTE In an active clause there cannot be predicate-object inversion.   This is because of the rule that if the patient (which occurs as object in an active sentence) comes before the verb then the verb must be passive.

EXERCISE 3

Some of the sentences below have inversion of subject and predicate or of
  agent and predicate. In some there is no inversion.
* If no inversion occurs mark structures: 'no inversion'. If inversion occurs
  state whether it is 'subject-predicate inversion' or 'predicate-agent
  inversion'.
* Label major components of the clause as appropriate. Clause components
  occurring in the exercise which are discussed in other sections are:
  subject, predicate, object, secondary object, agent, recipient. Any phrase
  indicating place, time, manner and so on should be labelled *adverb.*
* Translate the sentences. Do not translate with inversion if it would
  produce a clumsy sentence in English.

Example
Dengan mudah di sini dapat diperoleh kendaraan tradisional.
→   subject-predicate inversion

Dengan mudah	**di sini**	**dapat diperoleh**	**kendaraan tradisional.**
adverb	*adverb*	*predicate*	*subject*

Traditional vehicles can be obtained easily here.

John sampai di Jakarta setelah makan siang di Puncak.
→   no inversion

John	**sampai**	**di Jakarta**	**setelah makan siang di Puncak.**
subject	*predicate*	*adverb*	*adverb*

John arrived in Jakarta after having lunch in Puncak.

1.   **Di lapangan terbang disediakan ruangan tunggu.**

2.   **Pada hari itu tercipta suatu negara Indonesia merdeka.**

3.   **Tanah itu oleh orang lain dianggap mahal.**

4.   **Tugas itu harus dikerjakan selekas mungkin oleh semua anggota.**

5.   **Oleh orang tuanya Siti diberi cincin emas.**

6.   **Kepada yang lapar akan diberikan makanan.**

7.   **Oleh orang kota petani-petani itu dikirimi uang.**

8.   **Minggu lalu Muji ditawari pekerjaan oleh pemilik toko itu.**

9.   **Pak Kardi oleh dokter disuruh pergi ke rumah sakit.**

10.   **Sudah diselesaikannya pekerjaan itu.**

25   RELATIVE CLAUSES

A   Defining relative clauses

We can indicate precisely who or what we are talking about by putting a clause after a noun. The clause is preceded by **yang** and is called a *defining relative clause*, commonly called simply a relative clause. **Yang** links the relative clause to the preceding noun, the head noun of the phrase, and corresponds to 'who, which, that' in English. The relative clause derives from a basic clause (one which can stand alone as a sentence) whose subject corresponds to the head of the noun phrase in which the relative clause occurs. In the following example the basic clause and the relative clause derived from it are underlined:

> **Wanita itu bekerja dengan saya.**   <u>**Wanita itu duduk dekat jendela.**</u>
> That woman works with me.   That woman is sitting near the window.
>
> →   **Wanita <u>yang duduk dekat jendela</u> bekerja dengan saya.**
>   The woman who is sitting near the window works with me.

Basic clause:	
subject	predicate
Wanita itu	**duduk dekat jendela.**
Noun phrase:	
head noun	relative clause
wanita	**yang duduk dekat jendela**

EXERCISE 1

Each of the following constructions contains a relative clause.
- Translate each sentence into Indonesian.
- Underline the relative clause in each sentence.

Example:
The people that are gathering in front of the door have to move.
> →   **Orang <u>yang berkumpul di depan pintu</u> harus pindah.**

1. The child who fell from the tree had to be taken to the doctor.
2. People that are lazy will not get work.
3. The people who didn't get a seat were very angry.
4. The dog which bit Mary belongs to our neighbour.
5. My friend who works in the bank will call by tonight.
6. The child that is standing there is Ali.

•   The head noun can stand as actor or patient of the verb in the relative clause.

When it stands as actor the verb in the relative clause must be active (with prefix **meN-** if it is transitive), just as in the free clause from which it comes:
> **Orang itu membersihkan kamar.** → **orang yang membersihkan kamar**
>
> That person cleaned the room. → the person who cleaned the room

When the head noun stands as patient the verb must be passive, as it is in the free clause from which it comes:
> **Kamar itu sudah dibersihkan.** → **kamar yang sudah dibersihkan**
>
> That room has been cleaned. → the room which has been cleaned

In English the verb in a relative clause is frequently active, even though the head noun stands as patient to it. In fact a passive verb often sounds quite unnatural in English, as it would in the second example below. In Indonesian the verb *must* be passive in such case:
> **rumah yang dibangun Pak Dani**
>
> the house which Mr Dani built *or* the house which was built by Mr Dani
>
> **bis yang dinaikinya ke kota**
>
> the bus which she took to town (literally: the bus which was taken by her to town)

•   In English 'who, which, that' can sometimes be left out, along with the relevant form of 'to be', where that would occur. In Indonesian **yang** can *never* be omitted before a relative clause:
> **Celana yang dibelinya terlalu kecil.**
>
> The trousers (which) he bought are too small.
>
> **Orang yang berkumpul di depan pintu harus pindah.**
>
> The people (who are) gathering in front of the door have to move.

NOTE As in English, a relative clause in Indonesian can be used even when the person or thing being spoken about has already been identified. In this case it gives extra information about the person or thing and is called a non-defining relative clause. Commas are usually placed before and after a non-defining relative clause:
> **Istri Pak Ali, yang berasal dari Kalimantan, tidak suka tinggal di kota besar.**
>
> Mr. Ali's wife, who comes from Kalimantan, doesn't like living in the big city.

A number of non-defining relative clauses are included in exercises.

EXERCISE 2

- Translate the following sentences into Indonesian.
- Select an active or passive verb in the relative clause as required.

1.   The man who sold this car to me lives in Kebayoran.
2.   The house they bought last year is near the river.
3.   The movie Geoffrey Rush starred in was *Shine*.
4.   The meeting that was cancelled last night will be held next week.
5.   My neighbour, who was taken to hospital last week, is now home again.
6.   The demonstrators who threw stones were chased away by the police.
7.   The vegetables mother bought this morning have already been eaten.
8.   The secretary helping Mr Asdi began work at seven o'clock this morning.
9.   The woman who bought these vegetables is my mother.
10.   The parcel he sent last week still hasn't arrived.

- Passive constructions in relative clauses are type one or type two passives, just as in basic clauses [see section 4B]. Third person pronoun agents can still be in either type. In English it is not usual for a passive verb to occur in such constructions:

surat yang ditulis (oleh) ayah saya
the letter written by my father *or* the letter my father wrote
surat yang saya tulis
the letter written by me *or* the letter I wrote
surat yang dia tulis *or* **surat yang ditulisnya/surat yang ditulis olehnya**
the letter written by her *or* the letter she wrote

EXERCISE 3

- Translate each of the following sentences into Indonesian.
- Use the correct voice for the verb in the relative clause.
- If the verb is passive choose either passive type one or type two as required.
- Give both passive types where this is possible.

1.   The ambulance we called came quickly.
2.   I have read all the books which Mochtar Lubis has written.
3.   The dictionary she bought isn't very expensive.
4.   Most of the people who attended the meeting supported our proposal.
5.   John's father, who works in the hospital, has bought a new car.
6.   The class Mr Amir teaches is very quiet.

7.   The man who offered us work owns a clothing company.

8.   The sate I've cooked is still too hot.

9.   The house they bought is next door to Alan's house.

10.   The packet that Mrs Halimah sent was very heavy.

NOTE   A relative clause may be followed by **itu**. In the following sentence the relative clause **yang saya hadiri** 'which I attended' is followed by **itu**, which marks the head noun **rapat** 'meeting':

Rapat yang saya hadiri <u>itu</u> sangat membosankan.
That meeting I attended was very boring.

In such cases **itu** occurs in the original noun phrase into which the relative clause is inserted:

Saya menghadiri rapat.   **Rapat <u>itu</u> sangat membosankan.**
I attended a meeting.   That meeting was very boring.

The relative clause is placed before **itu** because **itu**, when it occurs, is always the final word in a noun phrase [see section 3D].

Normally, however, **itu** would be omitted following the relative clause because the thing we are talking about is now identified by the defining relative clause:

Rapat yang saya hadiri sangat membosankan.
The meeting I attended was very boring.

•   If the relative clause contains a passive type two construction the rule that nothing can come between the actor and verb still holds. Thus in the following example **harus** 'must' has to come before the actor, **kamu**:

Pakaian yang harus kamu cuci di keranjang itu.
The clothes you must wash are in that basket.

•   Sometimes a relative clause derives from a basic clause having a different voice. For instance, if the head noun corresponds to the object of an active verb then the verb in the relative clause will have to be passive. In the following example **rapat** 'meeting' is the object of the verb **menghadiri** 'attend' in the basic clause. As **rapat** is the head noun to the relative clause, the verb must be passive:

Ayah menghadiri rapat itu tadi malam.
Father attended the meeting last night.

→   **rapat yang dihadiri ayah tadi malam ...**
the meeting which father attended last night ...

•   If the head noun corresponds to a noun which follows an intransitive verb or occurs in a prepositional phrase after an intransitive verb, then the intransitive verb must be replaced by a passive transitive verb in the relative clause. In the following example the basic clause has an intransitive verb **cinta** followed by a prepositional phrase **kepada gadis itu**. The head noun, **gadis**, corresponds to the noun in the prepositional phrase. Therefore the verb plus preposition in the basic clause must be replaced by the passive transitive verb **dicintai** in the relative clause:

Ali cinta kepada gadis itu.
Ali loves that girl.

→   **gadis yang dicintai Ali ...**
the girl who Ali loves ...

EXERCISE 4

In each number below there are two sentences, each consisting of a basic clause.

- Combine the two sentences by changing the second sentence to a relative clause and placing it into the first sentence at the appropriate place.
- Replace an intransitive verb by a transitive verb and make any other necessary changes.
- Translate your constructions.
- Note: Be sure to form the relative clause from the second sentence, by placing it within the first sentence at the correct place, putting **yang** before it and making any necessary changes, as in the example. Be sure to change active to passive where necessary.

Examples
Pantai itu dekat Cairns. Keluarga saya berkunjung ke pantai itu tahun lalu.

→   **Pantai yang dikunjungi keluarga saya tahun lalu dekat Cairns.**
The beach my family visited last year is near Cairns.

Saya naik bis. Bis itu berhenti dekat rumah saya.
→   **Saya naik bis yang berhenti dekat rumah saya.**
I catch a bus which stops near my place.

1.   **Kereta api berangkat pada jam dua. Kamu harus naik kereta api itu.**
2.   **Perempuan itu adik saya. Kamu baru bertemu dengan perempuan itu.**
3.   **Mahasiswa itu tinggal di asrama. Asrama itu tidak jauh dari universitas.**
4.   **Dokter itu ramah sekali. Dia memeriksa anak-anak saya.**
5.   **Robyn kawin dengan orang Jawa. Orang Jawa itu sudah lama tinggal di Australia.**
6.   **Pengarang itu baru berumur 27 tahun. Dia menulis buku ini.**
7.   **Hutan itu indah sekali. Mereka masuk hutan itu.**

8.   **Tetangga itu meninggal kemarin. Kami kagum terhadap tetangga itu.**
9.   **Film itu lucu sekali. Kamu akan melihat film itu besok.**
10. **Rapat itu sangat membosankan. Dia menghadiri rapat itu tadi malam.**
11. **Barang itu harus dibuang. Saya tidak menjual barang itu.**
12. **Masalah itu penting sekali. Kita harus berpikir tentang masalah itu.**

•   The subject noun is the only noun which can precede the verb, except that a pronoun agent also precedes a passive verb. The English construction 'The coffee John was sold was already cold' has two nouns before the verb 'was sold': 'coffee' and 'John'. 'Coffee' is the subject of the main verb 'was already cold', while 'John' is the subject of the verb in the relative clause 'was sold'. In Indonesian both the verb in the relative clause and the main verb must have the same subject; 'coffee' has to be the subject of both the relative clause verb 'was sold' and of the predicate of the main clause 'was already cold'. 'John' must be indicated in a phrase after the verb:

Kopi yang dijual kepada John sudah dingin.
The coffee John was sold was already cold/The coffee that was sold to
John was already cold.

NOTE   Normally **yang** cannot precede a noun. Relative clauses with a noun usually only occur when the speaker wants to distinguish a person from others with the same characteristics, usually the same name:
Soeharto yang presiden Soeharto who was president (and not some other Soeharto)

Relative clauses indicating location, corresponding to relative clauses with 'where' in English, do not begin with **yang**. The more traditional construction begins with **tempat**:
Pabrik tempat mereka bekerja tidak jauh dari sini.
The place where they work isn't far from here.

The word **tempat** is commonly replaced with **di mana**, although some people regard this as unacceptable:
pabrik di mana mereka bekerja the factory where they work

EXERCISE 5

•   Translate the following sentences into Indonesian.
•   Be sure to place only one noun before the verb in the relative clause (with the exception of the agent).

1.   The child I bought the book for was very happy.
2.   The child who the book was bought for was very happy.

3.   The person the letter was sent to has moved to Bandung.
4.   The person who you sent the letter to has moved to Bandung.
5.   The person she sent the letter to has moved to Bandung.
6.   The person Mary sent the letter to was very happy.
7.   The person who was sent the letter by Mary was very happy.
8.   The letter Mary was sent was very brief.
9.   The skirt mother chose Mary was green.
10.   The skirt Mary was chosen was green.
11.   The girl the skirt was chosen for is named Mary.
12.   The work I was offered was not difficult.
13.   The work the secretary was offered was not difficult.
14.   The secretary the work was offered to is very diligent.
15.   The man that work was given to is my father.
16.   The man the sate was cooked for is my father.

B   Adjectives in relative clauses

An adjective can directly follow a noun, as discussed in Section 13B:
   rumah besar a big house

It can also be preceded by **yang**:
   rumah yang besar a big house

Use of **yang** separates the adjective from the noun and gives emphasis to it. This occurs, for instance, when a contrast is made:
   Mereka tinggal di rumah yang besar, bukan rumah yang kecil.
   They live in a big house, not a small house.

Following **yang** an adjective is a relative clause. If the adjective is accompanied by other components of the adjective phrase then usually **yang** must occur:
   rumah yang sangat besar a very big house
   anak yang tidak begitu sopan a child who isn't very polite

Conjoined adjectives must also be preceded by **yang**:
   anak yang rajin dan pandai a hard-working and clever child

If the adjective is accompanied by **paling** or **ter-**, both meaning 'most', **yang** need not occur:
   kelompok (yang) paling kuat *or* **kelompok (yang) terkuat**
   the strongest group

EXERCISE 6

•   Translate the following sentences into Indonesian.
•   If **yang** can occur optionally place it in parentheses.

1.   His wife is a beautiful and clever woman.
2.   He buys a new car every year.
3.   Who is the fastest runner?
4.   I bought a coat which is too long.
5.   His family wants to move to a bigger town.
6.   His father works in a large factory.
7.   I always buy inexpensive clothes.
8.   People who are already tired can rest now.
9.   They want to live in a town that is smaller than Jakarta.
10.   Tokyo is the most expensive city in the world.

> **NOTE**   Some sequences of noun + adjective can have idiomatic meaning as well as literal meaning. Thus **kamar kecil** can mean 'toilet' or 'little room'; **orang tua** can mean 'parents' or 'old people'. If **yang** is placed before the adjective it can only have the literal meaning: **kamar yang kecil** 'a little room'; **orang yang tua** 'old people'.

C   Possessive relative clauses

A relative clause which refers to something possessed, and which corresponds to a construction with 'whose' in English, is formed with **yang ....-nya**:

> **wisatawan <u>yang paspornya dicuri</u>**
> the tourist <u>whose passport was stolen</u>

A *possessive relative clause* (underlined in number 3. below) derives from a topic-comment clause (the first sentence in 2. below – see unit 26), which itself derives from a basic clause (the first sentence in 1. below):

1.   **Paspor wisatawan itu dicuri. Dia melapor ke polisi.**
      That tourist's passport was stolen. He reported to the police.
2.   **Wisatawan itu paspornya dicuri. Di melapor ke polisi.**
      That tourist, his passport was stolen. He reported to the police.
3.   **Wisatawan <u>yang paspornya dicuri</u> melapor ke polisi.**
      The tourist whose passport was stolen reported to the police.

1.	subject		predicate
	head noun	possessor	
	Paspor	**wisatawan itu**	**dicuri.**
	The passport	of that tourist	was stolen.
2.	topic	comment	
	Wisatawan itu	**paspornya dicuri.**	
	That tourist	his passport was stolen.	
3.	head noun	possessive relative clause	
	wisatawan	**yang paspornya dicuri**	
	the tourist	whose passport was stolen	

EXERCISE 7

Each number below contains two sentences, each consisting of a single clause.
*   Combine the two sentences into a single sentence which contains a possessive relative clause.
*   Translate your constructions.

Examples

Paspor wisatawan itu dicuri. Dia melapor ke polisi.

→   **Wisatawan yang paspornya dicuri melapor ke polisi.**

The tourist whose passport was stolen reported to the police.

Saya menginap dengan keluarga Jawa. Anak keluarga itu bekerja di Darwin.

→   **Saya menginap dengan keluarga Jawa yang anaknya bekerja di Darwin.**

I stayed with a Javanese family whose son works in Darwin.

1. **Kecantikan gadis itu dikagumi. Dia akan menjadi peragawati.**
2. **Harga lukisan itu tinggi. Lukisan itu dijual kepada orang kaya.**
3. **Tinggi teman saya hampir dua meter. Dia menjadi juara loncat tinggi.**
4. **Payung guru itu hilang. Dia kehujanan ketika pulang.**
5. **Dosen marah kepada mahasiswa itu. Karangan mahasiswa itu hilang.**
6. **Anak saya diajar oleh Pak Hadi. Rumah Pak Hadi tidak jauh dari rumah saya.**
7. **Rambut siswa itu terlalu panjang. Dia disuruh pergi ke tukang cukur.**
8. **Buku pengarang itu diterbitkan tahun lalu. Dia menerima hadiah.**
9. **Dia memiliki perkebunan di daerah itu. Tanah daerah itu subur sekali.**
10. **Rumah keluarga itu terbakar habis. Mereka dibantu oleh para tetangga.**

*   Often a possessive relative clause corresponds to an English construction containing 'with' rather than 'whose':

Gadis yang rambutnya panjang itu teman saya.

That girl with the long hair (= whose hair is long) is my friend.

The 'with' construction in English contains an adjective plus a noun. It can be used where the corresponding 'whose' construction has an adjective in its predicate, as in the above example.

NOTE   A **yang ...-nya** construction can correspond to several other constructions in English. Most common is the formal construction with 'of which':
Dia membeli mobil yang harganya tiga puluh ribu dollar.
He bought a car, the price of which (= whose price) was $30,000.

EXERCISE 8

- Translate the following constructions.
- Use possessive relative clauses.

Example
Mother is angry at the children with the dirty clothes.
→   **Ibu marah pada anak-anak yang pakaiannya kotor.**

1. That man with the big car is very rich.
2. The boy with the sore tooth had to go to the dentist.
3. The house with the big yard is Mr. Johnson's.
4. I repaired the chair with the broken leg.
5. Who is that woman with the funny hat?
6. He married the singer with the beautiful voice.

- As in other relative clauses, if there is a verb in a possessive relative clause it must be passive if the head noun stands as patient to it. In the following example **mobil** is the patient of the verb **meminjam**:
Anda meminjam mobil orang itu.
You borrowed that person's car.

So in the possessive relative clause the verb must be passive because the patient precedes it:
Siapa nama orang yang mobilnya Anda pinjam?
What is the name of the person whose car you borrowed?

EXERCISE 9

- Translate the following sentences into Indonesian.
- Use passive verbs where required.

1. I work with a man whose father sells fish at the market.
2. The man whose wife we took to hospital was very grateful.
3. The neighbour whose child broke my window will pay for new glass.
4. Adjat, whose father owns an import company, works in a bank.
5. The lady whose window was broken by that child scolded his parents.
6. The soccer player whose shoes were stolen has complained to his team manager.

7.   The school principal praised the teacher whose pupil won the writing competition.
8.   This morning I met the painter whose picture my father bought last year.

26 TOPIC-COMMENT CLAUSES

A The topic: a way of focusing attention

Topic-comment clauses are one of the ways to focus attention on a particular noun phrase. This phrase is taken from the basic clause and placed before it, becoming the *topic*. The rest of the clause is then a *comment* on the topic. The subject noun phrase of the original clause contains a possessor, underlined in the following example:

Nama <u>sopir itu</u> Pak Ali.
The name <u>of that driver</u> is Mr Ali.

subject		predicate
head	possessor	
Nama	**sopir itu**	**Pak Ali.**

The possessor, **sopir itu** in the above example, becomes the topic, going to the beginning of the construction. Its place after the subject noun is marked by **-nya**:

Sopir itu namanya Pak Ali.
As for that driver, his name is Mr Ali.

topic	subject	predicate
	head-topic marker	
Sopir itu	**nama-nya**	**Pak Ali.**

This sentence could also be translated 'Concerning that driver, his name is Mr Ali'. This conveys the force of the Indonesian construction, although it is quite stilted (while the Indonesian construction is not). Alternatively it could be translated 'That driver, his name is Mr Ali'. It could even be translated in the same way as the basic clause, although out of context this does not capture the force of the Indonesian. Topic-comment clauses occur frequently in Indonesian.

The topic is always marked within the subject by **-nya,** even if it is plural:

Keluarga itu anjingnya tertabrak mobil.
As for that family, their dog was hit by a car.

Most people only allow topic-comment constructions if the topic is third person. Some people place a comma after the topic: **Sopir itu, namanya Pak Ali.** A clause with **-nya** as possessor can be changed to a topic-comment clause:

Namanya Pak Ali. His name is Mr Ali.
→ **Dia namanya Pak Ali.** As for him, his name is Mr Ali.

EXERCISE 1

- Translate each of the following sentences.
- Change each sentence into a topic-comment construction.
- Translate the topic-comment constructions. (Sometimes the translation will need to be the same as in the original sentence to avoid an unnatural English construction.)

Example

Wajah Jakarta sudah mulai berubah.

→   The face of Jakarta has begun to change.

Jakarta wajahnya sudah mulai berubah.

As for Jakarta, its face has begun to change.

1.   **Anak Bu Halim lima orang.**
2.   **Ongkos perjalanan itu $1.000.**
3.   **Suara kelompok itu makin kuat.**
4.   **Penghasilan mereka besar sekali.**
5.   **Rumah tetangga saya terbakar tadi malam.**
6.   **Gaji pegawai-pegawai ini tidak akan naik.**
7.   **Penduduk negeri itu miskin sekali.**
8.   **Jalan-jalan kota itu tidak terurus.**

B   Emphasising the predicate

The components of the topic-comment clause are shown in the following example:

topic	comment
Jakarta	**wajahnya sudah mulai berubah.**
Jakarta	its face has begun to change.

This construction indicates that the speaker is focusing attention on Jakarta. The important thing about Jakarta is that its face is beginning to change.

Within the comment the subject usually precedes the predicate:

subject	predicate
wajahnya	**sudah mulai berubah**

Sometimes the predicate can be given extra focus or emphasis by being placed before the subject; this is called subject-predicate inversion [see section 24A]:

predicate	subject
sudah mulai berubah	**wajahnya**

The whole sentence is then:

topic	comment	
	predicate	subject
Jakarta	**sudah mulai berubah**	**wajahnya.**

Jakarta sudah mulai berubah wajahnya.
As for Jakarta, its face has begun to change.

As in the above example, it is difficult to catch this change in emphasis in the English translation; the Indonesian construction gives special emphasis to the fact that change in Jakarta has began to occur.

The subject and predicate are most likely to change places if the subject is something inalienably possessed. This means that the subject is part of or an innate quality of the topic. In the first example below subject-predicate inversion would only rarely occur and then only with special intonation; Pak Ali's wife is not inalienably possessed. In the second example inversion is common; Pak Ali's eyes are something inalienably possessed - they are a part of Pak Ali:

Pak Ali istrinya dioperasi.
Mr Ali's wife was operated on.
Pak Ali matanya dioperasi.
Pak Ali dioperasi matanya.
Mr Ali's eyes were operated on.

Subject-predicate inversion in topic-comment clauses is very frequent in cases where something is inalienably possessed; misunderstanding is very unlikely. In other cases inversion is rarer because the listener could misunderstand what the speaker means.

EXERCISE 2

- Change the following into topic-comment constructions.
- If subject-predicate inversion is likely - in cases of inalienable possession - give this form as well.
- Translate your sentences into English, in any of the ways outlined above.

1. **Kesabaran Abidin sudah habis.**
2. **Berat anak itu sudah dua puluh kilo.**
3. **Anak mereka belum bersekolah.**
4. **Istri Pak Hanafi tidak bekerja.**

5. **Nama jalan itu Jalan Sutomo.**
6. **Ayah Narti pergi ke Inggris.**
7. **Kantor ayah saya di Jalan Senopati.**
8. **Rasa ayam kampung enak.**
9. **Umur Natasha 24 tahun.**
10. **Kebenaran berita itu belum terbukti.**

NOTE In informal speech the topic is often preceded by **kalau** 'as for':
Kalau Pak Yanto, anaknya sudah kawin.
As for Mr Yanto, his children are already married.

EXERCISE 3

Each of the following sentences consists of a basic clause. Some cannot be converted to topic-comment clauses because the subject does not contain a possessor.

- Translate each sentence into English.
- Change sentences into topic-comment clauses if possible.

1. **Penduduk desa itu banyak.**
2. **Mobil besar itu kepunyaan Pak Ali.**
3. **Jumlah sekolah pada waktu itu masih sangat sedikit.**
4. **Jalan Sutomo selalu penuh dengan kendaraan.**
5. **Buah pohon kami enak sekali.**
6. **Buku sejarah Indonesia itu sekarang di perpustakaan.**
7. **Anak perempuan Bu Dewi diangkat menjadi kepala kantor.**
8. **Pikirannya kolot.**

A   Nominalised defining relative clauses

Yang can be used before adjectives and verbs within a noun phrase. In this function it introduces a relative clause [see sections 25A & B]:

mobil yang biru itu that blue car
orang yang duduk di situ the person sitting there

In Indonesian and English a noun with a relative clause can sometimes be omitted if clear from context. In English the noun is often replaced by 'one', whereas in Indonesian there is no replacement, the phrase thus beginning with **yang**:

yang biru itu that blue one
yang duduk di situ the one sitting there

In such cases the relative clause takes the place of the noun and is called a *nominalised relative clause*. Such clauses are very frequent in Indonesian, the noun commonly being omitted if the thing being referred to is clear from the context:

(Mobil) yang mana mobil Anda?   **Yang biru itu.**
Which (car) is yours?   That blue one.

In some contexts other translations are suitable. If more than one person is referred to then 'those (who)' may be most appropriate:

Yang belajar keras akan lulus; yang malas tidak akan lulus.
Those who study hard will pass; those who are lazy will not pass.

A translation with 'what' is sometimes more appropriate if the thing referred to is inanimate:

Yang dia baca koran *Kompas*.
What she's reading is the newspaper *Kompas*.

As in other relative clauses, a verb in a nominalised relative clause must be passive if the deleted noun stands as patient to it. In the first example below the head noun stands as actor so the verb is active. The noun is deleted in the second sentence. In the next sentence the noun stands as patient so the verb is passive; the noun is deleted in the last sentence:

Orang yang menolong saya Pak Ali.
The person who helped me was Mr Ali.
Yang menolong saya Pak Ali.
The one who helped me was Mr Ali.
Orang yang saya tolong Pak Ali.
The person I helped was Mr Ali.

Yang saya tolong Pak Ali.
The one I helped was Mr Ali.

EXERCISE 1

- Answer the following questions using nominalised relative clauses.
- Use the word provided in parentheses in your answer.
- Translate your constructions.

Example
Siapa yang sedang membersihkan kamar itu? (Steve)
→   **Yang sedang membersihkan kamar itu Steve.**
The one cleaning that room is Steve.

1.   **Siapa yang menyanyikan lagu itu? (Iwan Fels)**
2.   **Siapa yang mengemudikan bis itu? (Rizal)**
3.   **Siapa yang Anda temui tadi malam? (Alice)**
4.   **Apa yang dia cari? (buku catatannya)**
5.   **Apa yang Anda perlukan? (bensin)**
6.   **Siapa yang melihat dari jendela? (sekretaris saya)**
7.   **Apa yang mengganggu mereka? (nyamuk)**
8.   **Siapa yang mengetok pintu tadi? (tukang pos)**

- In a nominalised relative clauses **yang** can be followed not only by a verb but also adjective phrases and other word classes, including **ini** and **itu**: **yang ini** 'this one', **yang itu** 'that one', and **mana**: **yang mana** 'which one?' [see section 33D].

EXERCISE 2

- Translate the following into Indonesian.
- Underline the nominalised relative clauses in your translations.

Example
There are many political parties in Australia. The biggest are the Liberal Party and the Labor Party.
→   **Di Australia banyak partai politik. Yang terbesar adalah Partai Liberal dan Partai Buruh.**

1.   Do you like the expensive ones or the cheap ones?
2.   I don't like the small ones.
3.   Take that small suitcase; I'll take this heavier one.
4.   Ali: There are a lot of newspapers here. Which one would you like to read?
      Hasan: This one.

5.   This glass must be replaced with a clean one.
6.   The ones who haven't left yet can go tomorrow.
7.   Ali: Is this your car?
     Hasan: No. My car is that green one.
8.   The one who bought this book was my uncle.
9.   This building is not as tall as that one.
10. He isn't my uncle. My uncle is the one sitting in the front.

B   Nominalised possessive relative clauses

Possessive relative clauses [see section 25C] can also be nominalised. The first
sentence below contains a possessive relative clause following the head noun. In
the second sentence the head noun is deleted, leaving a *nominalised possessive
relative clause*:

Wisatawan <u>yang paspornya dicuri</u> melapor ke polisi.
The tourist whose passport was stolen reported to the police.
<u>Yang paspornya dicuri</u> melapor ke polisi.
The one whose passport was stolen reported to the police.

As with other relative clauses such constructions occur in situations where the
thing being referred to is clear, for instance in answer to questions:

Wartawan mana yang melapor ke polisi?   **Yang paspornya dicuri.**
Which journalist reported to the police?   The one whose passport
                                               was stolen.

English often uses 'the one with …' where Indonesian uses a nominalised
possessive relative clause [see also section 25C]:

Yang rambutnya panjang itu teman saya.
That one with the long hair (= whose hair is long) is my friend.

EXERCISE 3

The subject in each of the following sentences is a nominalised possessive
   relative clause.
•   Translate the sentences into Indonesian.
•   Underline the nominalised relative clause in each Indonesian sentence.

   Example
   The one whose mother teaches at my school is very lazy.
   →   **<u>Yang ibunya mengajar di sekolah saya</u> malas sekali.**

1.   There are many cities in Indonesia. The one whose population is the
     biggest is Jakarta.
2.   The one whose car was stolen lives near me.

3.   The one with lots of children (= whose children are many) comes from Queensland.
4.   Those whose farms were flooded have been helped by the government.
5.   The one with the red roof (= whose roof is red) is my house.
6.   The one whose father works in this shop is named Budi.
7.   The one whose house burned down was helped by the neighbours.
8.   The one whose salary is the lowest works the hardest.

A The copula

The word **adalah** is sometimes called a *copula* or *link verb*. It serves to link a subject and predicate if the predicate is a noun or noun phrase, just as the verb 'to be' does in English:

Ayah Tomo <u>adalah</u> pegawai Bank Indonesia.
Tomo's father <u>is</u> an employee of the Bank of Indonesia.

subject	(copula)	predicate
noun phrase		noun phrase
Ayah Tomo	**(adalah)**	**pegawai Bank Indonesia.**

Adalah is always optional but is very unlikely to occur in short constructions like **Ayah guru** 'Father is a teacher'. It is most common in noun clauses where either the subject or predicate is long, for instance if the subject contains a relative clause:

Orang yang menyelenggarakan konperensi ini <u>adalah</u> tenaga staf
        bagian tata usaha universitas.
The people who organised this conference <u>are</u> staff of the university's
        administration section.

It also serves to break up a string of nouns and add a smoothness to the construction:

Ikan paus adalah binatang laut.
The whale is a sea creature.

EXERCISE 1

- Insert **adalah** in the following sentences.
- Translate the sentences into English.

1. **Penari itu anak Pak Lukman.**
2. **Orang yang duduk di situ ayah saya.**
3. **Ini hak kita semua.**
4. **Gajah binatang yang sangat besar.**
5. **Indonesia sebuah kepulauan.**
6. **Wanita yang kawin dengan kakak saya guru sekolah menengah.**
7. **Hotel Sabang hotel yang paling murah di kota ini.**
8. **Bu Rodiah sekretaris Pak Bambang.**

> **NOTE** The word **ialah** has the same meaning as **adalah**, they are interchangeable except that **ialah** is less common and only occurs after third person subjects:
>
> **Ikan paus ialah binatang laut.** The whale is a sea creature.
>
> Some people use **adalah** and **ialah** if the predicate is an adjective:
>
> **Mobil-mobil seperti itu adalah/ialah sangat mahal.**
> Cars like that are very expensive.
>
> However, many Indonesians regard putting copulas before adjectives as being ungrammatical.

B   *Adalah* before verbal nouns

Adalah is common if the predicate is a verbal construction acting as a noun. In English such verbs are usually called *gerunds* or *verbal nouns*:

Tugas saya adalah <u>menjual koran</u>.
My task is <u>selling newspapers</u>.

In the above sentence **menjual koran** 'selling newspapers' is functioning as a noun. The subject, **tugas saya** 'my task', is not someone or something that does the action. The subject and predicate are in an *equative* relationship; the construction states that the person or thing expressed by the predicate is the same as the person or thing expressed by the subject. Such constructions usually contain **adalah**; often they sound awkward without it. On the other hand, in a verbal clause like **Saya menjual koran** 'I sell newspapers', **adalah** cannot occur between the subject and predicate.

EXERCISE 2

- Insert **adalah** wherever it can occur in the following constructions.
- Translate the constructions into English.

Examples
Keinginan Hani mempunyai rumah besar.
→   **Keinginan Hani adalah mempunyai rumah besar.**
   Hani's wish is to own a big house.

Hani ingin mempunyai rumah besar.
→   (**adalah** cannot occur)
   Hani wishes to own a big house.

1.   **Pekerjaannya setiap hari memasak di dapur.**
2.   **Kesenangan kami bermain sepak bola.**
3.   **Dul suka menangkap ikan.**

4.   **Banyak turis berlibur di Bali.**
5.   **Kami senang bermain sepak bola.**
6.   **Pekerjaan Dul menangkap ikan.**
7.   **Pekerja-pekerja itu setiap hari memasak di dapur.**
8.   **Rencana saya berlibur di Bali.**
9.   **Teman saya membeli mobil Mercedes.**
10.   **Kehendak saya membeli mobil Mercedes.**

NOTE   In some situations the verb **merupakan** can occur instead of **adalah** or **ialah**:
Rawa Bening <u>adalah/ialah</u> pusat tenaga listrik untuk daerah itu.
Rawa Bening <u>merupakan</u> pusat tenaga listrik untuk daerah itu.
Rawa Bening is the centre for electric power for that region.

Nevertheless, **merupakan** is not a copula; it is a verb and can be negated by **tidak**, whereas **adalah** is not a verb and cannot be preceded by **tidak**. As **adalah** comes before a noun it can be replaced by **bukan**:
Rawa Bening <u>tidak merupakan</u> pusat tenaga listrik untuk daerah itu.
Rawa Bening <u>bukan</u> pusat tenaga listrik untuk daerah itu.
Rawa Bening is not the centre for electric power for that region.

C *Adalah* after nominalised relative clauses

Transitive verbal clauses can sometimes be changed into noun clauses by changing the subject, the verb and everything else in the clause except the object, to a nominalised relative clause [see section 27A.]. The object of the original clause then becomes the predicate. Such constructions are equative because the subject refers to the same thing as the predicate; **adalah** can therefore occur optionally between the subject and predicate:

Dia membaca koran *Kompas*.
She is reading the newspaper *Kompas*.

→   **Yang dibacanya (adalah) koran *Kompas*.**
What she's reading is the newspaper *Kompas*.

Verbal clause:		
subject	predicate (verb)	object
Dia	**membaca**	**koran *Kompas*.**
Noun clause:		
subject		predicate (noun)
Yang dia baca	**(adalah)**	**koran *Kompas*.**

Note that when **yang** refers to the patient of the verb, as in the example above, the verb must be passive [as discussed in section 27A].

EXERCISE 3

- Change the following verbal clauses into noun clauses according to the model above.
- Insert **adalah** in the appropriate place.
- Translate your sentences.

Example

Pak Sastro menulis buku sejarah Indonesia tahun lalu.

→ **Yang ditulis Pak Sastro tahun lalu adalah buku sejarah Indonesia.**

What Mr Sastro wrote last year was an Indonesian history book.

1. **Ayah saya membeli mobil baru kemarin.**
2. **Nelayan itu menangkap dua ikan hiu.**
3. **Saya mencari restoran yang baik.**
4. **Ilmuwan itu menemukan zat baru.**
5. **Pemilik pabrik menawarkan pekerjaan kepada Anton.**
6. **Pemilik pabrik menawari Anton pekerjaan.**
7. **Pelayan mengambil segelas air.**
8. **Pelayan mengambilkan Anton segelas air.**

29   NOMINALISED PREDICATE CLAUSES

A   Nominalising predicates

Some verbal predicates can be nominalised by having **-nya** attached to them. The subject of the original clause then becomes a possessor. So from the clause:

Beberapa jalan ditutup.

Several roads were closed.

we can derive the *nominalised predicate clause*:

ditutupnya beberapa jalan

the closure of several roads

```
Basic clause:
    subject              predicate
    Beberapa jalan       ditutup.

Nominalised predicate clause:
    noun                 possessor
    ditutupnya           beberapa jalan
```

The nominalised predicate clause (underlined in the following example) is a kind of noun phrase and forms part of a larger clause:

Lalu lintas macet karena <u>ditutupnya beberapa jalan</u>.

The traffic is jammed because of <u>the closure of several roads</u>.

Adjectives can be nominalised in the same way as verbs. This is especially common with adjectives indicating measurements. Thus the adjective **tinggi** 'tall, high' can be used as a noun meaning 'height': From **Orang itu tinggi** 'That person is tall' is derived the nominalised construction **tingginya orang itu** 'the height of that person'. These forms usually occur in clauses whose predicate states what the measurement is:

Tingginya orang itu hampir dua meter.

That person's height is almost two metres.

EXERCISE 1

The underlined part in the following sentences is a nominalised predicate clause.
- Translate the whose sentence.
- Give the basic clause from which the nominalised clause derives.
- Translate the basic clause.

Example

Keadaan ini disebabkan karena <u>miskinnya orang tua mereka</u>.

→   This situation is caused by the poverty of their parents.

Orang tua mereka miskin.

Their parents are poor.

1.   **Mereka menunggu <u>datangnya barang-barang dari luar negeri</u>.**
2.   **Mereka ingin tahu tentang <u>tenggelamnya kapal itu</u>.**
3.   **Pemerintah melarang <u>dibentuknya partai baru</u>.**
4.   **<u>Meningkatnya jumlah anak di Indonesia</u> sungguh luar biasa.**
5.   **Wartawan itu mewawancarai pilot tentang <u>jatuhnya pesawat itu dekat Bandung</u>.**
6.   **Dengan <u>dipindahkannya terminal ke lokasi baru</u> para sopir bus merasa dirugikan.**
7.   **<u>Dalamnya kolam ini</u> tiga meter.**
8.   **<u>Meninggalnya Taufan</u> membuat teman-temannya sangat sedih.**
9.   **<u>Beratnya koper ini</u> sepuluh kilogram.**
10.   **<u>Dibangunnya pabrik itu</u> mengganggu ketenangan kota.**
11.   **<u>Turunnya harga beras</u> menggembirakan rakyat.**
12.   **<u>Meletusnya gunung api itu</u> sudah lama diramalkan.**

B   Nominalised predicates with more than one component

In these constructions it is the whole predicate which is nominalised, not just the verb or adjective. Thus components of the predicate preceding the verb or adjective, such as **tidak** 'not' and **sudah** 'already', can also appear. In the following adjective clause:

Pengaruh dialek Jakarta dalam bahasa Indonesia besar.

The influence of Jakarta dialect on Indonesian is <u>great</u>.

the predicate **besar** 'great' can be expanded to **makin besar** 'increasingly great':

Pengaruh dialek Jakarta dalam bahasa Indonesia <u>makin besar</u>.

The influence of Jakarta dialect on Indonesian is <u>increasingly great</u>.

This can now be nominalised, with the original subject becoming a possessor:

<u>makin besarnya pengaruh dialek Jakarta dalam bahasa Indonesia</u>

the increasing extent of the influence of Jakarta dialect on Indonesian

and be placed in a larger clause:

Salah satu perkembangan ialah <u>makin besarnya pengaruh dialek Jakarta dalam bahasa Indonesia</u>.

One of the developments is the increasing extent of the influence of Jakarta dialect on Indonesian.

If there is another component of the predicate before the verb or adjective a literal translation into English is often difficult, requiring a paraphrase to be used. Thus in the above example **makin besarnya** is translated 'the increasing extent'. In the following sentence the nominalised predicate **terlalu jauhnya** literally means 'the too farness' or 'the being too far'. A literal translation is given in parentheses, followed by a more natural translation:

> **Dia mengeluh tentang <u>terlalu jauhnya</u> rumahnya dari pusat pertokoan.**
>
> (He complained about the <u>too-farness</u> of his house from the shopping centre.)
>
> He complained about his house being too far from the shopping centre.

EXERCISE 2

- Translate the following sentences, using natural English constructions.
- Give the basic clause from which the nominalised clause derives.
- Translate the basic clause.

> *Example*
> **Dia mengeluh tentang terlalu jauhnya rumahnya dari pusat pertokoan.**
> →   He complained about his house being too far from the shopping centre.
> **Rumahnya terlalu jauh dari pusat pertokoan.**
> His house is too far from the shopping centre.

1. **Ini menunjukkan tidak adanya efisiensi kerja.**
2. **Kami sudah mendengar tentang sangat mundurnya kebebasan pers di sana.**
3. **Dia bertanya tentang telah terbitnya buku itu.**
4. **Dewan Keamanan menyerukan segera diakhirinya perang itu.**
5. **Stagnasi dapat dilihat dari tidak berubahnya struktur perekonomian.**
6. **Polisi cemas akan terus berlangsungnya pencurian di daerah itu.**
7. **Pemberitaan mengenai akan lepasnya provinsi itu dari Republik Indonesia mengkhawatirkan mereka.**

C Nominalised adjectives with and without -*nya*

Word-for-word translations of constructions with nominalised adjectives of measure are often clumsy in English. We usually use an adjective like 'tall' rather than a noun like 'height'. So we are more likely to say 'That person is two metres tall' than 'The height of that person is two metres':

> **Tingginya orang itu hampir dua meter.**
> That person is almost two metres tall.

If we are referring to first or second person **-nya** does not occur on the nominalised adjective of measure; so we say **tinggi saya, tinggi saudara** 'my height, your height':

Tinggi saya hampir satu setengah meter.
I am almost one and a half metres tall.

If the name of a third person is used **-nya** is optional:

Tinggi Tomo hampir satu setengah meter. *or*
Tingginya Tomo hampir satu setengah meter.
Tomo is almost one and a half metres tall.

In asking a question about a measurement **berapa** is used:

Tingginya berapa? *or* **Berapa tingginya?**
How tall is he?/What is his height?

EXERCISE 3

- Translate the following sentences into Indonesian.
- Use the nominalised adjectives of measure given in parentheses.

Example
How heavy are you/How much do you weigh? (**berat**)
→   **Beratmu berapa?**

1. This road is four metres wide. (**lebar**)
2. This plank is two and a half metres long. (**panjang**)
3. I weigh fifty seven kilos. (**berat**)
4. The distance of my house from the school is one kilometre. (**jauh**)
5. How tall is Mary? (**tinggi**)
6. The river is almost three metres deep here. (**dalam**)
7. The size (area) of Mr Sardi's farm is five hectare. (**luas**)
8. How long is this ladder? (**panjang**)
9. This suitcase weighs about ten kilos. (**berat**)
10. The speed of the car was 100 kilometres an hour/The car was travelling at 100 km/h. (**cepat**)

NOTE   **Tingginya** is used for 'tall/high' for the height of someone or something from top to bottom, but for the height of something above the ground, such as a plane in the sky, **ketinggian** is used:

Ketinggian pesawat itu sembilan ribu meter.   That plane is 9,000 metres high.

For age **umur** is used:

Umurmu berapa? How old are you?

D   Comparison with *peN-...-an* and *ke-...-an* nouns

A number of nominalised verbs have similar meanings to **peN-...-an** or **ke-...-an** nouns. Thus the following two sentences have the same meaning:

Keadaan ini disebabkan karena <u>miskinnya</u> orang tua mereka.
Keadaan ini disebabkan karena <u>kemiskinan</u> orang tua mereka.
This situation is caused by the poverty of their parents.

NOTE Nominalised predicates and corresponding derived nouns cannot always replace each other. The nouns cannot occur together with other predicate components, such as **tidak** and **sudah**, which nominalised predicates can take, as discussed in section 29B.

Also, the nominalised predicate must have a possessor, deriving from the subject of the original clause. **PeN-...-an** and **ke-...-an** nouns often occur without a possessor. Thus **dibangunnya** cannot replace **pembangunan** in the following:

Pembangunan sekarang terjadi di mana-mana.
Development is now occurring everywhere.

EXERCISE 4

- Rewrite the following sentences, replacing the nominalised predicate with the appropriate **peN-...-an** or **ke-...-an** noun.
- Translate the sentences.
- Note: You will need to use a good dictionary.

Example
Dia bertanya tentang dibangunnya pabrik itu.
→   **Dia bertanya tentang pembangunan pabrik itu.**
      He asked about the building of that factory.

1.   **Dia bertanya tentang datangnya bantuan dari luar negeri.**
2.   **Dia bertanya tentang naiknya harga beras.**
3.   **Dia bertanya tentang dicurinya uang itu.**
4.   **Dia bertanya tentang diumumkannya keputusan panitia.**
5.   **Dia bertanya tentang diperiksanya barang-barang itu.**
6.   **Dia bertanya tentang berangkatnya duta besar.**
7.   **Dia bertanya tentang matinya perampok itu.**
8.   **Dia bertanya tentang meningkatnya jumlah anak di Indonesia.**
9.   **Dia bertanya tentang dipindahkannya terminal ke lokasi baru.**
10.   **Dia bertanya tentang inginnya mereka mendapat kemerdekaan.**

A   Basic identifying clauses

One method for focusing attention on a particular element in a clause is to use an *identifying clause*.

The following basic clause is a neutral statement:
>**Orang itu mencuri dompet saya.**
>That person stole my wallet.

If we want to focus attention on **orang itu** 'that person', to make it clear that it was he and not someone else who was involved, we can make it the predicate. The rest of the clause, beginning with **yang**, becomes the subject. The predicate precedes the subject:
>**Orang itu yang mencuri dompet saya.**
>It was that person who stole my wallet.

This construction has the force of an English sentence like 'It was that person (and not someone else) who stole my wallet', or 'That is the person who stole my wallet'. Note that the subject is a nominalised relative clause [see section 27A].

Because the predicate comes first and because it receives focus it very frequently takes **-lah**. This attaches to the last word of the predicate phrase:
>**Orang itulah yang mencuri dompet saya.**
>It was that person who stole my wallet.

Basic clause:	
subject	predicate
Orang itu	**mencuri dompet saya.**
Identifying clause:	
predicate	subject (nom rel clause)
Orang itu(lah)	**yang mencuri dompet saya.**

- Translate the following sentences into English.
- Change each sentence into an identifying clause.
- Attach **-lah** to the end of the predicate.
- Translate each identifying clause.

Example

Kamar ini harus dihias untuk pesta.

→   This room must be decorated for the party.
Kamar inilah yang harus dihias untuk pesta.
This is the room which must be decorated for the party.

1. **Pak Bagio dipilih sebagai pemimpin partai.**
2. **Tetangga saya membantu Ali.**
3. **Kereta api itu cepat sekali.**
4. **Pak Siregar tinggal di rumah ini.**
5. **Anak saya menang.**
6. **Piring-piring ini belum dicuci.**
7. **Menteri Pendidikan berbicara dalam rapat itu.**
8. **Lukisan ini akan saya jual.**

NOTE   Although **-lah** is attached to predicates in exercises here it is not obligatory. In speech especially it is often omitted:
Mobil hitamlah yang mereka pilih.
Mobil hitam yang mereka pilih.
It was the black car which they chose.

However, **-lah** is commonly used in identifying clauses in writing, but also in speech if the speaker wants to strongly emphasise the point.

Identifying clauses have a distinctive intonation pattern, which cannot be indicated effectively in print. It involves the predicate taking extra stress and sentence final intonation, as if it were occurring at the end of the sentence.

EXERCISE 2

- Translate the following sentences into Indonesian using identifying clauses.
- In each case make the underlined word the predicate. This may require the sentence to be modified, such as an active verb becoming passive, as in the example.
- Translate your sentences.

Example

They chose <u>the black car</u>.

→   **Mobil hitamlah yang dipilih oleh mereka.**
It was the black car which they chose.

1. <u>My mother</u> chose this colour.
2. <u>Mr Johnson</u> teaches Mary and Tom.
3. Mother bought <u>a red umbrella</u>.

4. <u>My younger sister</u> is sitting under the tree.
5. I don't like <u>him</u>.
6. He is reading <u>a sports magazine</u>.
7. Father called <u>Dr Sutomo</u> when mother became ill.
8. <u>This door</u> has to be locked every night.
9. <u>They</u> chose her as leader.
10. <u>Only John</u> can help me.

B Nominalised relative clauses within identifying clauses

A nominalised relative clause [see section 27A] can occur as predicate of an identifying clause. In this case both predicate and subject are nominalised relative clauses, beginning with **yang**:

Yang kecillah yang tidak saya sukai.
It is the small one which I don't like.

The nominalised relative clause can be **yang ini** 'this one' or **yang itu** 'that one':

Yang inilah yang tidak saya sukai.
It is this one that I don't like.

EXERCISE 3

•   Translate the following sentences.

1. It is the blue one that is most expensive.
2. It is the big one that I've already read.
3. It is this one which you must wear.
4. It is that one which angered me.
5. It's the one waiting over there who wants to meet you.
6. It's the biggest one that I want to eat.
7. This is the one that he's looking for.
8. This is the one that is damaged.

C Negation in identifying clauses

Because the predicate in an identifying clause is a noun phrase it is negated with **bukan**. A negative word always comes before a predicate; this identifies the predicate as the first phrase in an identifying clause:

Bukan orang itu yang mencuri dompet saya.
It wasn't that person who stole my wallet.

In the following construction **tidak** *follows* **yang**; it occurs within the second phrase - the subject - rather than preceding it and thus does not mark the phrase as a predicate:

Yang inilah yang tidak saya sukai.
It is this one which I don't like/This is the one I don't like.

If **bukan** occurs **-lah** is not used.

EXERCISE 4

- Translate the following constructions into Indonesian, using identifying clauses.

    1.   I wasn't the one who wrote that letter.
    2.   It was John who wasn't chosen as leader.
    3.   It wasn't my child who won.
    4.   Budi lives near me. It is Mr Siregar who doesn't live in my street.
    5.   It wasn't this one which I chose.
    6.   This isn't the one they are looking for.
    7.   This is the one that isn't damaged.
    8.   This isn't the painting I'm going to sell.

31   ADJECTIVES WITH COMPLEMENTS

When functioning as a predicate some adjectives can be followed by a verbal clause functioning as a complement.

A   Complements with a passive verb

In one type of construction the verb in the complement is passive and the adjective describes the way the subject undergoes the action stated by the verb:

subject	predicate	complement
noun phrase	adjective	verb
Tulisan Anda	**sulit**	**dibaca.**

Tulisan Anda sulit dibaca.
Your writing is hard to read.

In the example above **tulisan Anda** 'your writing' stands as patient of the verb 'read'; the verb must therefore be in its passive form **dibaca**. This rule does not apply in English, in which the verb is usually active, as in the above example.

Only a limited number of adjectives can occur in this construction, the commonest being **sulit** and **sukar** 'difficult', **mudah** 'easy', and **enak** 'pleasant, tasty'. Others are **baik** 'good', **pantas** and **sesuai** 'appropriate, suitable' and **menarik** 'interesting'. The verb can optionally be preceded by **untuk**:
> **Jawaban pejabat itu tidak mudah (untuk) dimengerti.**
> The official's answer was not easy to understand.

The verb can have an agent phrase. The English equivalent does not have an agent; instead a phrase introduced by 'for' is used:
> **Jawaban pejabat itu tidak mudah (untuk) dimengerti oleh wartawan.**
> The official's answer was not easy for the journalist to understand.

Passive type two occurs if the actor is a first or second person pronoun [see section 4B]:
> **Kata-kata ini sukar saya ingat.** *or* **Kata-kata ini sukar untuk saya ingat.**
> These words are hard for me to remember.

EXERCISE 1

- Translate the following sentences into Indonesian.

1. This computer is easy to use.
2. Your question is hard for us to answer.
3. The pickpocket was not easy for the police to catch.
4. His house will not be hard for you to find.
5. This custom is hard for foreigners to understand.
6. That skirt is not appropriate for Mary to wear.
7. This sate is pleasant/tasty to eat.
8. This book is suitable for children to read.

- The adverbs **terlalu** 'too' and **cukup** 'enough' can precede the adjective; in this case numerous other adjectives can occur in this construction, such as **mahal** 'expensive'. The verb must be preceded by **untuk** if **terlalu** or **cukup** occurs:

  Sepatu ini terlalu mahal untuk kami beli.
  These shoes are too expensive for us to buy.

B   Complements with an active verb

Another type of construction indicates that the subject has enough of a quality to perform an action, in which case the adjective is preceded by **cukup**, or too much of a quality to perform it, in which case the adjective is preceded by **terlalu**. Since the subject performs the action the verb is active. The verb must be preceded by **untuk**:

  Dia cukup pandai untuk lulus ujian.
  She's clever enough to pass the exam.
  Dia terlalu malas untuk menolong kami.
  He is too lazy to help us.

EXERCISE 2

- Translate the following sentences into Indonesian.
- Choose active or passive voice for the verb as required.

1. This box is too heavy for me to lift.
2. These mangos are not yet ripe enough to eat.
3. This music is pleasant to hear.
4. I am too busy to go to lectures today.
5. Pramoedya Ananta Toer's books are interesting to read.
6. Unfortunately she isn't well enough to go to the party.
7. Sorry, I am too tired to help you.

8.   This water is too dirty to drink.
9.   He is rich enough to buy a Mercedes.
10. This shirt is already dry enough to wear.

Following some transitive and intransitive verbs **untuk**, **supaya** and **bahwa** can introduce complement clauses.

A *Untuk*

Untuk introduces a complement - an **untuk** clause - which has no subject. The **untuk** clause has no subject expressed because usually it would be the same as the subject of the main clause. When it introduces a complement **untuk** is usually not translated in English:

> **Kelly memutuskan untuk pergi.**
> Kelly decided to go.

main clause		complement	
subject	verb		verb
Kelly	**memutuskan**	**untuk**	**pergi.**

In the above example Kelly is subject of the main verb, **memutuskan**, and of the verb in the complement, **pergi**.

B *Supaya*

Supaya introduces a complement - a **supaya** clause - which has a subject:

> **Dia ingin supaya kami menolong dia.**
> He wishes that we help him/He wants us to help him.

As in the above example, **supaya** is sometimes translated 'that' and sometimes not translated; this depending to some extent on the particular English verb. **Supaya** complements follow transitive and intransitive verbs of intent; that is, the subject of the main verb intends (asks, orders and so on) someone else to perform an action.

> **NOTE** **Agar** has the same meaning as **supaya** but is more formal and is mainly used in writing:
> **Dia ingin agar kami menolong dia.** He wishes that we help him.

EXERCISE 1

- Fill in the blank space with **untuk** or **supaya** as appropriate.
- Translate the sentences into English.

1.   **Guru mengusulkan _____ saya pergi ke dokter.**
2.   **Kami berencana _____ berlibur pada akhir tahun.**
3.   **Saya berpesan _____ dia menjaga anak-anak.**
4.   **Mereka bersedia _____ menurunkan harga.**
5.   **Dia memutuskan _____ memberitahu saya.**
6.   **Dia menginstruksikan _____ sopir membawa tamunya ke hotel.**
7.   **Polisi mengimbau _____ warga tetap tinggal di dalam rumah.**
8.   **Dia menolak _____ menyebut nama-nama mereka.**
9.   **Dia minta _____ kami meminjaminya uang.**
10. **Die berniat _____ menemani saya.**

• Following a transitive main verb the subject of the **supaya** clause is identical to the object in the main clause. Either the object of the main verb or the subject of the **supaya** clause is omitted:

   Dia menyuruh saya supaya pergi.
   Dia menyuruh supaya saya pergi.
   He ordered me to go.

main clause			complement			
subject	verb	object			subject	verb
Dia	**menyuruh**	**saya**	**supaya**			**pergi.**
Dia	**menyuruh**		**supaya**		**saya**	**pergi.**

In the first sentence above the complement clause has no subject. In this case **untuk** can be used instead of **supaya**:

   Dia menyuruh saya untuk pergi.
   He ordered me to go.

If a transitive clause has an object expressed, followed by a **supaya** complement or **untuk** complement, it can be changed to the passive. The object of the active clause becomes the subject of the passive and is placed before the verb. The complement remains after the main clause:

   Saya disuruhnya untuk/supaya pergi.
   I was ordered by him to go.

If a **supaya** complement occurs with a subject then if the main clause is made passive the whole **supaya** clause must follow the passive verb:

   Disuruhnya supaya saya pergi.
   He ordered that I go.

EXERCISE 2

•   Change the following sentences from active to passive.
•   Omit the subject of the active sentence.
•   Translate your sentences.

Example

Dia menyuruh saya supaya pergi.

→   **Saya disuruh supaya pergi.**

I was ordered to go.

1. **Dokter menganjurkannya supaya berobat di Australia.**
2. **Dokter menganjurkan supaya dia berobat di Australia.**
3. **Dia mendesak pemerintah untuk memperkuat sensor terhadap film-film kekerasan.**
4. **Dia menyarankan supaya mereka kawin.**
5. **Dia menghimbau supaya Presiden mencabut keputusan menteri itu.**
6. **Dia memerintahkan saya untuk mengembalikan uang itu.**
7. **Dia mengusulkan supaya saya belajar di universitas ini.**
8. **Dia memanggil mereka untuk mengambil bagian dalam perundingan.**

NOTE   **Untuk** and **supaya** can often be omitted, although this occurs more frequently following some verbs than others:

Dia bermaksud pergi. *or* **Dia bermaksud untuk pergi.** He intends to go.

Dia menyuruh saya pergi. He ordered me to go.

Clauses introduced by **untuk** and **supaya** can occur in positions other than as complements. For instance, they can occur as subordinate clauses. A complement is always obligatory as the sentence is incomplete without it. Thus **untuk pergi** cannot be omitted from the sentence **Dia memutuskan untuk pergi.** He decided to go.

Subordinate clauses can be omitted, leaving a grammatically complete structure. In the following examples the main clause, which can occur alone, is underlined:

<u>**Dia pergi ke toko**</u> **untuk membeli gula dan mentega.**

<u>He went to the shop</u> (in order) to buy sugar and butter.

<u>**Dia belajar keras**</u> **supaya dia bisa lulus ujian.**

<u>She studied hard</u> so that she could pass the exam.

As above, **untuk** introduces a subordinate clause of purpose without a subject and is translatable 'to, in order to' and **supaya**, meaning 'so that, in order that', introduces a subordinate clause of purpose with a subject. **Untuk** and **supaya** cannot be omitted when introducing subordinate clauses.

The rules covering the details of their use are complex and cannot all be discussed here. Students should observe the ways they are used by native speakers.

C *Bahwa*

Bahwa translates 'that' and introduces a clause after transitive and intransitive verbs which report such things as what happened, what someone said or what a situation is:

Saya tahu bahwa dia sakit.
I know that he is sick.

Sometimes transitive and intransitive counterparts (which usually have the same translation in English) can both be followed by **bahwa**:

Dia sadar/menyadari bahwa dia telah ditipu.
He was aware that he had been tricked.

Bahwa can usually be omitted, just as 'that' can in English:

Saya tahu (bahwa) dia pencuri.
I know (that) he is a thief.

Introducing a complement **supaya** can sometimes be translated 'that'. However, it must be distinguished from **bahwa**. **Supaya** occurs after verbs of intent, that is verbs which indicate a command, wish, desire and so on. **Bahwa** occurs after reporting verbs, that is verbs which relate what someone said, thought and so on.

EXERCISE 3

- Translate the following sentences into Indonesian.
- Use the word in parentheses for the verb.
- Choose **supaya** or **bahwa** as appropriate.

1. I almost forgot that I have to meet Tony today. (**lupa**)
2. He answered that I must go. (**menjawab**)
3. Mr Trisno desires that his daughter marries a rich man.(**bercita-cita**)
4. He requested that we attend the meeting. (**memohon**)
5. We believe that we can win. (**percaya**)
6. I acknowledge that I need help. (**mengakui**)
7. The lecturer advised that I go to his lecture. (**menyarankan**)
8. He explained that he was late because his car broke down.
   (**menjelaskan**)

33   QUESTIONS

A Yes-no questions

Yes-no questions are questions which require 'yes' or 'no' as an answer. In Indonesian such a question has the same word order as a statement. It differs in having interrogative intonation and optionally being preceded by **apa** or **apakah**. **Apa(kah)** simply announces that what follows is a question:

Ini buku Anda?
Apa(kah) ini buku Anda?
Is this your book?

Apa also means 'what?':
Apa ini?
What is this?

When **apa** indicates that what follows is a question it can always be omitted and has no translation in English. When it means 'what?' it cannot be omitted.

EXERCISE 1

- In each of the following sentences indicate whether **apa** (i) can be omitted, by giving the sentence without it, or (ii) cannot be omitted, by writing (No).
- Translate the sentences into English.

Examples
Apa ini kantor Bapak?
→   **Ini kantor Bapak?**
       Is this your office?

Apa binatang itu?
→   (No)   What is that animal?

1.   **Apa warna bunga itu?**
2.   **Apa hari ini panas?**
3.   **Apa perbedaan antara kedua cerita itu?**
4.   **Apa dia pandai?**
5.   **Apa kamu sudah makan?**
6.   **Apa nama kota itu?**
7.   **Apa itu binatang?**
8.   **Apa kedua cerita itu berbeda?**
9.   **Apa itu bunga?**
10.   **Apa itu nama kota?**

B Specific questions

A question in Indonesian usually has the same word order as a statement. Intonation or the presence of **apa(kah)** marks yes-no questions. *Specific questions* require specific information, not 'yes' or 'no' as an answer. They contain a *question word*, such as **apa** 'what?' or **siapa** 'who?'. These words are not placed first unless they are the subject. When they are the object they occur after the verb; they do not go first as do 'who?' and 'what?' in English:

Saudara membantu <u>siapa</u> hari ini?
<u>Who</u> are you helping today?
Saudara menulis <u>apa</u>?
<u>What</u> are you writing?

subject	predicate	object
Saudara	**menulis**	**surat.**
You	are writing	a letter.
Saudara	**menulis**	**apa?**
You	are writing	what? = What are you writing?

When **apa** or **siapa** is the subject it comes before the verb. In active sentences **siapa** is optionally followed by **yang**; many people prefer to always put **yang** after **apa**:

Siapa (yang) membaca koran?
Who is reading the newspaper?
Apa yang mengganggu mereka?
What is annoying them?

EXERCISE 2

- Translate the following sentences into Indonesian.
- Place the question word in its correct position in the sentence.
- Give transitive verbs in the active form.

1. I would like to drink tea; what would you like to drink?
2. Who are you ringing?
3. Who wrote this letter?
4. Who are you helping?
5. Who did you meet at the market this morning?
6. What did mother buy for me?
7. What frightened them?
8. What will we eat at the restaurant tonight?
9. Who is helping you?
10. What did you make with that wood?

> **NOTE**   A construction with **apa** as object must be distinguished from a construction which begins with **apa(kah)** to indicate that it is a question. If **apa** is the object it cannot be omitted; if it is a question indicator it is optional:
> **Kamu mau membaca apa?** What do you want to read?
> **Apa kamu mau membaca.** *or* **Kamu mau membaca?** Do you want to read?

•   If **siapa** or **apa** is the subject and the predicate is a noun phrase **yang** does not occur and the ordering of subject and predicate is free:
Siapa anak itu *or* **Anak itu siapa?**
Who is that child?

When **siapa** follows a noun it is possessive, meaning 'whose': **anak siapa?** 'whose child?'. When **apa** follows a noun it means 'what (sort of)?': **buku apa?** 'what (sort of) book?'

EXERCISE 3

•   Translate the following sentences into English.

1.   **Kamu adik siapa?**
2.   **Kamu siapa?**
3.   **Adik kamu siapa?**
4.   **Sepatu apa ini?**
5.   **Ini sepatu apa?**
6.   **Ini sepatu siapa?**
7.   **Siapa adik kamu?**
8.   **Adik siapa kamu?**
9.   **Sepatu siapa ini?**
10.   **Apa ini sepatu?**

•   In English 'who' and 'what' usually only follow a preposition in very formal language, as in 'With what did he write?'. Usually we put the question word at the beginning of the sentence and the preposition last: 'What did he write with?' In Indonesian **siapa** and **apa** must immediately follow the preposition (just as in formal English). The sequence of preposition plus question word cannot be separated, although the whole phrase can often either precede the subject or follow the predicate:
Dia menulis <u>dengan apa</u>?
<u>Dengan apa</u> dia menulis?
<u>What</u> did he write <u>with</u>?

Once again, the word order in a question is the same as in a statement:

subject	predicate	prepositional phrase	
Dia	**menulis**	**dengan pena.**	
She	wrote	with a pen.	
Dia	**menulis**	**dengan apa?**	
She	wrote	with what? = What did she write with?	

The question word **mana** 'where?' follows one of the three locative prepositions **di** 'at', **ke** 'to' or **dari** 'from'. Here also the preposition and question word cannot be separated as they usually are in English:

Dia datang <u>dari mana</u>?

<u>Where</u> did she come <u>from</u>?

EXERCISE 4

- Translate the following sentences into Indonesian.
- Place the question word in its correct position.
- Give transitive verbs in the active form.

1. Who did Narti go with?
2. Who is this coffee for?
3. Who did the teacher give the book to?
4. Where did she go to?
5. What is he crying for?
6. What did father dig the hole with?
7. Where did he bring the books from?
8. Who is this letter from?
9. What does he work so hard for?
10. Who do you work with?

C Question words in identifying clauses

If a question word is the object it occurs after an active verb, not before it as in English:

Dia membaca <u>apa</u>?

<u>What</u> did he read?

If we want to focus attention on the question word we put it first and place **yang** after it. The verb cannot be active as it usually is in English; it must be passive. Thus to focus on **apa** in the above sentence the following construction is used:

Apa yang dia baca? *or* **Apa yang dibacanya?**

What did she read? (literally: What (was it) that was read by her?)

As in the above example, the translation in English usually has an active verb; it would be very unusual in English to say 'What was read by her?'. The Indonesian construction is actually an identifying clause [see section 30A], in which the question word is the predicate, placed before the subject to receive focus.

The question word can also occur within a noun phrase asking 'what thing?' or 'whose thing?'. In this case also to focus attention on it we make the phrase containing it the predicate in an identifying clause. In the first sentence below **mobil apa?** 'what car?' is the object in a basic active clause. In the second sentence it is the predicate in an identifying clause:

> **Pak Hadi membeli <u>mobil apa</u>?**
> **<u>Mobil apa</u> yang dibeli Pak Hadi?**
> <u>What car</u> did Mr Hadi buy?

EXERCISE 5

- Change the following active clauses into identifying clauses, with the question word as predicate.
- Translate your constructions into English.

> *Example*
> **Anda menemui siapa kemarin?**
> →   **Siapa yang Anda temui kemarin?**
>   Who did you meet yesterday?

1.   **Umar sedang membaca apa?**
2.   **Ibu mencuci apa?**
3.   **Saudara mencari siapa?**
4.   **Kamu paling menyukai warna apa?**
5.   **Kamu meminjam buku siapa tadi?**
6.   **Kamu membeli buku apa?**
7.   **Kita akan menonton film apa?**
8.   **Pak Hadi memanggil siapa?**
9.   **Mereka menunggu siapa?**
10.   **Orang itu memesan apa?**
11.   **Mereka menyewa rumah siapa?**
12.   **Kamu memikirkan apa?**

- In section 3B it is stated that some intransitive verbs can be followed by a preposition, such as **Pak Basri cinta kepada istrinya** 'Mr Basri loves his wife'. Some others can be directly followed by a noun phrase, called a complement:

> **Mereka belajar bahasa Perancis.**
> They are studying French.

In such cases the prepositional phrase or complement can be replaced by a question word:

Mereka belajar apa?
What are they are studying?
Pak Basri cinta kepada siapa?
Who does Mr Basri love?

Because the verbs are intransitive the cannot be changed to passives. To do this the corresponding transitive verbs must be used. Thus instead of intransitive **belajar**, transitive passive **dipelajari** is used; instead of intransitive **cinta akan**, transitive passive **dicintai** is used. The construction must be converted to an identifying clause, with the question word as predicate:

Apa yang dipelajari mereka?
What are they studying?
Siapa yang dicintai Pak Basri?
Who is loved by Mr Basri?

EXERCISE 6

- Change the following questions into identifying clauses with the question word as predicate.
- Translate your sentences into natural English.

    Example
    Mereka ingin bertemu dengan siapa?
    →   **Siapa yang ingin mereka temui?**
        Who do they want to meet?

    1.   **Mereka percaya kepada siapa?**
    2.   **Kamu suka apa?**
    3.   **Dia kenal akan siapa di sini?**
    4.   **Kamu berharap akan apa?**
    5.   **Mereka tahu apa?**
    6.   **Dia menikah dengan siapa?**

D   Questions with *yang mana*

Yang mana? means 'which?':
    Dia tinggal di rumah yang mana?
    Which house does he live in?

If **yang mana** occurs in the first phrase in the clause **yang** is obligatory unless the following phrase begins with **yang**. The following phrase must begin with **yang** if it contains a passive verb, because the construction is an identifying clause [see section 30A]:

Buku mana yang akan kamu beli? *or* **Buku yang mana yang akan kamu beli?**
Which book are you going to buy?

The following phrase optionally begins with **yang** if it contains an active verb:
Guru yang mana mengajar kelas ini?
Guru (yang) mana yang mengajar kelas ini?
Which teacher teaches this class?

Yang is also optional before the second phrase if it contains an intransitive verb or word of another class, such as an adjective, except that it cannot occur before a phrase beginning with a noun.

To ask 'which one?' or just 'which?' without a noun **yang mana** occurs alone, being nominalised [see section 27A]:
Yang mana mobil Anda?
Which one/Which is your car?

In this situation **yang** is still optional if the following phrase also begins with **yang**:
(Yang) mana yang akan kamu beli?
Which one will you buy?

EXERCISE 7

- Translate the following sentences into Indonesian.
- Place **yang** in parentheses where it is optional.
- If the verb is transitive use active or passive in Indonesian as indicated in parentheses.
- If 'active' or 'passive' is not indicated use an intransitive verb or other word class as appropriate.

Example
Which house did he build? (active)
→   **Dia membangun rumah yang mana?**

1.   Which city do they come from?
2.   Which one is Tomo?
3.   Which teacher wrote this history book? (active)
4.   Which coat did you choose? (passive)
5.   Which one did you borrow? (active)
6.   Which one did you see? (passive)
7.   Which shop sells umbrellas? (active)
8.   Which one is Tomo's house?

9.   Which journalist wrote this article? (active)
10.   Which one is best?
11.   Which chair did she sit in?
12.   Which shoes will you wear? (passive)
13.   Which magazine did Dewi buy? (passive)
14.   Which one helped you? (active)

E   *Apa* and *berapa*

'What?' is sometimes **apa** in Indonesian and sometimes **berapa**.

When we ask a question whose answer is a *name* we use **apa**. For instance, 'What day (did something happen)?' requires a name as the answer; therefore **apa** is used in the question:

Hari apa saudara akan pergi ke dokter?

What day are you going to the doctor?

When we ask a question whose answer is a *number* the question word is **berapa** rather than **apa,** although 'what?' is used in English. So when we ask 'What year (did something happen)?' the expected reply will be a number, requiring **berapa** in the question:

Tahun berapa saudara akan pergi ke Indonesia?

What year are you going to Indonesia?

•   When **berapa** *follows* a noun, as in the above example, it means 'what?, which?'. When it *precedes* a noun it means 'how many?':

Berapa tahun saudara tinggal di Jakarta?

How many years did you live in Jakarta?

'What time?' is usually **jam berapa**, literally 'what hour?':

Jam berapa saudara mulai bekerja?

What time do you begin work?

Berapa is also used in questions with 'how?', such as 'How tall are you?' [as discussed in section 29C].

EXERCISE 8

•   Translate the following sentences into Indonesian.
•   Your translation of each sentence will have **apa** following a noun, **berapa** following a noun or **berapa** preceding a noun.

1.   How many hours do you work a day?
2.   What movie did you see?

3.   What page did you read?
4.   What floor is her office on?
5.   How many pages did you read?
6.   What month were you born?
7.   How many days a week do you go to the office?
8.   What class are you in this year?
9.   What colour is that flower?
10.   How many classes do you teach?
11.   How many months did you live in Jakarta?
12.   What is your phone number?
13.   What street is your house in?
14.   What number is your house?
15.   What time do you usually wake up?

F   Sentence tags

In sentences like: 'It was hot yesterday, wasn't it?' and 'He's sick, isn't he?', the question at the end is usually to seek confirmation from the listener (if the speaker is uncertain of the truth of the statement) or to seek agreement from the listener (when the speaker knows the statement is correct). It is called a *sentence tag*. In Indonesian **bukan** is used. A positive answer can begin with **ya**, while a negative answer begins with **bukan** if a noun is being negated, otherwise with **tidak** or **belum**:

Sri cantik, bukan?	Sri's pretty, isn't she?
Ya, dia cantik.	Yes, she is.
Tidak, dia tidak cantik.	No, she isn't.

In everyday speech usually only the short answer is given:

Dia guru, bukan?	He's a teacher, isn't he?
Bukan.	No (he's not).

> **NOTE**   In everyday speech **ya** is commonly used as a sentence tag in place of **bukan**: **Dia cantik, ya?** She's pretty, eh?

EXERCISE 9

- Translate the following sentences into Indonesian.
- Follow your translations with the appropriate negative responses.

Example
You've eaten, haven't you?
→   **Kamu sudah makan, bukan?   -   Belum.**

1.   It's hot today, isn't it?
2.   He's clever, isn't he?
3.   Budi is your younger brother, isn't he?
4.   You arrived yesterday, didn't you?
5.   You've read this book, haven't you?
6.   Today is Monday, isn't it?
7.   This is John's house, isn't it?
8.   They are going to leave tomorrow morning, aren't they?
9.   They've already left, haven't they?
10.   Your name is Anthony, isn't it?

NOTE   In English 'not' does not occur in the tag if it occurs in the main clause. In Indonesian **bukan** still occurs:

   Anda tidak punya mobil, bukan? You don't have a car, do you?

In Indonesian an answer to such a question is with **ya** if what is said is correct. Thus the answer to the above question is **ya** if you do not have a car, where in English 'no' is used:

   Anda tidak punya mobil, bukan? You don't have a car, do you?
   Ya (saya tidak punya mobil). No (I don't have a car).

G   Indirect questions

A question can be placed within a statement, taking the place of a noun. Questions placed within statements are called *indirect questions*. The word order within the question remains unchanged. The question **kapan dia akan pindah?** 'When will he move?' can occur after **tahu** 'know':

   Saya tidak tahu <u>kapan dia akan pindah</u>.
   I don't know <u>when he will move</u>.

The rule that if the patient is mentioned first the verb must be passive also holds in indirect questions:

   Saya tidak tahu <u>apa yang dibawanya</u>.
   I don't know <u>what he's carrying</u>.

An indirect yes-no question must be preceded by **apa** or **apakah**. The question (**Apa**) **mereka sudah pergi?** 'Have they gone yet?' becomes an indirect question in the following statement:

   Saya tidak tahu apa mereka sudah pergi.
   I don't know if/whether they've gone yet.

EXERCISE 10

- Translate the following sentences into Indonesian.
- Give the indirect question as a direct question.
- Translate the direct question.

Example
I don't know why he didn't come.
→ **Saya tidak tahu mengapa dia tidak datang.**
  Mengapa dia tidak datang?
  Why didn't he come?

1. I don't know who that person is.
2. I don't know if/whether he can come tomorrow.
3. I don't know what John is reading.
4. I don't know who Alice met this morning.
5. I don't know how he could succeed.
6. I don't know where he came from.
7. I don't know whether she lives here or not.
8. I don't know when she came here.
9. I don't know what mother bought.
10. I don't know where we will go tomorrow.
11. I don't know what time this office opens.
12. I don't know who came with Alice.
13. I don't know who Alice came with.
14. I don't know which is their house.

> **NOTE** Where an indirect yes-no question begins with 'if' (or 'whether') in English it does not begin with **kalau** in standard Indonesian but with **apa(kah)**:
> **Dia bertanya <u>apakah</u> mereka setuju atau tidak.**
> She asked <u>if</u> they agree or not.

H   Questions with -*kah*

We can mark a sentence as a question by using **-kah**. It is always optional and is mainly used in writing and formal speech.

If the question begins with **apa**, which also signals that what follows is a question, **-kah** attaches to it. It otherwise attaches to another word, which is then usually placed first in the question:
Apakah Anda mau ikut?
Maukah Anda ikut?
Do you want to come along?

If the predicate is a phrase, such as an adjective phrase, **-kah** attaches to the final word of the phrase, with the whole phrase being placed first in the question:

Terlalu gemukkah dia?

Is he too fat?

If the predicate contains a temporal or a modal **-kah** can attach either to that word or to the verb, depending on which one the question is being asked about:

Akankah dia pergi?

Akan pergikah dia?

Will she go?

If there is a question word **-kah** attaches to it. If the question word is part of a phrase the whole phrase comes first:

Siapakah orang itu?

Who is that person?

Tahun berapakah kamu lahir?

What year were you born?

EXERCISE 11

- Translate the following sentences into Indonesian.
- Attach **-kah** to the underlined word.
- If **apakah** can occur give the form of the question with this word as well.

Example

Did she <u>fall</u>?

→   **Jatuhkah dia?**

Apakah dia jatuh?

1. Has she <u>gone</u> yet?
2. Has she <u>already</u> gone?
3. <u>Where</u> did those children go?
4. Do I <u>have to</u> study today?
5. <u>What</u> time does the plane leave?
6. Are you <u>sick</u>?
7. <u>Who</u> did you meet?
8. <u>Whose</u> book did you borrow?
9. Do you <u>agree</u>?
10. <u>May</u> I come in?
11. <u>What</u> is she reading?
12. Do you <u>know</u> that person's name?

Indefinite pronouns indicate that a person or thing is being spoken about without a particular person or thing being identified.

A   Question word plus *saja*

Question words can be combined with **saja** to indicate someone or something indefinite, corresponding to English expressions with 'any'. The main forms include **siapa saja** 'anyone (at all)', **apa saja** 'anything (at all)', and **kapan saja** 'any time':

> **Siapa saja boleh ikut.**
> Anyone can come along.
> **Singgah di rumah kapan saja!**
> Call in any time!

In some contexts **apa saja** is more appropriately translated 'whatever' and **kapan saja** as 'whenever'.

The form **di mana saja** translates '(at/in) anywhere', **ke mana saja** translates '(to) anywhere' and **dari mana saja** translates 'from anywhere':

> **Taruh barang itu di mana saja!**
> Put those things anywhere!
> **Tikus masuk dari mana saja.**
> Rats come in from anywhere.

Following a noun **mana saja** means 'any' and answers a question with **yang mana** 'which?', while **apa saja** means 'any (sort of)' and answers a question with **apa** 'what (sort of)?':

> **Kalau libur kami menginap di hotel mana saja.**
> When on holiday we stay in any hotel at all.
> **Saya suka membaca buku apa saja.**
> I like reading any sort of book at all.

> **NOTE**   In more formal language **pun** can replace **saja**:
> **Siapa saja boleh ikut** *or* **Siapa pun boleh ikut.** Anyone can come along.
> **Kamu boleh datang kapan pun kamu mau.** You can come whenever you like.

Instead of occurring as subject of a passive verb **siapa saja** and **apa saja** occur as predicate in an identifying clause, in which the following subject begins with **yang** [see also section 30A]:

Apa saja yang dibelinya selalu mahal.
Anything he buys is always expensive/Whatever he buys is always
  expensive.

EXERCISE 1

- Translate each of the following sentences, using a question word + **saja**.

1. I can work with anyone at all.
2. Borrow any book at all (any book you like)!
3. You can borrow a book any time.
4. Anywhere (wherever) he goes his dog always follows.
5. You can drink anything (you like).
6. These things can be bought at any market at all.
7. Those things can be bought anywhere.
8. Whatever she wears is beautiful.
9. Anyone he meets is always polite to him.
10. Anything he says is always true.
11. Don't forget to take money wherever you go.
12. Anyone invited to Tomo's party is happy to go.

EXERCISE 2

- Answer the following questions.
- Use the appropriate question word + **saja**, relating to the underlined word or phrase.
- Translate your sentences.

Example
Boleh saya datang ke rumahmu <u>besok</u>?
→   **Kamu boleh datang ke rumah saya kapan saja.**
     You can come to my place any time.

1. **Boleh saya datang dengan <u>teman saya</u>?**
2. **Boleh saya membaca <u>majalah</u>?**
3. **Boleh saya membaca majalah <u>ini</u>?**
4. **Boleh saya pergi ke <u>bioskop</u>?**
5. **Boleh saya bermain dengan <u>bola ini</u>?**
6. **Boleh saya duduk di <u>sini</u>?**
7. **Boleh saya bertanya kepada <u>Bu Mina</u>?**
8. **Boleh saya pergi ke bioskop <u>besok</u>?**

B   Question word plus *saja* in questions

When phrases like **apa saja** occur in questions they indicate plurality; that is, an expectation on the part of the person asking the question that the answer will contain reference to more than one thing:

> **Harry akan menemui siapa saja?**
> Who will Harry meet?

The questioner assumes Harry will meet more than one person. A typical answer will probably refer to a number of people, such as:

> **Harry akan menemui Richard, Bruce dan Carlo.**
> Harry will meet Richard, Bruce and Carlo.

However, if Harry is only going to meet one person the answer may be:

> **Harry akan menemui Richard saja.**
> Harry will just meet Richard.

Note that the English question word does not indicate plurality. However, the Indonesian constructions can sometimes be translated in a way that makes plurality explicit. Thus in the above question **siapa saja** might alternatively be translated 'which people?'.

EXERCISE 3

The following statements are answers to questions.
* Make up questions which would receive these answers.
* In each case use the appropriate question word plus **saja** to elicit the underlined words.
* Translate your questions.

> *Example*
> **Mereka menjual papaya, pisang dan jeruk.**
> →   **Mereka menjual buah-buahan apa saja?**
>   What fruit do they sell?

1.   **Saya harus menjemput tamu-tamu itu.**
2.   **Mereka tinggal di pulau Jawa, Bali dan Lombok.**
3.   **Kita memerlukan gula, garam dan kopi.**
4.   **Mahasiswa itu berasal dari Korea, Jepang dan Cina.**
5.   **Warta berita disiarkan jam lima, jam enam dan jam setengah delapan.**
6.   **Bus ini berhenti di Garden City, Coorparoo dan Stones Corner.**
7.   **Nama anak Pak Rudi adalah Narti, Sigit dan Pomo.**
8.   **Mereka membicarakan masalah politik dan ekonomi tadi malam.**

C *Tidak* plus reduplicated question word

Equivalent to English expressions like 'no one, not anyone' and 'nothing, not anything' are phrases in Indonesian with **tidak** followed by the appropriate question word reduplicated: **tidak siapa-siapa** 'no one', **tidak apa-apa** 'nothing' and **tidak di/ke/dari mana-mana** '(at/to/from) nowhere'. **Tidak** is usually separated from the question word by a verb:

Saya tidak membeli apa-apa.
I didn't buy anything.
Saya tidak pergi ke mana-mana.
I didn't go anywhere.

In the above examples in both English and Indonesian the negative word comes before the verb. In English the negative can alternatively be put after the verb: 'I bought nothing', 'I saw no one'. This cannot be done in Indonesian; **tidak** must come before the verb. However, the combinations do occur in short answers where the verb is omitted:

Kamu sudah membeli apa? - Tidak apa-apa.
What have you bought?   - Nothing.

NOTE   Tidak apa-apa can translate 'nothing' or 'it doesn't matter', depending on context. The latter can be in response to an apology, for instance:
Maaf, saya terlambat. Sorry, I'm late.
Tidak apa-apa. It doesn't matter/That's alright.

EXERCISE 4

- Translate the following questions and answers, choosing appropriate phrases from those discussed above.

    1. Who did you go to town with yesterday?
        I didn't go with anyone.
    2. Where are you going?
        I'm not going anywhere.
    3. What does she know?
        She doesn't know anything/She knows nothing.
    4. Who do you want to sell that car to?
        I don't want to sell it to anyone.
    5. Who did Johnny hit?
        He didn't hit anyone.
    6. Where has that lady ever sung?
        She hasn't yet sung anywhere.
    7. Where have you just come from?
        I haven't come from anywhere.

8. What did she write the letter with?
    She didn't write with anything.
9. Who did you see?
    I saw no one.
10. Where have you been?
    I've been nowhere.

> **NOTE**   As well as following **tidak** the phrase (**di/ke/dari**) **mana-mana** can occur in positive statements, meaning '(at/to/from) everywhere'. This contrasts with (**di/ke/dari**) **mana saja**, which means 'anywhere' [see section 34A]:
> **Kamu boleh duduk <u>di mana saja</u>, terserah.** You can sit <u>anywhere</u>, it's up to you.
> **Kini gedung-gedung tinggi terdapat <u>di mana-mana</u>.** Nowadays tall buildings are found <u>everywhere</u>.

*   While reduplicated forms follow verbs the forms **apa saja** and **mana saja** follow nouns:
    Saya tidak membeli apa-apa. I didn't buy anything.
    Saya tidak membeli buku apa saja. I didn't buy any book at all.

D   'No one' and 'nothing' as subject

The forms **siapa-siapa** and **apa-apa** have to follow the predicate and so cannot occur as subjects. Equivalent to 'no one' and 'nothing' as subject are **tidak seorangpun** 'no one' and **tidak satupun** 'nothing'. The difference is shown by the following pair:
    Saya tidak mengenal siapa-siapa di sini.
    I don't know anyone here.
    Tidak seorangpun mengenal saya di sini.
    No one knows me here.

It is common for **yang** to follow the subject forms:
    Tidak seorangpun yang mengenal saya di sini.
    No one knows me here.

> **NOTE**   **Tak** is frequently used in writing instead of **tidak** before **seorangpun** and **satupun** and some people write **pun** as a separate word:
> **Tak seorang pun tersenyum kepadanya.** No one smiled at him.

EXERCISE 5

*   Translate the following sentences into Indonesian.

1. He didn't want to help anyone.

2. Nothing interested her.
3. She didn't eat anything.
4. We didn't eat anywhere.
5. We didn't eat at any restaurant.
6. We didn't go anywhere.
7. We didn't go to any beach.
8. No one was seen there.
9. Nothing was stolen.
10. The police didn't arrest anyone at the disco last night.
11. I didn't buy anything at the shop.
12. I didn't buy any clothes at the shop.
13. No one wanted to help him.
14. No one can run as fast as Soeprapto.

35   IMPERATIVES

A   Transitive and intransitive imperatives

An *imperative* sentence is used when we tell or order someone to do something:

Datang ke sini!
Come here!
Tutup pintu!
Shut the door!

If the imperative verb is intransitive it has the same form as in a statement. So if it has prefix **ber-** or **meN-** this remains. If the verb is transitive the prefix **meN-** drops. Thus **meN-** remains if the verb is intransitive, like **menyanyi** 'sing' (base **nyanyi**), but drops if the verb is transitive, like **buka** 'open' (which is **membuka** in a statement):

Menyanyi sekarang!
Sing now!
Buka pintu ini!
Open this door!

NOTE   In writing -lah is frequently added to the verb in an imperative:
Bukalah pintu ini! Open this door!

Use of **-lah** is less frequent in these constructions in spoken Indonesian.

Imperatives are not necessarily strong commands. They can be anything from polite suggestions to orders, depending on tone of voice and non-linguistic indicators.

EXERCISE 1

- Translate the following sentences into Indonesian.
- Use the base given in parentheses for the verb.
- Add the appropriate prefix to the verb or none, as required, and add any required suffix to the verb.

Examples
Stop here! (**henti**)
→   **Berhenti di sini!**

Fill in this form! (**isi**)
→   **Isi formulir ini!**

1.   Write a letter to mother! (**tulis**)

2.   Buy bread and sugar! (**beli**)
3.   Call in at my place tomorrow! (**singgah**)
4.   Speak slowly! (**bicara**)
5.   Leave tomorrow! (**angkat**)
6.   Cross over here! (**seberang**)
7.   Give this letter to Tom! (**beri**)
8.   Swim near the shore! (**renang**)
9.   Sit in this chair! (**duduk**)
10.   Stay at my place tonight! (**inap**)
11.   Clean this room at once! (**bersih**)
12.   Send me a letter every week! (**kirim**)

NOTE   Suffixed pronouns **-ku**, **-mu** and **-nya** cannot be used on verbs in imperative sentences. Full pronouns must be used instead:
  Kamu menjemputnya *or* **Kamu menjemput dia.** You meet him.
but **Jemput dia!** Meet him!

Where 'it' occurs as object in English, in Indonesian imperatives either the noun is repeated or the object is not mentioned, as in the imperative on the second line below, because **-nya** cannot occur:
  Buku ini bagus. Saya sudah membacanya. This book is good. I've read it.
  Buku ini bagus. Baca! This book is good. Read it!

B   Negative imperatives with *jangan*

We tell someone not to do something by using **jangan** 'don't':
  Jangan naik bus!
  Don't go by bus!

When an intransitive verb follows **jangan** any prefix is retained. If the verb is transitive some people retain prefix **meN-** while others omit it. For most purposes it can be regarded as optional:
  Jangan baca buku itu sekarang!
  Jangan membaca buku itu sekarang!
  Don't read that book now!

EXERCISE 2

- Translate the following sentences into Indonesian.
- Use the base given in parentheses for the verb.
- Add the appropriate prefix to the verb or none, as required. If a prefix occurs optionally give both possible forms.

Examples

Don't go to the pictures today.

→ **Jangan pergi ke bioskop hari ini!**

Don't meet them at the airport!

→ **Jangan jemput/menjemput mereka di bandar udara!**

1. Don't smoke in this room! (**rokok**)
2. Don't wear that shirt! (**pakai**)
3. Don't sleep in class! (**tidur**)
4. Don't dance here! (**tari**)
5. Don' play on the road! (**main**)
6. Don't wash these clothes! (**cuci**)
7. Don't shop at that market! (**belanja**)
8. Don't come in! (**masuk**)
9. Don't take that newspaper! (**ambil**)
10. Don't write your name in this book! (**tulis**)

C Passive imperatives

Imperatives with transitive verbs are often expressed in the passive in Indonesian. The verb has prefix **di-** even though the order is directed at second person ('you'). The construction thus contains a suggestion of being directed at a third person. It is therefore rather indirect and so less forceful or abrupt than an imperative with an active verb, containing a sense of 'it is to be done!', rather than 'you do it!', although this is sometimes difficult to reflect in the English translation:

Barang itu ditaruh di sini saja!

Just put those things here! (Those things are to be put here!)

In a negative passive the subject can precede **jangan**, precede the verb or follow the verb:

Jendela ini jangan dibuka!
Jangan jendela ini dibuka!
Jangan dibuka jendela ini!

Don't open this window! (This window is not to be opened!)

EXERCISE 3

• Transform the following active imperatives into passives.
• Translate your sentences.

Example

Jangan meminjami mereka barang berharga!

→   **Jangan mereka dipinjami barang berharga!**

Don't lend them valuable things!

1.   **Bawa buku ini ke perpustakaan!**
2.   **Jangan memakai kemeja itu di kebun!**
3.   **Bersihkan kamar ini sebelum ibu pulang!**
4.   **Matikan lampunya sebelum tidur!**
5.   **Jangan mengganggu tamu kalau ia mau tidur!**
6.   **Jangan menyerahi saya tugas yang berat!**
7.   **Jangan mengeposkan surat itu!**
8.   **Simpan pakaian ini di lemari!**
9.   **Jangan menutup pintu ini!**
10.   **Jangan membelikan anak ini pakaian mahal!**

D   Polite imperatives

There are numerous ways of softening an imperative in Indonesian, just as there are in English. One way is to use a word meaning 'please'. There are a number of these words. When they are used with transitive verbs prefix **meN-** is dropped but prefixes remain on intransitive verbs. Two words translating English 'please' are the following.

The word **silakan** is used when we invite someone to do something for their own benefit:

Silakan ambil kue.

Please take a cake.

We can use **tolong** when we request someone to do something for our benefit:

Tolong carikan saya tempat duduk.

Please find me a seat.

EXERCISE 4

- Translate the following sentences into Indonesian.
- Choose **silakan** or **tolong** to translate 'please' as appropriate.

1.   Please sit down.
2.   Please have a cup of coffee. (literally: Please drink coffee.)
3.   Please guard these suitcases.
4.   Please get me a clean shirt.
5.   Please fix this bike.
6.   Please come in.

7.   Please iron this shirt.
8.   Please have a swim if you're hot.
9.   Please rest if you are tired.
10.   Please put the car in the garage.

NOTE There are a number of other words similar in function to **tolong**. The most frequent is **coba**:
Coba duduk baik-baik! Please sit properly!

Most people only allow **tolong** with transitive verbs, whereas **coba** can also be used with intransitive verbs, as in the above example. **Coba** is almost always used by seniors to juniors and does not make a request for the speaker's benefit.

36   EXCLAMATIONS

Exclamations express the speaker's feelings, usually of surprise, anger, or strong emotion, at some event or situation. Exclamations can be interjections, which are usually single words, or sentences. Exclamatory sentences can consist of **bukan main**, **alangkah** or **betapa** plus adjective-**nya**. They are often translated into English as 'How + adjective!' or, less formally, with expressions like 'Gosh, it's + adjective':

Bukan main besarnya!
How big it is!
Alangkah ramainya jalan ini!
How busy this street is/Gosh, this street's busy!
Betapa kagetnya orang itu!
How startled those people were!

NOTE   In informal speech the adjective + **-nya** often occurs alone, usually following an interjection:
Aduh, kotornya jalan ini! Oh, this road's dirty!
Wah, mahalnya! Gosh, it's expensive!

EXERCISE 1

The following sentences are statements about a characteristic someone or
  something has.
* Change the statements into exclamations, using **bukan main**.
* Translate your sentences.

Example
Orang itu kuat.
→   **Bukan main kuatnya orang itu!**
    How strong that man is!

1.   **Pegawai itu sibuk.**
2.   **Kucing itu gemuk.**
3.   **Politisi itu sombong.**
4.   **Kantor itu kacau.**
5.   **Sambal ini pedas.**
6.   **Hawa panas hari ini.**

EXERCISE 2

- Translate the following sentences into English.

1. **Betapa kagetnya orang itu ketika kami masuk!**
2. **Betapa kecewanya Dewi melihat kelakuan anaknya!**
3. **Alangkah lancarnya anak itu membaca!**
4. **Alangkah enaknya jika liburan diperpanjang!**
5. **Alangkah mahalnya barang-barang itu!**
6. **Alangkah indahnya taman yang kami kunjungi kemarin!**

Ellipsis is the omission of a word or phrase, usually because it is clear from context. Most classes of words can be omitted in some contexts. This section looks at ellipsis of pronouns. Often a pronoun can be omitted in Indonesian where it is required in English. Nevertheless, there are clear rules as to when a pronoun can and cannot be omitted.

When a person being spoken about is clear from context a pronoun is then used to refer to that person. Since the person we are talking about is identified as John in the first sentence below we refer to him by a pronoun in the next sentence:

John masuk kamar. Lalu <u>dia</u> duduk.
John came into the room. Then <u>he</u> sat down.

For most Indonesians **mereka** and **dia** can only refer to humans. There are therefore no pronouns for animals and things unless **-nya** can occur, as possessive 'its, their' or as object in an active sentence or agent in a passive sentence. Otherwise, when a thing is clear from context usually there is nothing corresponding to 'it' in English:

Dasi ini bagus. Boleh saya pinjam?
This tie is attractive. Can I borrow [it]?
Burung-burung itu akan makan padi. Lebih baik diusir.
Those birds will eat the rice. [They]'d better be driven off.

EXERCISE 1

- Translate the following sentences into Indonesian.
- Use pronouns in Indonesian where possible.

1. I bought those bananas yesterday but they've already been eaten by the children.
2. This tea is too sweet. I don't like it.
3. I went to John's house but he had already left.
4. We need patience if we wish to succeed.
5. I can't wear this coat because it is too small.
6. I'm going to wash these clothes so they are clean for the party tomorrow.
7. The car is good but its door is damaged.
8. I bought it yesterday.

NOTE   While **ia** and **mereka** were not possible for reference to non-humans in the past, the practice of using them is gradually appearing in Indonesian, possibly under the influence of English.

•   In Indonesian, as in English, pronouns refer to someone who has already been mentioned or is clear from context. In Indonesian pronouns can be omitted in some positions where they must be expressed in English.

First and second person pronouns can sometimes be omitted if it is clear who is being referred to, even if that person has not been mentioned. For instance, it may be clear that reference is to 'you', as in the following imperative and question:

Duduk kalau cape. Sit down if [you] are tired.

Mau ikut? Do [you] want to come along?

It will be clear if a person is referring to himself or herself, even if what they say may not indicate this removed from any context:

Boleh masuk?

May [I] come in?

A sentence may consist of a main clause and a subordinate clause. A subordinate clause is introduced by a conjunction, such as **karena** 'because', **kalau** 'if', **ketika** 'when'. The subject of a subordinate clause can be omitted whether it precedes of follows the main clause, if it identifies the same person as the subject of the main clause. In the following **karena (dia) sakit** is a subordinate clause of reason:

Ali tidak pergi ke sekolah karena sakit.

Karena sakit, Ali tidak pergi ke sekolah.

Ali didn't go to school because [he] was sick.

If the person is identified in the subordinate clause it can be replaced by a pronoun in the main clause. However, the pronoun cannot be omitted in this case:

Karena Ali sakit, <u>dia</u> tidak pergi ke sekolah.

Because Ali was sick <u>he</u> didn't go to school.

Possessive pronouns can also be omitted if it is clear who is meant, as when referring to something possessed by the subject:

Saya mau mencuci tangan.

I want to wash [my] hands.

EXERCISE 2

•   Translate the following sentences into Indonesian.

•   Omit pronouns where possible. Assume context makes it clear who is being referred to.

1.   When Mr Idrus arrived home he immediately had lunch.
2.   If you are late you'll have to wait outside.
3.   Drink some water if you're thirsty.
4.   Do you want to sell your car?
5.   We need patience if we wish to succeed.
6.   Sorry, I'm late because I missed the bus.
7.   May I have a glass of water?
8.   Please have a swim if you are hot.
9.   When we arrived in Jakarta we took a taxi to the hotel.
10.   When Jack arrived in Jakarta he took a taxi to the hotel.
11.   Although she's old she's still healthy.
12.   We are tired. When can we go home?
13.   I'd help them if I was rich.
14.   When he arrived home Mr Idrus immediately had lunch.
15.   When did you arrive?
16.   We were very cold last night because we forgot to take warm clothes.
17.   I didn't go to work today because I was sick.
18.   I didn't go to work today because she was sick.
19.   The children brushed their teeth before they went to bed.
20.   Return that book after you've finished reading it.

KEY TO EXERCISES

1   PREFIXES

EXERCISE 1

1.	**mengajar**	8.	**menggaruk**
2.	**membeli**	9.	**mendengar**
3.	**mengolah**	10.	**menyanyi**
4.	**melihat**	11.	**menyerah**
5.	**merasa**	12.	**mengirim**
6.	**memakai**	13.	**meminta**
7.	**mencoba**	14.	**menjual**

EXERCISE 2

1.	'marry' **me- + nikah**	9.	'wait' **me- + nanti**
2.	'stab' **men- + tikam**	10.	'gape' **me- + nganga**
3.	'accompany' **meng- + antar**	11.	'choose' **mem- + pilih**
4.	'become small' **meng- + kecil**	12.	'welcome' **meny- + sambut**
5.	'cook' **me- + masak**	13.	'flame' **me- + nyala**
6.	'spell' **meng- + eja**	14.	'fill' **meng- + isi**
7.	'consider' **meng- + anggap**	15.	'chat' **meng- + obrol**
8.	'brush' **meny- + sikat**	16.	'plant' **men- + tanam**

EXERCISE 3

1.	**menyedot-nyedot**	7.	**menjadi-jadi**
2.	**mengulang-ulang**	8.	**mengomong-omong**
3.	**memijat-mijat**	9.	**menulis-nulis**
4.	**menggaruk-garuk**	10.	**membaca-baca**
5.	**meminta-minta**	11.	**mengarang-ngarang**
6.	**memutar-mutar**	12.	**mencari-cari**

EXERCISE 4

1. **mengecek, mencek** 'to check'
2. **mengetik, mentik** 'to type'
3. **mengebom, membom** 'to bomb'
4. **mengerem, merem** 'apply brakes'
5. **mengelap, melap** 'wipe with cloth'
6. **mengedor, mendor** 'shoot'

EXERCISE 5

1.	**terserah** 'it's up to you'	6.	**pelajaran** 'lesson'
2.	**beterbangan** 'flying about'	7.	**bepergian** 'go on a trip'
3.	**pekerja** 'worker'	8.	**berkeras** 'persist'
4.	**terasa** 'felt'		
5.	**bekerja** 'work'		

2   NOUN AFFIXES

EXERCISE 1

1. He threatened the shop assistant.
    Ancamannya didengar banyak orang.
    His threat was heard by many people.
2. She painted her father.
    Lukisan itu akan digantung di dinding kantor.
    The painting will be hung on the office wall.
3. Sandra chose a red dress.
    Teman-temannya menggemari pilihannya.
    Her friends admired her choice.
4. Rusli tried to answer the questions of the police.
    Sayang, jawabannya tidak meyakinkan polisi.
    Unfortunately, his answers did not convince the police.
5. Siti is always complaining.
    Keluhannya menjengkelkan rekan-rekannya.
    Her complaints irritate her colleagues.
6. Because he was thirsty he had to drink a lot.
    Dia mengambil minuman itu dari kulkas.
    He took the drink from the fridge.
7. The children are forbidden to leave the house.
    Larangan itu berlaku sampai besok.
    The prohibition is in force until tomorrow.
8. They collected folk stories on the island of Sulawesi.
    Kumpulan cerita itu akan diterbitkan di Australia.
    The collection of stories will be published in Australia.
9. The artists exhibited their paintings at Taman Ismail Marzuki.
    Pameran itu dikunjungi banyak orang.
    The exhibition was visited by many people.
10. Bambang has been saving his money in this bank for years.
    Sekarang tabungannya sudah banyak.
    Now his savings are substantial.

EXERCISE 2

1. Many people know he is brave.
    Banyak orang tahu tentang keberaniannya.
    Many people know about his bravery.
2. Many people know he has gone.
    Banyak orang tahu tentang kepergiannya.
    Many people know about his departure.
3. Many people know he has succeeded.
    Banyak orang tahu tentang keberhasilannya.
    Many people know about his success.
4. Many people know he has failed.
    Banyak orang tahu tentang kegagalannya.
    Many people know about his failure.

5. Many people know he is healthy.
    Banyak orang tahu tentang kesehatannya.
    Many people know about his health.
6. Many people know he has won.
    Banyak orang tahu tentang kemenangannya.
    Many people know about his victory.

EXERCISE 3

1. The rioters burned his office last year.
    Pembakaran kantornya terjadi tahun lalu.
    The burning of his office happened last year.
2. The committee announced its decision this morning.
    Pengumuman keputusannya terjadi tadi pagi.
    The announcing of its decision occurred this morning.
3. The minister opened the program in the main hall.
    Pembukaan acara terjadi di ruangan utama.
    The opening of the program took place in the main hall.
4. Poor people suffer everywhere.
    Penderitaan orang miskin terjadi di mana-mana.
    The suffering of poor people happens everywhere.
5. Harry stole the gold last year.
    Pencurian emas itu terjadi tahun lalu.
    The theft/stealing of the gold happened last year.
6. Police questioned the thief yesterday.
    Pemeriksaan pencuri itu terjadi kemarin.
    The questioning of the thief happened yesterday.
7. The people who possess weapons must register them at this office.
    Pendaftaran senjata harus terjadi di kantor ini.
    The registering of weapons must take place in this office.
8. He translated my book last year.
    Penerjemahan buku saya terjadi tahun lalu.
    The translating of my book took place last year.

EXERCISE 4

The following include possible answers to the questions.
1. What time do you begin work?
    Pekerjaan saya mulai jam delapan pagi.
    My work begins at 8 in the morning.
2. In what year did they meet?
    Pertemuan mereka terjadi dua tahun lalu.
    Their meeting occurred two years ago.
3. What did he ask about?
    Pertanyaannya tentang kesehatan kita.
    His question was about our health.
4. When did he request our help?
    Permintaannya diterima minggu lalu.
    His request was received last week.

5.   When did they divorce?
      Perceraian mereka terjadi dua tahun lalu.
      Their divorce happened two years ago.
6.   Where did they oppose their enemy?
      Perlawanan itu terjadi di daerah perbatasan.
      The opposition was in the border region.
7.   Where did they fight?
      Perkelahian mereka terjadi di luar rumah.
      Their fight occurred outside the house.
8.   What year did the workers begin to be active?
      Pergerakan buruh mulai tahun 1895.
      The labour movement began in 1895.

EXERCISE 5

1.   **Kemiskinan rakyat di daerah itu sangat menyedihkan.**
2.   **Tabungannya belum cukup untuk membeli rumah.**
3.   **Penyatuan bangsa sudah bertahun-tahun ditunggu.**
4.   **Apa perbedaan antara kedua kata ini?**
5.   **Pemilihan umum akan diadakan bulan Maret tahun depan.**
6.   **Jawaban yang kami terima tidak memuaskan.**
7.   **Pertemuan antara kedua perdana menteri akan berlangsung di Jakarta.**
8.   **Kami mengalami kesulitan ketika kami memohon visa.**
9.   **Pembangunan gedung-gedung tinggi terjadi dimana-mana.**
10.   **Ibu belum pulang dari pusat pertokoan.**
11.   **Borobudur adalah bangunan yang sangat tua.**
12.   **Sebelum membeli karpet kita harus tahu ukuran kamar.**

EXERCISE 6

1.   **kebersihan** 'cleanliness'
      All the citizens are proud of the cleanliness of their city.
2.   **nyanyian** 'song'
      I've just heard a *dangdut* song on the radio.
3.   **pemeriksaan** 'inspection/inspecting, examination'
      The inspection of the luggage took about three hours.
4.   **perbuatan** 'action(s), behaviour'
      His actions embarrassed his parents.
5.   **perumahan** 'housing'
      She lives in a housing complex not far from here.
6.   **ukiran** 'carving', **lukisan** 'painting'
      He returned from Bali with a lot of carvings and paintings.
7.   **kedatangan** 'arrival'
      The arrival of the leader was welcomed by the people.
8.   **permohonan** 'request, application'
      Our request to become members will be granted.
9.   **perjanjian** 'agreement'
      Indonesia and Australia will make a new agreement.
10.   **buatan** 'make; product' : **buatan Australia** 'made in Australia; Australian made'
      The Holden car is made in Australia.

11.   **pembuatan** 'making, manufacture, construction (of something)'
The construction of the bridge had to be stopped because of the rain.
12.   **pertanyaan** 'question'
Our lecturer couldn't answer the difficult question.

EXERCISE 7

1.   Who guards that shop?
Penjaga toko itu Pak Ali.
The guard of that shop is Mr Ali.
2.   Who owns that shop?
Pemilik toko itu Pak Ali.
The owner of that shop is Mr Ali.
3.   Who sings that song?
Penyanyi lagu itu Pak Ali.
The singer of that song is Mr Ali.
4.   Who leads that party?
Pemimpin partai itu Pak Ali.
The leader of that party is Mr Ali.
5.   Who founded that party?
Pendiri partai itu Pak Ali.
The founder of that party was Mr Ali.
6.   Who translated that book?
Penerjemah buku itu Pak Ali.
The translator of that book was Mr Ali.
7.   Who trains that sportsman?
Pelatih olahragawan itu Pak Ali.
The trainer of that sportsman is Mr Ali.

3   TRANSITIVE AND INTRANSITIVE VERBS

EXERCISE 1

1.   The pilot landed his plane safely. (T)
2.   We have to report to the immigration office. (I)
3.   That volcano erupted several years ago. (I)
4.   We reported the theft to the police. (T)
5.   I want to check the truth of that story. (T)
6.   The plane landed safely. (I)
7.   Since the accident his health has got steadily worse. (I)
8.   Andi writes a letter to his mother every week. (T)
9.   His father died last year. (I)
10.   He held my hand tightly. (T)

EXERCISE 2

1.   **menghadiri** 'attend' (T)
2.   **berkumpul** 'assemble, gather' (I)
3.   **menyerahkan** 'surrender, hand over' (T)
4.   **menyembunyikan** 'hide (something)' (T)
5.   **menyerah** 'surrender, give in' (I)

6.   **pindah** 'move' (I)
7.   **hadir** 'be present' (I)
8.   **melambai** 'wave' (I)
9.   **melambaikan** 'wave (something)' (T)
10.   **tumbuh** 'grow' (I)
11.   **menaikkan** 'raise, cause (something) to go up' (T)
12.   **bergerak** 'move, be in motion' (I)
13.   **bersembunyi** 'hide' (I)
14.   **naik** 'rise, go up' (I)

EXERCISE 3

Note: Sometimes a slightly different translation is appropriate for intransitive and transitive verbs. In such cases alternatives are given, separated by slashes.

1.   **Andi akan menikahi tunangannya bulan depan.**
      Andi is going to marry his fiancee next month.
2.   **Mengapa polisi mendatangi rumah Anda tadi malam?**
      Why did the police come to/visit your house last night?
3.   **Anda ingin menanyakan apa?**
      What do you want to ask about?
4.   **Banyak turis mengunjungi pantai ini pada masa liburan.**
      Lots of tourists visit this beach in the holiday season.
5.   **Kita tidak perlu memikirkan hal itu.**
      There's no need for us to think about that matter.
6.   **Mereka mengagumi kepala desa.**
      They admire the village head.
7.   **Tamu mengadukan pelayanan yang kurang baik.**
      The customers complained about the poor service.
8.   **Mereka menyadari bahaya di tempat itu.**
      They are aware of/realise the danger in that place.
9.   **Saya tidak mempercayai cerita itu.**
      I don't believe that story.
10.   **Saya tidak mau meniduri kasur ini karena kotor.**
      I don't want to sleep on this mattress because it's dirty.
11.   **Kami menggemari makanan Jepang.**
      We are fond of Japanese food.
12.   **Jangan menduduki kursi ibu!**
      Don't sit on/occupy mother's chair.

EXERCISE 4

1.   The meeting dispersed.
      Polisi membubarkan rapat.
      The police dispersed the meeting.
2.   The children kept away from the snake which came into the house.
      Ibu menjauhkan anak-anak dari ular yang masuk rumah.
      Mother kept the children away from the snake which came into the house.
3.   Siti woke at six o'clock.
      Ibu membangunkan Siti jam enam.
      Mother woke Siti at six o'clock.

4. The bus stopped in front of the school building.
   Sopir menghentikan bis di depan gedung sekolah.
   The driver stopped the bus in front of the school building.
5. The students assembled in the school yard.
   Pak guru mengumpulkan siswa-siswa di halaman sekolah.
   The teacher assembled the students in the school yard.
6. The people united when the enemy attacked their country.
   Pemimpin baru menyatukan rakyat ketika musuh menyerang negerinya.
   The new leader united the people when the enemy attacked their country.
7. Telephone communication with the town was cut off.
   Kaum pemberontak memutuskan hubungan telepon dengan kota itu.
   The rebels cut off telephone communication with the town.
8. The light is on.
   Saya menyalakan lampu.
   I turned on the light.
9. The University of Indonesia campus has moved to Depok.
   Pemerintah sudah memindahkan kampus Universitas Indonesia ke Depok.
   The government has moved the University of Indonesia campus to Depok.
10. The bomb exploded on the road.
    Teroris meledakkan bom itu di jalan.
    The terrorists exploded the bomb on the road.

4   ACTIVE AND PASSIVE VERBS

EXERCISE 1

1. My mother advised Ann.
   Ann dinasihati oleh ibu saya.
   Ann was advised by my mother.
2. Mochtar Lubis wrote this book.
   Buku ini ditulis oleh Mochtar Lubis.
   This book was written by Mochtar Lubis.
3. The attendant will take those suitcases to the room.
   Koper-koper itu akan dibawa ke kamar oleh pelayan.
   Those suitcases will be taken to the room by the attendant.
4. Ted telephones Mandy every day.
   Mandy ditelepon oleh Ted setiap hari.
   Mandy is telephoned by Ted every day.
5. She shut the window.
   Jendela ditutup oleh dia.
   The window was shut by her.
6. Gladys welcomed the guest.
   Tamu disambut oleh Gladys.
   The guest was welcomed by Gladys.
7. Halimah opened all the presents.
   Semua hadiah dibuka oleh Halimah.
   All the presents were opened by Halimah.

8.   That child annoyed them.
Mereka diganggu oleh anak itu.
They were annoyed by that child.

9.   They will accompany us to the airport.
Kami akan diantar ke bandar udara oleh mereka.
We will be accompanied to the airport by them.

10.   Mr Iwan put those things in the kitchen.
Barang itu diletakkan di dapur oleh Pak Iwan.
Those things were put in the kitchen by Mr Iwan.

EXERCISE 2

1.   **di-** This work must be finished immediately.
2.   **di-** His father was born in Yogyakarta 40 years ago.
3.   **di-** The meeting was cancelled by the committee because it rained.
4.   **meN-** He's going to the railway station to collect his friend.
5.   **meN-** They rejected my suggestion.
6.   **di-** I was ordered to go.
7.   **meN-** That region produces timber.
8.   **di-** His bike was stolen last night.
9.   **meN-** They are still looking for work.
10.   **di-** Cakes baked by mother are always very tasty.
11.   **di-** The discussions will be continued in May.
12.   **meN-** Farida has invited lots of people to her party.

EXERCISE 3

1.   Tuti has read the letter.
Surat itu sudah dibaca oleh Tuti.

2.   They don't understand my advice.
Nasihat saya tidak dimengerti oleh mereka.

3.   Utomo threw that stone.
Batu itu dilempar oleh Utomo.

4.   They will establish a new party.
Partai baru akan didirikan oleh mereka.

5.   All the people in the village have heard that story.
Cerita itu sudah didengar oleh semua orang di desa.

6.   They have eaten the rice.
Nasi itu sudah dimakan oleh mereka.

7.   Who washed this shirt?
Kemeja ini dicuci oleh siapa?

8.   He has to drink this milk.
Susu ini harus diminum olehnya.

EXERCISE 4

1.   **Kamar saya sudah dibersihkan oleh pembantu.**
My room has been cleaned by the servant.

2.   **Apa pekerjaannya sudah mereka selesaikan?** *or* **Apa pekerjaannya sudah diselesaikan mereka?**
Have they finished their work?

3. **Hal ini harus saya pikirkan.**
   I have to think about this matter.
4. **Mengapa mereka dipanggil Pak Basuki?**
   Why were they called by Mr Basuki?
5. **Di mana tas ini Anda beli?**
   Where did you buy this bag?
6. **Barang ini tidak boleh kamu ambil.**
   You are not allowed to take these things.
7. **Tasnya dia tinggalkan di mobil** *or* **Tasnya ditinggalkannya di mobil.**
   He left his bag in the car.
8. **Tomo akan kita antar ke dokter.**
   We will to take Tomo to the doctor.
9. **Harga beras akan dinaikkan oleh pemerintah.**
   The price of rice will be raised by the government.
10. **Kartu yang indah dipilih oleh anak itu untuk ibunya.**
    The child chose a beautiful card for her mother.
11. **Film itu sudah saya lihat.**
    I've already seen that movie.
12. **Surat itu mau mereka kirim hari ini** *or* **Surat itu mau dikirim mereka hari ini.**
    They want to send that letter today.

EXERCISE 5

1. **Saya tidak diundang ke pesta Farida.**
2. **Apa kamar ini dibersihkan setiap hari?**
3. **Uangnya dicuri dari kamarnya.**
4. **Meja sudah dipindah ke kamar lain.**
5. **Anak-anaknya dilarang keluar rumah.**
6. **Buku-buku ini harus dikembalikan ke perpustakaan.**
7. **Barang macam itu dapat dibeli di pasar mana saja.**
8. **Dia dipilih sebagai pemimpin partai.**
9. **Masalah ini dibicarakan minggu lalu.**
10. **Rapat itu dihadiri banyak orang.**

EXERCISE 6

1. **Pupuk itu digunakan di sawah.**
2. **Mengapa dia sudah pindah ke Cairns?**
3. **Mengapa pariwisata tidak dikembangkan di negeri itu?**
4. **Mengapa lukisan itu dipindahkan dari ruang tamu?**
5. **Harga bensin dinaikkan bulan lalu.**
6. **Para pengungsi terbang ke Pontianak dengan pesawat Cessna.**
7. **Pupuk itu berguna bagi para petani.**
8. **Harga bensin naik bulan lalu.**
9. **Para pengungsi diterbangkan ke Pontianak dengan pesawat Cessna.**
10. **Ekonomi negeri itu berkembang dengan pesat.**

EXERCISE 7

1. I read my children a story every night.
   Anak saya saya bacakan cerita setiap malam.

2.   He named his child Utomo.
      Anaknya dinamainya Utomo *or* **Anaknya dia namai Utomo.**
3.   I don't lend them valuables.
      Mereka tidak saya pinjami barang berharga.
4.   Who will call me a taxi?
      Saya akan dipanggilkan taksi oleh siapa?
5.   The secretary sent her a letter yesterday.
      Dia dikirimi sekretaris surat kemarin.
6.   I will make you (a cup of) coffee.
      Anda akan saya buatkan kopi.
7.   We chose Ratna an umbrella for her journey.
      Ratna kami pilihkan payung untuk perjalanannya.
8.   My father will pay the cost of the taxi there for us.
      Kita akan dibayarkan ongkos taksi ke sana oleh ayah saya.
9.   Supardi gave Irawati a gold ring.
      Irawati diberi cincin emas oleh Supardi.
10.   They haven't offered us work yet.
      Kami belum ditawari pekerjaan oleh mereka *or* **Kami belum mereka tawari pekerjaan.**

5   INTRANSITIVE VERBS

EXERCISE 1

1.   **tenggelam** 'sink'
2.   **lupa** 'forget'
3.   **meledak** 'explode'
4.   **berdoa, mendoa** 'pray'
5.   **mendidih** 'boil'
6.   **berdiri** 'stand'
7.   **batuk, berbatuk** 'cough'
8.   **memekik** 'scream, yell'
9.   **jemur** 'dry in the sun' (**menjemur** is transitive)
10.   **menang** 'win'
11.   **berludah, meludah** 'spit'
12.   **menyerah** 'surrender'

EXERCISE 2

1.   **Gadis itu berambut panjang.**
      That girl has long hair.
2.   **Koper itu berisi pakaian.**
      That suitcase contains clothes.
3.   **Mereka beragama Islam.**
      Their religion is Islam.
4.   **Rumah ini berhalaman luas.**
      This house has a big yard.
5.   **Pak Usman beranak lima orang.**
      Mr Usman has five children.
6.   **Pak Pradeep berasal dari India.**
      Mr Pradeep comes (originates) from India.

7. **Gedung itu berlantai sembilan**
   That building has nine floors.
8. **Ikan ini berbau busuk.**
   This fish smells rotten.

EXERCISE 3

1. **Aminah bersepeda ke sekolah.**
   Aminah rides a bike to school.
2. **Apa dia sudah berkeluarga?**
   Does he have a family yet?
3. **Mereka berbahasa Indonesia dengan lancar.**
   They speak Indonesian fluently.
4. **Arif berumur 20 tahun.**
   Arif is 20 years old.
5. **Buku ini tidak berguna.**
   This book is of no use.
6. **Usahanya tidak berhasil.**
   His efforts didn't succeed.
7. **Orang kaya itu berumah dua.**
   that rich man has two houses.
8. **Tetangga saya selalu bertopi kalau keluar rumah.**
   My neighbour always wears a hat when he leaves the house.

6   *-KAN* AND *-I* VERBS

EXERCISE 1

1. He is free from jail.
   Gubernur membebaskannya dari penjara.
   The governor released him from jail.
2. That area is safe.
   Tentara mengamankan daerah itu.
   The army made that area safe.
3. This water is hot.
   Ibu sudah memanaskan air ini.
   Mother has heated this water.
4. This light has to be off before we go to bed.
   Kita harus mematikan lampu ini sebelum kita tidur.
   We have to turn this light off before we go to bed.
5. This sentence is correct.
   Guru membetulkan kalimat ini.
   The teacher corrected this sentence.
6. My work is light.
   Bantuannya meringankan pekerjaan saya.
   His help lightened my work.
7. His mother is angry.
   Anak nakal itu memarahkan ibunya.
   That naughty child angered his mother.
8. His tie is straight.
   Pak Yusuf meluruskan dasinya.
   Mr Yusuf straightened his tie.

EXERCISE 2

1. Are the customers satisfied with the service in this restaurant?
   Ya, pelayanan itu memuaskan.
   Yes, the service is satisfactory/satisfying.
2. Is Tommy sad because of the death of his cat?
   Ya, kematian kucingnya menyedihkan.
   Yes, the death of his cat is saddening.
3. Were they afraid watching the movie?
   Ya, film itu menakutkan.
   Yes, the movie was frightening.
4. Is Mrs Sulastri worried about her husband's illness?
   Ya, penyakit suaminya mengkhawatirkan.
   Yes, her husband's illness is worrying.
5. Is Henny disappointed with her exam results?
   Ya, hasil ujiannya mengecewakan.
   Yes, her exam results are disappointing.
6. Was mother glad to hear the news?
   Ya, kabar itu menggembirakan.
   Yes, the news was gladdening.
7. Are you pleased to receive that news?
   Ya, kabar itu menyenangkan.
   Yes, that news is pleasing.
8. Were they startled to hear the answer?
   Ya, jawaban itu mengagetkan.
   Yes, the answer was startling.

EXERCISE 3

1. They send their children to school in Rawamangun.
   The verb **menyekolahkan** 'send to school' is based on **sekolah** 'school'.
2. Mr Rahman chaired that meeting.
   The verb **mengetuai** 'to chair, convene' is based on **ketua** 'chairperson, convenor'.
3. All new students must register their names here.
   The verb **mendaftarkan** 'to register' is based on **daftar** 'list'.
4. The agreement between the two universities was signed by the two vice-chancellors.
   The verb **menandatangani** 'to sign' is based on **tandatangan** 'signature'.
5. The competition was sponsored by Toyota.
   The verb **mensponsori** 'to sponsor' is based on **sponsor** 'sponsor'.
6. The doctor treated his wound with antibiotics.
   The verb **mengobati** 'to treat medically' is based on **obat** 'medicine'.
7. The Torajans sacrifice many buffaloes every year.
   The verb **mengorbankan** 'to sacrifice' is based on **korban** 'sacrifice'.
8. The journalist wishes to interview the minister.
   The verb **mewawancarai** 'to interview' is based on **wawancara** 'interview'.
9. The town was blanketed in black smoke from that factory.
   The verb **menyelimuti** 'to cover' is based on **selimut** 'blanket'.
10. The youths/young people idolised the new singer.
    The verb **mendewakan** 'to idolise' is based on **dewa** 'deity, god'.

11.   The cunning lawyer cornered the witness.
       The verb **menyudutkan** 'to put in a corner' is based on **sudut** 'corner'.
12.   The police still do not know who masterminded the robbery.
       The verb **mendalangi** 'to mastermind' is based on **dalang** 'puppeteer'.
13.   The bomb injured ten people.
       The verb **melukai** 'to injure' is based on **luka** 'wound, injury'.
14.   The police kept the name of the informant a secret.
       The verb **merahasiakan** 'to keep (something) secret' is based on **rahasia** 'secret'.
15.   The group will stage a new play next month.
       The verb **mementaskan** 'to stage, perform on stage' is based on **pentas** 'stage'.

EXERCISE 4

1.   **Dia selalu dinasihati oleh orang tuanya.**
2.   **Pak Ali mewakili Indonesia dalam perundingan.**
3.   **Dia membuktikan bahwa dia tidak bersalah.**
4.   **Para olahragawan mensukseskan/menyukseskan Olimpiade Atlanta.**
5.   **Ola mengepalai kantor di Semarang.**
6.   **Petani-petani memasarkan sayur-sayurannya di kota.**
7.   **Pencuri itu dipenjarakan lima tahun.**
8.   **Pantai-pantai Bali dibanjiri dengan turis asing.**
9.   **Halamannya dipagari dengan bambu.**
10.   **Bung Karno mengilhami rakyat Indonesia selama masa revolusi.**

EXERCISE 5

1.   **Ari menaiki bis ke kota.** (**naik** go up; get on, ride on)
      Ali took the bus to town.
2.   **Toni menjatuhkan batu dari atap.** (**jatuh** drop)
      Toni dropped a stone from the roof.
3.   **Pengimpor itu mendatangkan barang dari Cina.** (**datang** come)
      The importer brought in goods from China.
4.   **Orang sakit diturunkan dari bis.** (**turun** go down)
      The sick person was taken off (lowered from) the bus.
5.   **Siti menduduki kursi ini.** (**duduk** sit)
      Siti is occupying this seat.
6.   **Saya selalu menjauhkan anak saya dari anjing itu.** (**menjauh** keep away)
      I always keep my children away from that dog.
7.   **Polisi mendatangi rumah perjudian.** (**datang** come)
      The police paid a call on the gambling place.
8.   **Anak itu pandai melompati pagar tinggi.** (**melompat** jump)
      That child is good at jumping over high fences.
9.   **Ayah memisahkan anak yang berkelahi.** (**berpisah** separate, part)
      Father separated the children who were fighting.
10.   **Pencuri itu dijatuhi hukuman lima tahun.** (**jatuh** fall)
      The thief was sentenced to five years jail. (literally: ...had imposed (dropped) on him a sentence of five years.)
11.   **Tuan rumah mendudukkan tamunya di ruang tamu.** (**duduk** sit)
      The host seated her guests in the lounge room.

12. **Mereka masih mendiami rumah ini. (berdiam di** reside in)
They still reside in/occupy this house.
13. **Saya selalu menjauhi anjing itu. (menjauh** keep away)
I always avoid/keep away from that dog.
14. **Susanto memulangkan jenazah ayahnya ke kampung. (pulang** return home)
Susanto brought his father's body home to the village.

EXERCISE 6

1. **meminjami** - I don't want to lend him my car.
2. **berikan** - Please give this book to him.
3. **menyerahi** - Don't give me heavy duties!
4. **mengirimi** - Who sent you these photos?
5. **menyerahkan** - Mr Sutrisno always gives heavy duties to other people.
6. **menghadiahkan** - The school principal presented an English dictionary to the cleverest student.
7. **menjuluki** - The English press nicknamed Margaret Thatcher 'The Iron Lady'.
8. **memberi** - Why do you want to give him this book?
9. **suguhi** - Minah, served the guests coffee!
10. **meminjamkan** - I don't want to lend my car to him.
11. **menyodorkan** - The bank presented/offered a new contract to their customers.
12. **menghadiahi** - The school principal presented the student with an English dictionary.

EXERCISE 7

1. The judge imposed a heavy sentence on the criminal.
Hakim menjatuhi penjahat hukuman berat.
The judge gave the criminal a heavy sentence.
2. When did he offer that help to you?
Kapan dia menawari kamu bantuan itu?
When did he offer you that help?
3. This stall offers sweet coffee to its customers.
Warung ini menyuguhi tamunya kopi manis.
This stall offers its customers sweet coffee.
4. He handed his guests coffee and cake.
Dia menyodorkan kopi dan biskuit kepada tamunya.
He handed coffee and biscuits to his guests.
5. God blessed/gifted the couple with a child.
Tuhan menganugerahkan seorang anak kepada suami istri itu.
God bestowed a child on the couple.
6. She gave Mrs Suparno her children for safekeeping.
Dia menitipkan anaknya kepada Ibu Suparno.
She entrusted her children to Mrs Suparno.

EXERCISE 8

1. **menghubungkan** - This new road will connect the city with the harbour.
2. **memuatkan** - The labourers loaded rice onto the truck.
3. **menyemprotkan** - This farmer sprays pesticide twice a week.
4. **menaburkan** - The girls scattered flowers along the road.
5. **menghindari** - The demonstrators tried to avoid the police.
6. **memuati** - The labourers loaded the truck with rice.
7. **menaburi** - She always sprinkles her food with salt.
8. **melumuri** - She smeared her body with oil.
9. **menyemproti** - This farmer sprays his vegetables twice a week.
10. **menghindarkan** - He managed to get his children away from the danger.
11. **menghubungi** - I will contact them tomorrow.
12. **melumurkan** - She smeared oil on her body.

EXERCISE 9

Dia is used as subject in each of the following sentences.

1. **Dia menuangkan kopi ke dalam cangkir.**
   Dia menuangi cangkir dengan kopi.
   (both:) He poured coffee into the cup.
2. **Dia meneteskan obat ke dalam matanya.**
   Dia menetesi matanya dengan obat.
   (both:) He dripped the medicine into his eyes.
3. **Dia menyiramkan air ke bunga.**
   He sprayed water onto the flowers.
   Dia menyirami bunga dengan air.
   He sprayed the flowers with water.
4. **Dia menyorotkan lampu santer ke dalam gang.**
   He shone the torch into the alley.
   Dia menyoroti gang dengan lampu santer.
   He lit up the alley with a torch.
5. **Dia membebankan banyak tugas baru kepada saya.**
   He loaded lots of new tasks on me.
   Dia membebani saya dengan banyak tugas baru.
   He burdened me with lots of new tasks.
6. **Dia menanamkan pohon mangga di lereng ini.**
   He planted mango trees on this slope.
   Dia menanami lereng ini dengan pohon mangga.
   He planted this slope with mango trees.
7. **Dia mengoleskan salep ke lukanya.**
   He smeared ointment on his wound.
   Dia mengolesi lukanya dengan salep.
   He smeared his wound with ointment.

EXERCISE 10

1. **Pak Warouw menanam(kan) pohon ini tiga tahun lalu.**
2. **Dia menyiram(i) bunga-bunga ini setiap hari.**
3. **Kita harus membicarakan hal ini besok.**
4. **Dia tidak mau memberi(kan) raportnya kepada ayahnya.**
5. **Kita akan menyumbang(kan) seratus dolar kepada para korban banjir.**

6.   **Pak Ahmed ditangkap karena meracuni istrinya.**
7.   **Saya menyurati ibu setiap minggu.**
8.   **Orang yang masuk perpustakaan harus menitip(kan) barangnya di loket.**
9.   **Saya meminjamkan pena kepada Titik dua minggu lalu.**
10.   **Saya tidak mau menyeberang(i) jalan ini karena lalu lintas terlalu padat.**
11.   **Tuan rumah melayani tamu-tamu sesudah mereka duduk.**
12.   **Kamu harus mengulang(i) latihan ini.**
13.   **Banjir bulan lalu merusak(kan) banyak desa.**
14.   **Polisi mengikut(i) pencuri ke rumahnya.**
15.   **Stasiun radio ini sering menyiarkan musik Indonesia.**
16.   **Saya akan mengantar(kan) Sally ke rumahnya.**

EXERCISE 11

1.   Dul stabbed his enemy's arm with a knife.
      Dul menikamkan pisau ke tangan musuhnya.
      Dul stabbed a knife into his enemy's arm/Dul used a knife to stab his enemy in the arm.
2.   Tomo covered his face with his hat.
      Tomo menutupkan topinya ke/pada mukanya.
      Tomo used his hat to cover his face.
3.   The eagle grasped the fish in its claws.
      Burung elang mencengkeramkan cakarnya pada ikan.
      The eagle fastened its claws on the fish.
4.   She rubbed her skin with soap.
      Dia menggosokkan sabun pada kulitnya.
      She rubbed the soap into her skin.
5.   She knocked/tapped on the table with her spoon.
      Dia mengetokkan sendoknya di meja.
      She beat her spoon on the table.
6.   Amie scratched her head with a pencil.
      Amie menggarukkan pensil di kepalanya.
      Amie used a pencil to scratch her head.
7.   She sliced the bread with a long knife.
      Dia mengiriskan pisau panjang pada roti.
      She sliced the bread with a long knife.
8.   The servant wiped the table with a dirty cloth.
      Pembantu menyekakan lap yang kotor pada meja.
      The servant wiped a dirty cloth over the table.
9.   The craftsman chopped the wood with his machete.
      Perajin memotongkan parangnya pada kayu itu.
      The craftsman used his machete to chop the wood.
10.   The doctor injected the patient's thigh with a new medicine.
      Dokter menyuntikkan obat baru ke paha pasien.
      The doctor injected a new medicine into the patient's thigh.

EXERCISE 12

1. That tailor sewed my shirt.
   Saya menjahitkan kemeja ke tukang jahit itu.
   I had my shirt sewn by that tailor.
2. This garage repaired my car.
   Saya mereparasikan mobil ke bengkel ini.
   I had my car repaired in this garage.
3. That new printery printed my invitation cards.
   Saya mencetakkan kartu undangan saya ke percetakan baru itu.
   I had my invitation cards printed by that new printery.
4. This family rents my house.
   Saya menyewakan rumah kepada keluarga ini.
   I rent (out) my house to this family.
5. The mill weighs the farmers' rice.
   Para petani menimbangkan beras ke penggiling itu.
   The farmers have their rice weighed at the mill.
6. Who checked your eyes?
   Kamu memeriksakan mata kepada siapa?
   Who did you have check your eyes?
7. That auctioneer will auction my house tomorrow.
   Saya akan melelangkan rumah saya pada pelelang itu.
   will have my house auctioned off by that auctioneer.
8. That doctor operated on Mrs Yusup's eyes.
   Ibu Yusup mengoperasikan mata ke dokter itu.
   Mrs Yusup had her eyes operated on by that doctor.

EXERCISE 13

1. **Bu Slamet memasakkan keluarganya nasi goreng.**
   Mrs Slamet cooked her family fried rice.
2. **Pak Hartono mencarikan anaknya sekolah.**
   Mr Hartono looked for a school for his children.
3. **Pak Budi membuatkan anaknya main-mainan.**
   Pak Budi made his children toys.
4. **Tono mengambilkan ayahnya koran.**
   Tono got/fetched his father the paper.
5. **Dia memanggilkan temannya dokter.**
   He called a doctor for his friend.
6. **Tuti mengiriskan ayah roti.**
   Tuti sliced the bread for father.

EXERCISE 14

1. Siti tidied up the room. (N)
2. Siti cleaned the room. (N)
3. Siti washed the clothes (for someone). (B)
4. Siti sent clothing. (N)
5. Siti requested money (for someone). (B)
6. Siti sewed (someone) a jacket. (B)
7. Siti chose (someone) a jacket. (B)
8. Siti offered work. (N)

9.   Siti opened the door (for someone). (B)
10.   Siti stole clothes (for someone). (B)

EXERCISE 15

1.   All Mr Sarif's proposals were agreed to. (N)
2.   The burglar who got into Mrs Suparno's house was beaten up by the village people. (R)
3.   The demonstrators pelted the journalists with stones and rubbish. (R)
4.   He lifted the suitcases one by one. (R)
5.   The naughty child wasn't game to face the school principal. (N)
6.   Who lent you this dictionary? (N)
7.   He was badly injured because he was stabbed repeatedly by the burglar. (R)
8.   Who wrote on this paper? (N)
9.   Mother is angry because Siti keeps biting her nails. (R)
10.   They repeatedly fetched stones from the river. (R)
11.   The manager wants to reduce the number of workers in his factory. (N)
12.   The secretary opened the letters before giving them to Mr Hadi. (R)

7   *PER-* VERBS

EXERCISE 1

1.   Security at the airport is tight.
      Polisi sudah memperketat penjagaan di bandar udara.
      Police have tightened security at the airport.
2.   His house is large.
      Kardi sudah memperbesar rumahnya.
      Kardi has enlarged his house.
3.   Their holiday was long
      Keluarga itu sudah memperpanjang liburannya.
      That family has lengthened (extended) their holiday.
4.   The meeting was brief.
      Ketua sudah mempersingkat rapat.
      The convenor has shortened the meeting.
5.   This knife is sharp.
      Bapak sudah mempertajam pisau ini.
      Father has sharpened this knife.
6.   That park is beautiful.
      Tukang kebun sudah memperindah taman itu.
      The gardener has beautified that park.
7.   His Indonesian is fluent.
      Mahasiswa itu sudah memperlancar bahasa Indonesianya.
      That student has improved (literally: made more fluent) his Indonesian.
8.   Her recovery was quick.
      Obat baru itu sudah mempercepat kesembuhannya.
      The new medicine has speeded up her recovery.

EXERCISE 2

1. **Saya mau membesarkan/memperbesar foto-foto ini.**
    I want to enlarge these photos.
2. **Sandiwara itu menyedihkan semua penonton.**
    The play saddened the whole audience.
3. **Lampu lalu lintas akan dipasang di perempatan ini untuk melancarkan/memperlancar lalu lintas.**
    traffic lights will be installed on this intersection to speed up (cause to flow smoothly) the traffic.
4. **Jalan ini akan dilebarkan/diperlebar.**
    This road is going to be widened.
5. **Sopir menghentikan bis di luar gedung sekolah.**
    The driver stopped the bus outside the school building.
6. **Anak-anak itu menjatuhkan batu ke dalam sungai.**
    The children dropped stones into the river.
7. **Bendera harus diturunkan setiap malam.**
    The flag must be lowered every night.
8. **Bank ini bersedia melunakkan/memperlunak syarat-syaratnya untuk nasabah baru.**
    This bank is willing to soften its terms for new customers.
9. **Tentara membebaskan kota itu dari kaum pemberontak.**
    The army freed the city from the rebels.
10. **Pedagang itu mendatangkan barang dari luar negeri.**
    That merchant brings in goods from overseas.

EXERCISE 3

1. **Tomo mengingatkan/memperingatkan adiknya supaya tidak bermain dekat jalan.**
2. **Dia mendengarkan musik dangdut.**
3. **Mereka mempertunjukkan tari-tarian baru tadi malam.**
4. **Mengapa kamu memperlakukan dia begitu?**
5. **Saya belum mengenalkan/memperkenalkan Titik kepada orang tua saya.**
6. **Saya ingin membandingkan/memperbandingkan semua mobil itu sebelum memilih satu.**
7. **Peta ini menunjukkan jalan ke Salatiga.**
8. **Dia memperdengarkan musik dangdut di pestanya.**
9. **Saya akan mempertimbangkan permohonan Anda.**
10. **Arif mempertanyakan keputusan wasit.**
11. **Dia menanyakan ongkos perjalanan ke Bali.**
12. **Dewi melakukan tugasnya dengan baik.**
13. **Maria menyiapkan/mempersiapkan laporan untuk kepala sekolah.**
14. **Universitas harus memperhitungkan biaya gedung baru.**

EXERCISE 4

1. **Mereka sedang memperbarui/membarui rumahnya.**
2. **Pemerintah sedang mempelajari usul mereka.**
3. **Mereka sudah memperlengkapi/melengkapi rumahnya dengan perabot baru.**

4. **Orang tua ingin mempertahankan tradisi lama.**
5. **Pemerintah tidak mau mempersenjatai rakyat.**
6. **Ibu Mamam mempersilakan/menyilakan tamu duduk.**
7. **Bangsa Indonesia memperingati Hari Kemerdekaan pada tanggal 17 Agustus.**
8. **Jenderal itu berhasil mempersatukan/menyatukan tentara.**

8 *TER-* VERBS

EXERCISE 1

1. This morning I locked the door.
   Sekarang pintu terkunci.
   Now the door is locked.
2. This morning I opened the window.
   Sekarang jendela terbuka.
   Now the window is open.
3. This morning waste from that factory polluted the river.
   Sekarang sungai itu tercemar.
   Now the river is polluted.
4. This morning all the visitors recorded (noted down) their names in the guest book.
   Sekarang nama semua pengunjung tercatat dalam buku tamu.
   Now the names of all the visitors are recorded in the guest book.
5. This morning the new students registered their names for this course.
   Sekarang nama mahasiswa baru terdaftar untuk kursus ini.
   Now the names of the new students are registered for this course.
6. This morning the rebels cut off communications with the capital.
   Sekarang hubungan dengan ibu kota terputus.
   Now communications with the capital are cut off.

EXERCISE 2

1. **Jangan naik mobil ke kota. Lalu-lintas di sana tidak teratur.**
   Don't go to town by car. The traffic there is disorganised.
2. **Saya minta pintu kantor ini dikunci sebelum Anda pulang.**
   I request this door be locked before you go home.
3. **Mengapa pintu toko itu terbuka lebar?**
   Why is the door of that shop open wide?
4. **Meja ini harus diatur sebelum tamu-tamu tiba.**
   This table must be set before the guests arrive.
5. **Obat ini mengandung zat yang terlarang.**
   This medicine contains a prohibited substance.
6. **Nama kepala sekolah tertulis di pintu kantornya.**
   The name of the school head is written on his office door.
7. **Meskipun dia sudah pulang pintu kantornya tidak terkunci.**
   Although he has gone home his office door isn't locked.
8. **Jangan lupa! Pintu toko harus dibuka sebelum jam delapan pagi.**
   Don't forget! The shop door must be opened before eight in the morning.
9. **Kata-kata yang kasar itu dengan sengaja dimuatnya dalam pidatonya.**
   He deliberately put those vulgar words in his speech.

10. **Pestisida itu dilarang oleh Departemen Kesehatan.**
   That pesticide is banned by the Health Department.
11. **Dalam harian *Kompas* tadi pagi termuat foto rombongan dari Hong Kong.**
   In *Kompas* this morning there was (lit: there was contained) a photo of the group from Hong Kong.
12. **Surat ini ditulis kemarin.**
   This letter was written yesterday.

EXERCISE 3

1. **terjamin** 'guaranteed' : stative
   Freedom of the press is guaranteed in that country.
2. **terlempar** 'thrown' : accidental
   The car driver was thrown to the road when his car struck a tree.
3. **terpesona** 'enticed, put under a spell' : accidental
   We are easily enticed by expensive goods.
4. **terbatas** 'limited' : stative
   His knowledge is very limited.
5. **tergelincir** 'slip' : accidental
   Tuti had to be taken to the doctor after she slipped on the stairs.
6. **tersepak** 'unintentionally kicked' : accidental
   The child cried when his was unintentionally kicked on the foot by his friend.
7. **tertinggal** 'left unintentionally' : accidental
   His book was left in the canteen (or more natural in English: He left his book in the canteen).
8. **tercantum** 'included' : stative
   Her name was not included in the list of people who passed the exam.

EXERCISE 4

1. **terjatuh** 'fell' : accidental
   Ali fell from the tree.
2. **(tidak) terangkat** 'can(not) be lifted' : abilitative
   They weren't able to lift the table.
3. **terbakar** 'caught fire, burned down' - accidental
   Whose house burned down yesterday?
4. **terkena** 'struck, subjected to' : accidental
   The rescue team distributed medicines to the village people who were caught in the flood.
5. **terdampar** 'be stranded, go aground' : accidental
   The local people tried to save the whale which was stranded on the beach.
6. **terpengaruh** 'influenced; affected' : accidental
   The local people won't be affected by the government decision.
7. **(tidak) terkendalikan** 'can(not) be controlled' : abilitative
   The anger of the demonstrators couldn't be controlled.
8. **termakan** 'accidentally eaten' : accidental
   My child accidentally ate the tablets.
9. **tertabrak** 'crashed into, struck' : accidental
   He died after being struck by a car.

10. **(tidak) terbaca** '(il)legible, can(not) be read' : abilitative
The writing in this book is too small to read.
11. **tersentuh** 'accidentally touched' : accidental
He cried out when the nurse touched his wound.
12. **(tidak) terhitung** '(un)countable, can(not) be counted' : abilitative
The number of stars in the sky can't be counted/is uncountable.

EXERCISE 5

1. Sorry, I ate your rice by mistake. : accidental
2. Were you able to eat such a large amount of rice? : abilitative
3. They were startled to hear that news. : accidental
4. Lunch is available in the dining room. : stative
5. He died as a result of being run over by a truck. : accidental
6. Their anger could not be controlled/was uncontrollable. : abilitative
7. The bus which fell into the gorge is now lying upside down. : stative
8. That news was (contained) in all the newspapers. : stative
9. Whose foot did he tread on? : accidental
10. Can his house be seen from here? : abilitative
11. We cannot complete that work. : abilitative
12. I woke up suddenly at four o'clock this morning. : accidental

9   *KE-...-AN* VERBS

EXERCISE 1

1. Didi had to move to another town after losing his job.
2. Unfortunately, we got caught in the rain when we went picnicking yesterday.
3. In that region many people don't have sufficient food.
4. She had an unexpected visitor while having a bath.
5. People who get bitten by a mosquito in that region sometimes are infected with malaria.
6. That poor woman; she was pickpocketed on the bus.
7. Ali was caught smoking by his mother. (**kedapatan** literally: 'be discovered (doing something bad), be found out')
8. Many farmers are starving because the harvest failed.
9. We were very cold/chilled last night because we forgot to take warm clothes.
10. Sorry, I'm late because I missed the bus. (literally: I was left behind by the bus.)

EXERCISE 2

1. **Karena gula habis saya harus pergi ke toko.**
Because sugar was used up I had to go to the shop.
2. **Jam tangan saya hilang waktu saya bermain di pantai.**
My watch got lost when I was playing at the beach.
3. **Tadi malam ada pencuri masuk rumah kami.**
Last night a thief got into our house.
4. **Karena kami kehabisan gula saya harus pergi ke toko.**
Because we ran out of sugar I had to go to the shop.
5. **Dompet Ani dicuri sementara dia makan di restoran.**
Ani's purse was stolen while she was eating in the restaurant.

6. **Saya kehilangan jam tangan waktu saya bermain di pantai.**
   I lost my watch while playing on the beach. (literally: I suffered the loss of my watch....)
7. **Polisi tahu Hamzah mencuri mobil itu.**
   The police know Hamzah stole that car.
8. **Ani kecurian dompet sementara dia makan di restoran.**
   Ani had her purse stolen while she was eating in the restaurant.
9. **Kakinya patah karena dia jatuh dari pohon.**
   His leg is broken because he fell from a tree.
10. **Kakinya patah karena dia kejatuhan pohon.**
    His leg is broken because he was hit by a falling tree. (literally: ...he was fallen on by a tree.)
11. **Kadang-kadang petani keracunan karena menggunakan terlalu banyak pestisida.**
    Sometimes farmers get poisoned (suffer poison) from using too much pesticide.
12. **Petani itu diracuni oleh istrinya.**
    The farmer was poisoned by his wife.
13. **Dia kematian ayah tahun lalu.**
    He lost his father last year. (literally: He suffered the death of his father...)
14. **Hamzah ketahuan mencuri mobil itu oleh polisi.**
    Hamzah is known to have stolen the car by the police.

10 *BER-...-KAN* VERBS

EXERCISE 1

1. **Dia bersenjatakan pedang.**
2. **Perkumpulan itu beranggotakan lebih dari seratus orang.**
3. **Rumah-rumah di desa itu berdindingkan bambu.**
4. **Dia beristrikan wanita Jawa.**
5. **Kebunnya berpagarkan pohon-pohon tinggi.**
6. **Lantai rumah mereka beralaskan tikar.**
7. **Partai politik itu berlambangkan bintang.**
8. **Bahasa Indonesia berasalkan dialek-dialek Melayu.**

11 *BER-...-AN* VERBS

EXERCISE 1

Note: A reduplicated base is given in parentheses where this frequently occurs.
1. **Anak-anak berdesak(-desak)an di halaman sekolah.**
2. **Kami belum berkenalan.**
3. **Kami sering berkirim(-kirim)an surat.**
4. **Rumah saya berhadapan dengan gereja.**
5. **Kedua rumah itu bersebelahan.**
6. **Kedua pemimpin itu berpelukan ketika bertemu.**
7. **Anak-anak itu berkejar(-kejar)an di halaman.**
8. **Kedatangannya bertepatan dengan hari libur.**
9. **Mereka berciuman di bawah pohon.**
10. **Sudah lama mereka bermusuhan.**

EXERCISE 2

1. **berserakan** 'scattered about' : Random
   This room is in a mess; papers are scattered everywhere.
2. **berlarian** 'run this way and that (of many people or things)' : Random
   The pupils were running about in the school yard.
3. **bersaingan** 'compete with each other' : Reciprocal
   Those two restaurants compete with each other/are in competition.
4. **bergantungan** 'hanging all about' : Random
   Flying foxes are hanging all through those trees.
5. **berloncatan** 'leap about (of many people or things)' : Random
   Because it has been raining for a long time the frogs are leaping about on the grass.
6. **berkasih-kasihan** 'love each other' : Reciprocal
   The two young people love each other.
7. **berpegangan tangan** 'hold each other's hand' : Reciprocal
   They are holding hands (with each other).
8. **berdatangan** 'coming one by one, in random manner' : Random
   The guests are beginning to turn up.
9. **bertaburan** 'scattered about' : Random
   Stars are scattered about the sky.
10. **berpandang(-pandang)an** 'gaze at each other' : Reciprocal
    Bob and Mary sat gazing at each other.

12 BASE-*MEN*- VERBS

EXERCISE 1

1. (R) Andi and Mina often telephone each other.
2. (E) Affairs/Anything to do with lifting I hand over to those who are stronger.
3. (R) All people must respect one another.
4. (R) Arif and his neighbours like to help each other.
5. (E) If you want to know about anything to do with dancing contact Mr Nyoman.
6. (R) Those two children are very naughty. They often fight and bite each other.
7. (R) They have been friends for a long time and they often visit each other.
8. (E) Julia wants to open a restaurant because she is an expert in cooking.
9. (E) My sister is going to do a course on (the art of) painting.
10. (R) In Indonesia people usually bargain with each other in the markets.
11. (E) If you want to become a farmer you must know everything about planting (growing crops).
12. (R) We don't correspond with each other any more.
13. (E) That lecturer teaches about composition (the art of writing).
14. (R) The army and the rebels were shooting at each other in the mountains.

13   NOUN PHRASES

EXERCISE 1

1.   This is a big house. (S)
2.   That town is big. (S)
3.   my clever teacher (N)
4.   Tomo's room is clean. (S)
5.   his old car (N)
6.   Siti is a good friend (S)
7.   That ugly building is tall. (S)
8.   That is a big town. (S)
9.   I am a clever teacher. (S)
10.   That tall building is ugly. (S)
11.   Siti's good friend (N)
12.   His car is old. (S)
13.   My teacher is clever. (S)
14.   Tomo's clean room (N)
15.   Siti's friend is good. (S)
16.   that big town (N)

EXERCISE 2

1.   This nurse is Detty.
2.   that lecturer of Budi's
3.   That doctor is my father.
4.   He is that child.
5.   This is Detty's nurse.
6.   this bag of yours
7.   that doctor of my father's
8.   that child of theirs
9.   That lecturer is Budi.
10.   this clever secretary of ours
11.   Detty is this nurse.
12.   That child is him.
13.   That is my father's doctor.
14.   This is our clever secretary.
15.   that child of his
16.   This secretary of ours is clever.
17.   Budi is that lecturer.
18.   This is your bag.

EXERCISE 3

1.   **Itu rumah besar.**
2.   **Rumah itu besar.**
3.   **rumah besar itu**
4.   **Rumah saya besar.**
5.   **Itu rumah besar saya.**
6.   **Rumah saya itu besar.**
7.   **rumah besar saya itu**
8.   **mobil mahal itu**
9.   **Itu mobil mahalnya.**
10.   **Itu mobil mahal.**
11.   **Mobilnya itu mahal.**
12.   **mobil mahalnya itu**
13.   **Mobil itu mahal.**
14.   **Mobilnya mahal.**

EXERCISE 4

1.   **toko buku mereka itu**
     that book shop of theirs
2.   **kantor bapak yang besar itu**
     that big office of father's
3.   **papan tulis kotor itu**
     that dirty blackboard
4.   **kemeja merah saya ini**
     this red shirt of mine
5.   **anak saya yang pandai**
     my clever child
6.   **buku yang ditulisnya itu**
     that book which he wrote
7.   **mobil Alex yang dicuri kemarin**
     Alex's car which was stolen yesterday

8. **anak perempuan yang cantik**
    a pretty girl (female child)
9. **celananya yang kotor**
    his dirty trousers
10. **kapal nelayan yang tenggelam**
    the fisherman's boat which sank
11. **paket berat yang dikirim dari Inggris**
    the heavy packet sent from England
12. **kamar duduk yang sempit ini**
    this narrow sitting room
13. **celana kotornya**
    his dirty trousers
14. **sepeda motor tukang kayu itu**
    that carpenter's motor bike

14   ADJECTIVE PHRASES

EXERCISE 1

1. **Jakarta lebih besar daripada Solo.**
2. **Solo lebih kecil daripada Jakarta.**
3. **Simon kurang pandai dari Alice.**
4. **Melbourne jauh lebih dingin dari Brisbane.**
5. **Rumah di Sydney tiga kali lebih mahal dari rumah di Brisbane.**
6. **Ali lima sentimeter lebih tinggi dari Tom.**
7. **Buku ini dua ratus halaman lebih panjang dari buku itu.**
8. **Jalan ini dua meter lebih lebar daripada jalan ke Bogor.**
9. **Pekerjaan Anda tidak lebih berat dari pekerjaan saya.**
10. **Pekerjaan saya tidak kurang berat daripada pekerjaan Anda.**
11. **Bahasa Indonesia Bob sedikit lebih lancar daripada bahasa Indonesia Jane.**
12. **Ratna dapat lari dua kali lebih cepat dari adiknya.**

EXERCISE 2

1. **Amir siswa yang terpandai di kelas ini.**
3. **Film mana yang paling menakutkan?**
3. **Tokyo adalah kota termahal di dunia.**
4. **Film mana yang terbaik minggu ini?**
5. **Kue ini yang termanis dari semua makanan di meja.**
6. **Buaya binatang yang paling berbahaya di Indonesia.**
7. **Bill Gates orang terkaya di dunia.**
8. **Ini buku yang paling menarik.**

EXERCISE 3

1. **Kamar saya sebersih kamar Henry.**
    Kamar saya sama bersihnya dengan kamar Henry.
2. **Apa Jakarta sebesar London?**
    Apa Jakarta sama besarnya dengan London?
3. **Dia tidak setua saya.**
4. **Pisang dan papaya sama enaknya.**

5.   **Melbourne hampir sebesar Sydney.**
6.   **Henry tidak sesopan adiknya.**
7.   **Kedua anak laki-laki itu sama nakalnya**.
8.   **Barang di Jakarta sekarang semurah barang di Singapura.**
     Barang di Jakarta sekarang sama murahnya dengan barang di Singapura.
9.   **Kota Yogyakarta seramai kota Semarang.**
     Kota Yogyakarta sama ramainya dengan kota Semarang.
10. **Rapat-rapat ini sama pentingnya.**

15   PREDICATE PHRASES

EXERCISE 1

1.   I <u>have just woken up</u>.
2.   <u>Have</u> you <u>ever been</u> to Europe?
3.   When we arrived all the other guests <u>were already seated</u>.
4.   Adrian always sings while <u>having a bath</u>.
5.   When I arrived at his house Tom <u>was still eating</u>.
6.   The lecture <u>had begun</u> when Paul arrived at the classroom.
7.   Alex <u>had just woken up</u> when his wife left for work this morning.
8.   I <u>am going to meet</u> them tomorrow.
9.   When I arrived at his house Tom <u>was eating</u>.
10. Has your friend <u>gone home yet</u>?
11. This rice <u>will be eaten</u> shortly.
12. That region <u>was once inhabited</u> but now it <u>is (already) empty</u>.
13. Every day Alex <u>only gets up</u> when his wife leaves for work. *or* Every day Alex <u>doesn't get up until</u> his wife leaves for work.
14. I <u>once heard</u> him give a speech.
15. It's now nine o'clock but he <u>is still having a bath</u>.

EXERCISE 2

1.   She <u>may</u> come in now.
2.   She <u>must be allowed to</u> come in now.
3.   She <u>is already allowed to</u> come in.
4.   If she comes tomorrow she <u>will be allowed to</u> come in.
5.   Martina <u>could already</u> swim before she was aged five.
6.   Martina <u>will be able to</u> swim before she's aged five.
7.   Martina is ten years old but she <u>can only just</u> swim.
8.   You <u>must be able to</u> swim if you want to become a policeman.
9.   If you call at my place too late at night I <u>will already be</u> asleep.
10. If you call at my place after eight o'clock I <u>will have already</u> eaten.
11. If you call at my place at seven I <u>will be</u> eating.
12. The audience <u>must already be</u> seated in the theatre before eight o'clock.
13. This kitchen <u>still has to</u> be cleaned.

16 NEGATIVES

EXERCISE 1

1. **Saya tidak malas.**
    I'm not lazy.
2. **Kota Jakarta tidak kecil.**
    Jakarta isn't small.
3. **Ayah saya bukan polisi.**
    My father is not a policeman.
4. **Bahasa Indonesia tidak sukar.**
    Indonesian isn't difficult.
5. **Ini bukan pena saya.**
    This isn't my pen.
6. **Ali bukan sopir.**
    Ali isn't a driver.
7. **Anak itu tidak mandi.**
    That child isn't having a bath.
8. **Kamar tidur saya tidak kotor.**
    My bedroom isn't dirty.
9. **Ani tidak tidur.**
    Ani isn't asleep.
10. **Tom bukan sekretaris.**
    Tom isn't a secretary.

EXERCISE 2

1. Has their teacher arrived yet? - **Belum.**
2. Is their teacher lazy? - **Tidak.**
3. Is their teacher English? - **Bukan.**
4. Are you tired? - **Tidak.**
5. Are you a farmer? - **Bukan.**
6. Have you been to America? - **Belum.**
7. Is that person your father? - **Bukan.**
8. Is that person waiting for the bus? - **Tidak.**
9. Has he been waiting for a long time? - **Belum.**

EXERCISE 3

1. Applicants do not have to be married.
2. Air stewardesses must be unmarried (literally: … must not yet be married.)
3. We never go there.
4. I will not take you to the cinema.
5. He still doesn't want to help us.
6. He still cannot be trusted.
7. He isn't sleeping at present.
8. I haven't eaten yet.
9. We have never been there.
10. They will not leave yet.
11. They don't have to leave yet.
12. Martina can't (isn't able to) swim yet.
13. We couldn't (were not allowed to) enter the theatre last night because we arrived late.
14. She can't speak Japanese.
15. I will never go there.
16. The city can no longer be seen from here because of the pollution.
17. Mr Soenjono is no longer a teacher.
18. You may not sit down before the teacher sits.
19. You can't (aren't allowed to) come in yet.
20. You still aren't allowed to come in.

EXERCISE 4

1. Saya datang ke sini bukan untuk menginap di hotel, tetapi untuk bergaul dengan orang setempat.
2. Bukan harga beras yang naik, melainkan harga barang-barang dari luar negeri.
3. Bukannya saya tidak mau membeli rumah baru, tetapi uang saya tidak cukup.
4. Saya pergi ke kota bukan untuk berbelanja, tetapi untuk bertemu dengan seorang teman.
5. Ketika ditangkap mereka bukannya menyerah, melainkan menyerang polisi dengan batu.
6. Dia jatuh bukan karena mabuk, tetapi karena jalan licin.
7. Bukan dia yang salah, melainkan saya.
8. Bukannya saya tidak mau berbicara dengan Anda, tetapi saya sangat sibuk sekarang.
9. Bukan saya tidak pandai berenang, tetapi airnya terlalu dingin.
10. Saya duduk bukan untuk istirahat, tetapi untuk membaca buku.

17 BARU

EXERCISE 1

1. Not until night time did I go to the office.
   Baru malam harinya aku pergi ke kantor.
2. The news was not heard until three o'clock.
   Berita itu terdengar baru pukul tiga.
3. This crisis will only pass after July.
   Krisis ini akan berlalu baru setelah bulan Juli.
4. Only after receiving the employees' promise did he pay the salaries.
   Baru sesudah menerima janji pegawai itu dia membayar gaji.
5. Not until the next day was the work commenced.
   Hari berikutnya baru pekerjaan itu dimulai.
6. Tony only went to sleep after his parents got home.
   Tony tidur baru sesudah orang tuanya pulang.
7. I'm not going to begin work until five o'clock.
   Saya baru akan mulai bekerja jam lima.
8. Not until the end of the year did the two farmers return to their village.
   Pada akhir tahun, baru kedua petani itu pulang ke desa.

18 PREPOSITIONS

EXERCISE 1

1. Mereka datang ke sini dari Jepang.
2. Anak-anak bermain di sebelah rumah.
3. Dia datang dari belakang rumah
4. Anak-anak lari ke seberang jalan.
5. Dia melemparkan bola dari atas gedung.
6. Kami menyimpan koper-koper tua itu di bawah rumah.
7. Dia mengusir anjing ke luar rumah.

8.   Apa rumah kita kelihatan dari sana?
9.   Anda boleh duduk di situ.
10.   Dia meletakkan makanan di atas meja.
11.   Dia mengambil pena dari dalam tasnya.
12.   Charlie mengambil bola dari bawah meja.

EXERCISE 2

1.   Kereta apa berangkat <u>pada</u> jam tiga.
2.   Mereka tinggal <u>di</u> Bandung.
3.   Nenek saya meninggal <u>pada</u> tahun 1981.
4.   Kata itu juga terdapat <u>pada</u> bahasa Perancis.
5.   Ada tiga sekretaris <u>di</u> kantor ayah saya.
6.   Dia duduk <u>di</u> kursi ini.
7.   <u>Pada</u> waktu malam dia selalu pulang.
8.   Ibunya meninggal <u>pada</u> akhir bulan Oktober.
9.   Kucing berbaring <u>di</u> lantai dapur.
10.   Ratna <u>di</u> rumah temannya sekarang.

EXERCISE 3

1.   Malcolm washed his hands <u>with</u> soap.
2.   The government declared war <u>on</u> the enemy.
3.   They travelled <u>by</u> ship.
4.   The climate in Hobart is very different <u>from</u> the climate in Jakarta.
5.   I'm rather worried <u>about</u> the danger to our traditions.
6.   We are grateful <u>for</u> your kindness.
7.   Java is divided <u>into</u> three provinces.
8.   They have a right <u>to</u> that house.
9.   The victory of the Australian team <u>over</u> Korea was very surprising.
10.   The government declared was <u>on</u> the enemy.
11.   Susan is annoyed <u>at</u> her younger brother.
12.   Their kindness <u>to</u> my family was very pleasing.
13.   Mother's love <u>for</u> her children is very strong.
14.   That person's prejudice <u>against</u> foreigners is extraordinary.

EXERCISE 4

1.   That help is very important <u>for</u> us.
2.   I don't know them.
3.   Indonesia is rich <u>in</u> oil.
4.   Ratna longs <u>for</u>/misses her father very much.
5.   I was angry <u>at</u> Allan.
6.   I don't believe <u>in</u>/trust him.
7.   They sang happily.
8.   Why are you suspicious <u>of</u> them?
9.   Indonesia consists <u>of</u> thousands of islands.
10.   We already know <u>about</u> that matter.
11.   Her writing is different <u>from</u> mine.

19   *ADA*

EXERCISE 1

1. Tomo ada pacar baru.
2. Ada pasar yang baik di Cikini?
3. Di mana ada hotel yang murah di kota ini?
4. Ada empat orang di taksi itu.
5. Apa (ada) banyak mahasiswa di universitas itu?
6. Saya tidak ada uang.
7. Ada rapat di sini tadi malam.
8. Ada ikan yang segar hari ini?
9. Apa ada becak di Australia?
10. Ibumu ada?
11. Ibu (ada) di dapur.
12. Tidak ada restoran di jalan ini.
13. Ada apa di tas ini?
14. Tidak (ada) banyak toko di sini.
15. Guru belum ada.

EXERCISE 2

1. Banyak barang di pasar hari ini; ada yang murah, ada yang mahal.
2. Tidak ada yang menolong dia waktu dia berangkat.
3. Saya tidak tahu mengapa dia marah; barangkali ada yang mengganggunya.
4. Saya mengajak mereka datang ke bioskop tapi tidak ada yang mau ikut.
5. Banyak turis tiba di Bali hari itu; ada yang berhenti di Denpasar, ada yang meneruskan ke Ubud.
6. Ada yang percaya padanya, ada yang tidak.
7. Ada yang berbau busuk di kulkas.
8. Tidak ada yang menjemput Tomo di bandar udara.
9. Saya tidak suka makanan ini; tidak ada yang bisa dimakan.
10. Sesudah pesta ada anak yang pulang, ada yang bermain di halaman belakang.

20   FUNCTIONS OF *-NYA*

EXERCISE 1

1. Agent
   The beggar was given money by him.
2. Object
   I bought it yesterday.
3. Possessor
   His wife was born in Solo.
4. Definitiser
   We went to the cinema last night. The movie was excellent.
5. Definitiser
   You haven't cleaned the house properly. The bathroom is still dirty.

6.   Linker
      My friend's mother works in Sarinah.
7.   Object
      Because Tom didn't want to work we told him to go away.
8.   Agent
      We were given this task by him. ·
9.   Linker
      Tuti's sister teaches at this school.
10.   Possessor
      Sardi wants to sell his car.
11.   Definitiser
      We had to take a taxi because the bus was late.
12.   Definitiser
      I want to have a bath but the water is too cold.

21   NUMBERS

EXERCISE 1

1.   **Ronny punya dua mobil.**
      Mobil Ronny dua.
2.   **Paman saya punya banyak teman.**
      Teman paman saya banyak.
3.   **Pak Ali punya lima belas kerbau.**
      Kerbau Pak Ali lima belas.
4.   **Dia punya hampir seratus ayam.**
      Ayamnya hampir seratus.
5.   **Saya punya lebih dari lima puluh buku.**
      Buku saya lebih dari lima puluh.
6.   **Joe punya dua adik laki-laki.**
      Adik laki-laki Joe dua.
7.   **Kami hanya punya sedikit uang.**
      Uang kami hanya sedikit.
8.   **Orang kaya itu punya tiga pertanian.**
      Pertanian orang kaya itu tiga.

EXERCISE 2

1.   **Dia mengirim kedua anaknya ke sekolah di Australia.**
2.   **Dua anak sedang bermain di jalan.**
3.   **Kelima anaknya sakit.**
4.   **Lima dari anaknya sakit.**
5.   **Tujuh (orang) teman menengok/menjenguk Allan di rumah sakit.**
6.   **Anaknya yang kedua sedang bersekolah di Australia.**
7.   **Ketujuh teman Allan menengok dia di rumah sakit.**
8.   **Anaknya yang kelima sakit.**
9.   **John adalah teman ketujuh yang menengok Allan di rumah sakit.**
10.   **Martin anak mereka yang pertama.**
11.   **Empat dari orang itu menolong saya.**
12.   **Keempat orang itu menolong saya.**

13. **Empat orang menolong saya.**
14. **Rumah yang keempat rumah saya.**

EXERCISE 3

1. **Surabaya kota kedua terbesar di Indonesia.** *or* **Surabaya kota terbesar (yang) kedua di Indonesia.**
2. **Kami berdua bekerja di kota.**
3. **Dia punya empat ekor anjing. Keempatnya besar.**
4. **Saya akan sibuk sekali selama ketiga minggu yang terakhir tahun ini.**
5. **Saya membeli tiga buku tadi pagi. Ketiganya mahal.**
6. **Kamu harus membaca kesepuluh halaman yang pertama di buku ini.**
7. **Mereka berempat bekerja di kota. Keempatnya naik kereta api ini.**
8. **Willy pemain ketiga yang terbaik di timnya.** *or* **Willy pemain terbaik yang ketiga di timnya.**
9. **Ada dua jalan ke desa itu. Keduanya baik.**
10. **Kamu bertiga boleh pergi sekarang.**
11. **Paman saya orang terkaya yang kelima di kota ini.**
12. **Ketiga anaknya yang pertama cantik sekali.**

EXERCISE 4

1. Mr Hasan teaches class four.
2. We had to work six hours yesterday.
3. Today we begin with lesson twenty.
4. She lives on floor seven.
5. He is eighty years old. (literally: His age is 80 years.)
6. We are going to move there on the fifteenth.
7. She's lived here for eight years.
8. We have finished twenty lessons in this book.
9. I've read page ten.
10. We began work at six o'clock yesterday.
11. We will leave on the 16th of April.
12. The Oxford dictionary consists of twelve volumes.
13. I want to borrow volume twelve.
14. Mr Hasan teaches four classes.
15. He was born in 1980.
16. I've read ten pages.

EXERCISE 5

1. **tiga perempat**
2. **dua perlima**
3. **tiga pertujuh**
4. **enam persepuluh**
5. **empat perlima**
6. **dua perseratus**
7. **seperdelapan**
8. **seperseratus**
9. **dua seperempat**
10. **tiga setengah**
11. **lima tiga persepuluh**
12. **enam sepertiga**

EXERCISE 6

1. **Dua pertiga mahasiswa di kelas ini perempuan.**
2. **Tiga perempat guru di sekolah ini punya mobil.**

3. Dia minum seperempat gelas air.
4. Tomo hanya bekerja dua setengah jam.
5. Dia tinggal di Bandung selama empat seperempat tahun.
6. Dia lari satu tigaperempat kilometer.
7. Umur Alice satu setengah tahun.
8. Saya sudah membaca satu setengah halaman.
9. Harganya hanya empat setengah dollar.
10. Saya sudah menunggu setengah jam.

22 ARITHMETIC

EXERCISE 1

1. Tiga tambah empat sama dengan tujuh.
2. Lima tambah empat sama dengan sembilan.
3. Dua puluh lima tambah tujuh belas sama dengan empat puluh dua.
4. Lima puluh tambah dua puluh tiga sama dengan tujuh puluh tiga.
5. Tiga kali tiga sama dengan sembilan.
6. Enam kali empat sama dengan dua puluh empat.
7. Tujuh kali lima sama dengan tiga puluh lima.
8. Sepuluh kali delapan sama dengan delapan puluh.
9. Enam kurang satu sama dengan lima.
10. Dua belas kurang tiga sama dengan sembilan.
11. Dua puluh kurang tiga sama dengan tujuh belas.
12. Seratus lima kurang dua belas sama dengan sembilan puluh tiga.
13. Delapan dibagi dua sama dengan empat.
14. Sembilan dibagi tiga sama dengan tiga.
15. Seratus dibagi lima sama dengan dua puluh.
16. Dua ratus dibagi empat sama dengan lima puluh.

23 REFLEXIVES

EXERCISE 1

1. Tamu memperkenalkan diri.
2. Anda harus menyesuaikan diri dengan situasi baru.
3. Saya mencoba menenangkan diri.
4. Sutan melepaskan diri dari tali.
5. Mereka mempersenjatai diri dengan pisau.
6. Irawati harus mengurusi diri sesudah suaminya meninggal.

EXERCISE 2

1. Aku tidak membela dia; aku membela diriku sendiri.
2. Dia menyalahkan dirinya sendiri.
3. Dia menulis tentang dirinya sendiri.
4. Bagaimana mereka dapat memerintah orang lain? Mereka belum dapat memerintah diri mereka sendiri.
5. Kamu selalu memikirkan dirimu sendiri.
6. Sebelum mengerti orang lain kita harus mengerti diri kita sendiri.

7. **Saya menujukan kata-kata itu kepada diri saya sendiri.**
8. **Joko membeli rokok itu tidak hanya untuk temannya tetapi juga untuk dirinya sendiri.**

EXERCISE 3

1. **Orang itu adalah ayah Arjuna sendiri.**
2. **Pak Umar membangun rumah ini sendiri.** *or* **Pak Umar sendiri membangun rumah ini.**
3. **Kita harus membersihkan rumah sendiri.** *or* **Kita sendiri harus membersihkan rumah.**
4. **Detty kembali ke desanya sendiri.**
5. **Kamu bertiga harus berbelanja sendiri.**
6. **Saya digigit oleh anjing saya sendiri.**
7. **Apa ini mobil Tomo sendiri?**
8. **Ini rumah saudara sendiri, bukan?**
9. **Mengapa bertanya kepada saya? Anda sudah tahu sendiri (*or* Anda sendiri sudah tahu) apa yang terjadi.**
10. **Saya sendiri sering pergi ke sana.**

24　WORD ORDER IN CLAUSES

EXERCISE 1

1. **Di atas gunung didirikan sebuah menara tinggi.**
   On top of the mountain was built a high tower.
2. **Sekitar pukul tiga datang seorang tetangga.**
   Around three o'clock there came a neighbour.
3. **Untuk melancarkan lalu lintas dipasang lampu lalu lintas.**
   To speed up the traffic traffic lights were installed.
4. **Bagi dia dibuat sepatu khusus.**
   For him were made special shoes.
5. **Tiap malam dipergelarkan tarian klasik Jawa.**
   Every night classical Javanese dances are performed.
6. **Di tokonya tersedia alat-alat modern.**
   In his shop are available modern implements.
7. **Di penjara itu meringkuk enam pengusaha yang melakukan kejahatan.**
   In the jail are confined six businessmen who committed crimes.
8. **Dari hutan terdengar suara harimau.**
   From the forest could be heard the sound of the tiger.

EXERCISE 2

1. **Lalu menyeberanglah dia.**
   Then over he crossed.
2. **Pada tahun 1928 diadakanlah suatu rapat besar yang dinamakan Kongres Pemuda.**
   In 1928 there was held a large meeting called the Youth Congress.
3. **Kira-kira tahun 1400 masuklah pengaruh Islam di Indonesia.**
   About the year 1400 the influence of Islam entered Indonesia.
4. **Pada hari itu terciptalah suatu Indonesia merdeka.**
   On that day there was created a free Indonesia.

5.   **Pasukan menghadang massa dan terdengarlah suara tembakan.**
     Troops intercepted the mob and there was heard the sound of shooting.
6.   **Ketika saya di Bandung datanglah surat dari isteri saya.**
     While I was in Bandung there came a letter from my wife.
7.   **Setelah hujan berhenti berangkatlah kami.**
     After the rain stopped we set off.
8.   **Tertipulah kamu!**
     You were tricked!

EXERCISE 3

1.   subject-predicate inversion
     Di lapangan terbang   disediakan   ruangan tunggu.
     adverb   *predicate*   *subject*
     At the aerodrome a waiting room has been prepared.
2.   subject-predicate inversion
     Pada hari itu   tercipta   suatu negara Indonesia merdeka.
     adverb   *predicate* *subject*
     On that day was created a free Indonesian nation.
3.   predicate-agent inversion
     Tanah itu   oleh orang lain   dianggap mahal.
     subject   *agent*   *predicate*
     That land is regarded as expensive by other people.
4.   no inversion
     Tugas itu   harus dikerjakan   selekas mungkin   oleh semua anggota.
     subject   *predicate*   *adverb*   *agent*
     That task needs to be done as soon as possible by all members.
5.   predicate-agent inversion
     Oleh orang tuanya   Siti   diberi   cincin emas.
     agent   *subject*   *predicate* *secondary object*
     By her parents Siti was given a gold ring.
6.   subject-predicate inversion
     Kepada yang lapar   akan diberikan   makanan.
     recipient   *predicate*   *subject*
     To the hungry will be given food.
7.   predicate-agent inversion
     Oleh orang kota   petani-petani itu   dikirimi   uang.
     agent   *subject*   *predicate* *secondary object*
     Those farmers are sent money by the city people.
8.   no inversion
     Minggu lalu   Muji   ditawari pekerjaan   oleh pemilik toko itu.
     adverb   *subject*   *predicate*   *agent*
     Last week Muji was offered work by the shop owner.
9.   predicate-agent inversion
     Pak Kardi   oleh dokter   disuruh pergi   ke rumah sakit.
     subject   *agent*   *predicate*   *adverb*
     Mr Kardi was told to go to hospital by the doctor.
10. subject-predicate inversion
     Sudah diselesaikan   -nya   pekerjaan itu.
     predicate   *-agent*   *subject*
     He has already finished that work.

25   RELATIVE CLAUSES

EXERCISE 1

1. Anak <u>yang jatuh dari pohon</u> harus dibawa ke dokter.
2. Orang <u>yang malas</u> tidak akan mendapat pekerjaan.
3. Orang-orang <u>yang tidak mendapat tempat duduk</u> marah sekali.
4. Anjing <u>yang menggigit Mary</u> kepunyaan tetangga kami.
5. Teman saya <u>yang bekerja di bank</u> akan singgah nanti malam.
6. Anak <u>yang berdiri di sana</u> Ali.

EXERCISE 2

1. Orang yang menjual mobil ini kepada saya tinggal di Kebayoran.
2. Rumah yang dibeli oleh mereka tahun lalu terletak dekat sungai.
3. Film yang dibintangi Geoffrey Rush berjudul *Shine*.
4. Rapat yang dibatalkan tadi malam akan diadakan minggu depan.
5. Tetangga saya, yang dibawa ke rumah sakit minggu lalu, sekarang sudah pulang.
6. Demonstran yang melemparkan batu diusir oleh polisi.
7. Sayur-sayuran yang dibeli oleh ibu tadi pagi sudah dimakan.
8. Sekretaris yang menolong Pak Asdi mulai bekerja pada jam tujuh tadi pagi.
9. Wanita yang membeli sayur-sayuran ini ibu saya.
10. Paket yang dikirimnya minggu lalu masih belum sampai.

EXERCISE 3

1. Ambulans yang kami panggil segera datang.
2. Saya sudah membaca semua buku yang dikarang oleh Mochtar Lubis.
3. Kamus yang dia beli tidak begitu mahal. *or* Kamus yang dibelinya tidak begitu mahal.
4. Kebanyakan orang yang menghadiri rapat mendukung usul kami.
5. Ayah John, yang bekerja di rumah sakit, sudah membeli mobil baru.
6. Kelas yang diajar Pak Amir tenang sekali.
7. Orang yang menawari kami pekerjaan mempunyai perusahaan pakaian.
8. Sate yang saya masak masih terlalu panas.
9. Rumah yang mereka beli di sebelah rumah Alan *or* Rumah yang dibeli mereka di sebelah rumah Alan.
10. Paket yang dikirim oleh Ibu Halimah berat sekali.

EXERCISE 4

1. Kereta api yang harus kamu naiki berangkat pada jam dua.
   The train you have to catch leaves at two o'clock.
2. Perempuan yang baru kamu temui (itu) adik saya.
   The woman you've just met is my sister.
3. Mahasiswa itu tinggal di asrama yang tidak jauh dari universitas.
   That student lives in a hostel which isn't far from the university.
4. Dokter yang memeriksa anak-anak saya ramah sekali.
   The doctor who checked my children was very friendly.

5. **Robyn kawin dengan orang Jawa yang sudah lama tinggal di Australia.**
   Robyn married a Javanese who has lived in Australia for a long time.
6. **Pengarang yang menulis buku ini baru berumur 27 tahun.**
   The writer who wrote this book is just 27 years old.
7. **Hutan yang dimasuki mereka indah sekali.**
   The forest they entered was very beautiful.
8. **Tetangga yang kami kagumi meninggal kemarin.**
   The neighbour we admired died yesterday.
9. **Film yang akan kamu lihat besok lucu sekali.**
   The movie you're going to see tomorrow is very funny.
10. **Rapat yang dihadirinya tadi malam sangat membosankan.**
    The meeting she attended last night was very boring.
11. **Barang yang tidak saya jual harus dibuang.**
    The goods I didn't sell have to be thrown out.
12. **Masalah yang harus kita pikirkan penting sekali.**
    The problem we have to think about is very important.

EXERCISE 5

1. **Anak yang saya belikan buku itu senang sekali.**
2. **Anak yang dibelikan buku itu senang sekali.**
3. **Orang yang dikirimi surat itu sudah pindah ke Bandung.**
4. **Orang yang Anda kirimi surat itu sudah pindah ke Bandung.**
5. **Orang yang dia kirimi surat itu sudah pindah ke Bandung.** *or* **Orang yang dikiriminya surat itu sudah pindah ke Bandung.**
6. **Orang yang dikirimi surat oleh Mary senang sekali.**
7. **Orang yang dikirimi surat oleh Mary senang sekali.**
8. **Surat yang dikirimkan kepada Mary singkat sekali.**
9. **Rok yang dipilih ibu untuk Mary berwarna hijau.**
10. **Rok yang dipilih untuk Mary berwarna hijau.**
11. **Gadis yang dipilihkan rok itu bernama Mary.**
12. **Pekerjaan yang ditawarkan kepada saya tidak sulit.**
13. **Pekerjaan yang ditawarkan kepada sekretaris tidak sulit.**
14. **Sekretaris yang ditawari pekerjaan itu rajin sekali.**
15. **Orang yang diberi/diserahi pekerjaan itu ayah saya.**
16. **Orang yang dimasakkan sate itu ayah saya.**

EXERCISE 6

1. **Istrinya perempuan yang cantik dan pandai.**
2. **Dia membeli mobil (yang) baru setiap tahun.**
3. **Siapa pelari (yang) paling cepat?**
4. **Saya membeli jas yang terlalu panjang.**
5. **Keluarganya mau pindah ke kota yang lebih besar.**
6. **Ayahnya bekerja di pabrik (yang) besar.**
7. **Saya selalu membeli pakaian yang tidak mahal.**
8. **Orang yang sudah capek boleh istirahat sekarang.**
9. **Mereka mau tinggal di kota yang lebih kecil dari Jakarta.**
10. **Tokyo adalah kota (yang) termahal di dunia.**

EXERCISE 7

1. **Gadis yang kecantikannya dikagumi akan menjadi peragawati.**
   The girl whose beauty is admired will become a model.
2. **Lukisan yang harganya tinggi dijual kepada orang kaya.**
   The painting whose price is high was sold to a rich person.
3. **Teman saya yang tingginya hampir dua meter menjadi juara loncat tinggi.**
   My friend who is nearly two metres tall is the high jump champion.
4. **Guru yang payungnya hilang kehujanan ketika pulang.**
   The teacher whose umbrella was lost got caught in the rain on the way home.
5. **Dosen marah kepada mahasiswa yang karangannya hilang.**
   The lecturer was angry at the student whose essay was lost.
6. **Anak saya diajar oleh Pak Hadi, yang rumahnya tidak jauh dari rumah saya.**
   My child is taught by Mr Hadi, whose house isn't far from mine.
7. **Siswa yang rambutnya terlalu panjang disuruh pergi ke tukang cukur.**
   The student whose hair was too long was told to go to the barber.
8. **Pengarang yang bukunya diterbitkan tahun lalu menerima hadiah.**
   The writer whose book was published last year received a prize.
9. **Dia memiliki perkebunan di daerah yang tanahnya subur sekali.**
   He owns a plantation in an area whose soil is very fertile.
10. **Keluarga yang rumahnya terbakar habis dibantu oleh para tetangga.**
    The family whose house was destroyed by fire were helped by the neighbours.

EXERCISE 8

1. **Orang yang mobilnya besar itu kaya sekali.**
2. **Anak yang giginya sakit harus pergi ke dokter gigi.**
3. **Rumah yang halamannya luas rumah Pak Johnson.**
4. **Saya memperbaiki kursi yang kakinya patah.**
5. **Siapa wanita yang topinya lucu itu?**
6. **Dia kawin dengan penyanyi yang suaranya bagus itu.**

EXERCISE 9

1. **Saya bekerja dengan orang yang ayahnya menjual ikan di pasar.**
2. **Orang yang istrinya kami bawa ke rumah sakit sangat berterima kasih.**
3. **Tetangga yang anaknya memecahkan kaca jendela saya akan membayar kaca baru.**
4. **Adjat, yang ayahnya mempunyai perusahaan impor, bekerja di sebuah bank.**
5. **Wanita yang jendelanya dipecahkan oleh anak itu memarahi orang tuanya.**
6. **Pemain sepak bola yang sepatunya dicuri sudah mengadu kepada manajer timnya.**
7. **Kepala sekolah memuji guru yang siswanya memenangkan lomba menulis.**
8. **Tadi pagi saya menemui pelukis yang lukisannya dibeli ayah saya tahun lalu.**

26   TOPIC-COMMENT CLAUSES

EXERCISE 1

1. Mrs Halim has five children.
   Bu Halim anaknya lima orang.
   Mrs Halim has five children. (literally: Mrs Halim, her children are five.)
2. The cost of that journey is $1,000.
   Perjalanan itu ongkosnya $1.000.
   That journey, its cost is $1,000.
3. The voice of that group is getting stronger.
   Kelompok itu suaranya makin kuat.
   That group, its voice is getting stronger.
4. Their income is very big.
   Mereka penghasilannya besar sekali.
   As for them, their income is very big.
5. My neighbour's house burned down last night.
   Tetangga saya rumahnya terbakar tadi malam.
   My neighbour, his house burned down last night.
6. The salary of these employees won't go up.
   Pegawai-pegawai ini gajinya tidak akan naik.
   As for these employees, their salary won't go up.
7. The inhabitants of that country are very poor.
   Negeri itu penduduknya miskin sekali.
   As for that country, its inhabitants are very poor.
8. The roads in that town are neglected (not looked after).
   Kota itu jalan-jalannya tidak terurus.
   That town, its roads are neglected.

EXERCISE 2

1. **Abidin kesabarannya sudah habis.**
   Abidin sudah habis kesabarannya.
   As for Abidin, his patience is at an end.
2. **Anak itu beratnya sudah dua puluh kilo.**
   Anak itu sudah dua puluh kilo beratnya.
   That child's weight is already twenty kilos.
3. **Mereka anaknya belum bersekolah.**
   Their children don't go to school yet.
4. **Pak Hanafi istrinya tidak bekerja.**
   Mr Hanafi's wife doesn't work.
5. **Jalan itu namanya Jalan Sutomo.**
   Jalan itu Jalan Sutomo namanya.
   The name of that street is Sutomo Street.
6. **Narti ayahnya pergi ke Inggris.**
   Narti's father went to England.
7. **Ayah saya kantornya di Jalan Senopati.**
   My father's office is in Senopati Road.
8. **Ayam kampung rasanya enak.**
   Ayam kampung enak rasanya.
   As for village chickens, their taste is delicious.

9.   **Natasha umurnya 24 tahun.**
      Natasha 24 tahun umurnya.
      Natasha's age is 24 years.
10.   **Berita itu kebenarannya belum terbukti.**
      Berita itu belum terbukti kebenarannya.
      That news, its truth has not yet been proved.

EXERCISE 3

1.   That village has many inhabitants.
      Desa itu penduduknya banyak.
2.   That large car is Mr Ali's.
3.   The number of schools at that time was still very small.
4.   Sutomo Street is always full of vehicles.
5.   The fruit on our tree is very tasty.
      Pohon kami buahnya enak sekali.
6.   That book on Indonesian history is now in the library.
7.   Mrs Dewi's daughter was promoted to office head.
      Bu Dewi anak perempuannya diangkat menjadi kepala kantor.
8.   His thoughts are old fashioned.
      Dia pikirannya kolot.

27   NOMINALISED RELATIVE CLAUSES

EXERCISE 1

1.   **Yang menyanyikan lagu itu Iwan Fels.**
      The one who sings that song is Iwan Fels.
2.   **Yang mengemudikan bis itu Rizal.**
      The one driving that bus is Rizal.
3.   **Yang saya temui tadi malam Alice.**
      The one I met last night was Alice.
4.   **Yang dia cari buku catatannya.**
      What he's looking for is his notebook.
5.   **Yang saya perlukan bensin.**
      What I need is petrol.
6.   **Yang melihat dari jendala sekretaris saya.**
      The one looking from the window is my secretary.
7.   **Yang mengganggu mereka nyamuk.**
      What is annoying them is mosquitoes.
8.   **Yang mengetok pintu tadi tukang pos.**
      The one who knocked on the door just now was the postman.

EXERCISE 2

1.   **Apa Anda suka <u>yang mahal</u> atau <u>yang murah</u>?**
2.   **Saya tidak suka <u>yang kecil</u>.**
3.   **Ambil koper yang kecil itu; saya mengambil <u>yang lebih berat ini</u>.**
4.   **Ali: Banyak koran di sini. Anda mau membaca <u>yang mana</u>?**
      Hasan: <u>Yang ini</u>.
5.   **Gelas ini harus diganti dengan <u>yang bersih</u>.**

6   **Yang belum berangkat** boleh pergi besok.
7.   Ali: **Apa ini mobil saudara?**
        Hasan: **Bukan. Mobil saya yang hijau itu.**
8.   **Yang membeli buku ini** paman saya.
9.   **Gedung ini tidak setinggi yang itu.**
10.   **Dia bukan paman saya. Paman saya yang duduk di depan.**

EXERCISE 3

1.   **Ada banyak kota di Indonesia. Yang penduduknya paling besar**
        Jakarta.
2.   **Yang mobilnya dicuri** tinggal dekat saya.
3.   **Yang anaknya banyak** berasal dari Queensland.
4.   **Yang pertaniannya kebanjiran** sudah dibantu oleh pemerintah.
5.   **Yang atapnya merah** rumah saya.
6.   **Yang ayahnya bekerja di toko ini** bernama Budi.
7.   **Yang rumahnya terbakar** dibantu oleh para tetangga.
8.   **Yang gajinya paling rendah** bekerja paling keras.

28 *ADALAH*

EXERCISE 1

1.   **Penari itu adalah anak Pak Lukman.**
        That dancer is Mr Lukman's daughter.
2.   **Orang yang duduk di situ adalah ayah saya.**
        The person sitting there is my father.
3.   **Ini adalah hak kami semua.**
        This is the right of all of us.
4.   **Gajah adalah binatang yang sangat besar.**
        The elephant is a very large animal.
5.   **Indonesia adalah sebuah kepulauan.**
        Indonesia is an archipelago.
6.   **Wanita yang kawin dengan kakak saya adalah guru sekolah menengah.**
        The woman who married my brother is a high school teacher.
7.   **Hotel Sabang adalah hotel yang paling murah di kota ini.**
        The Hotel Sabang is the cheapest hotel in this town.
8.   **Bu Rodiah adalah sekretaris Pak Bambang.**
        Mrs Rodiah is Mr Bambang's secretary.

EXERCISE 2

1.   **Pekerjaannya setiap hari adalah memasak di dapur.**
        His work every day is to cook in the kitchen.
2.   **Kesenangan kami adalah bermain sepak bola.**
        Our favourite pastime is playing soccer.
3.   (**adalah** cannot occur)
        Dul likes catching fish.
4.   (**adalah** cannot occur)
        Many tourists holiday in Bali.
5.   (**adalah** cannot occur)
        We like playing soccer.

6.   **Pekerjaan Dul adalah menangkap ikan.**
      Dul's work is catching fish.
7.   (**adalah** cannot occur)
      Those employees cook in the kitchen every day.
8.   **Rencana saya adalah berlibur di Bali.**
      My plan is to holiday in Bali.
9.   (**adalah** cannot occur)
      My friend bought a Mercedes.
10.   **Kehendak saya adalah membeli Mercedes.**
      My desire is to buy a Mercedes.

EXERCISE 3

1.   **Yang dibeli ayah saya kemarin adalah mobil baru.**
      What my father bought yesterday was a new car.
2.   **Yang ditangkap nelayan itu adalah dua ikan hiu.**
      What the fisherman caught was two sharks.
3.   **Yang saya cari adalah restoran yang baik.**
      What I'm looking for is a good restaurant.
4.   **Yang ditemukan ilmuwan itu adalah zat baru.**
      What that scientist discovered was a new substance.
5.   **Yang ditawarkan oleh pemilik pabrik kepada Anton adalah pekerjaan.**
      What the factory owner offered Anton was work.
6.   **Yang ditawari pekerjaan oleh pemilik pabrik adalah Anton.**
      The one who was offered work by the factory owner was Anton.
7.   **Yang diambil pelayan adalah segelas air.**
      What the waiter fetched was a glass of water.
8.   **Yang diambilkan segelas air oleh pelayan adalah Anton.**
      The one who was fetched a glass of water by the waiter was Anton.

29   NOMINALISED PREDICATE CLAUSES

EXERCISE 1

1.   They waited for the coming of goods from overseas.
      Barang-barang datang dari luar negeri.
      Goods came from overseas.
2.   They want to know about the sinking of the ship.
      Kapal itu tenggelam.
      The ship sank.
3.   The government prohibited the forming of new parties.
      Partai baru dibentuk.
      New parties were formed.
4.   The increase in the number of children in Indonesia is truly extraordinary.
      Jumlah anak di Indonesia meningkat.
      The number of children in Indonesia is increasing.
5.   The journalist interviewed the pilot about the crash of the plane near Bandung.
      Pesawat itu jatuh dekat Bandung.
      The plane crashed near Bandung.

6.   With the shifting of the terminal to a new location the bus drivers felt disadvantaged.
Terminal dipindahkan ke lokasi baru.
The terminal was shifted to a new location.

7.   The depth of this pool is three metres.
Kolam ini dalam.
This pool is deep.

8.   Taufan's death made his friends very sad.
Taufan meninggal.
Taufan died.

9.   The weight of this suitcase is ten kilograms.
Koper ini berat.
This suitcase is heavy.

10.   The building of the factory disturbed the peace of the town.
Pabrik itu dibangun.
The factory was built.

11.   The fall in the price of rice delighted the people.
Harga beras turun.
The price of rice fell.

12.   The eruption of that volcano has long been predicted.
Gunung api itu meletus.
That volcano erupted.

EXERCISE 2

1.   This indicates that there is no work efficiency.
Efisiensi kerja tidak ada.
Work efficiency doesn't exist.

2.   We have heard about the great decline in freedom of the press there.
Kebebasan pers di sana sangat mundur.
Freedom of the press there has very much declined.

3.   He asked about that book having already appeared.
Buku itu telah terbit.
That book has already appeared.

4.   The Security Council called for the immediate end to the war.
Perang itu segera diakhiri.
The war was immediately ended.

5.   Stagnation can be seen from the unchanging economic structure.
Struktur perekonomian tidak berubah.
The economic structure does not change.

6.   The police are worried about the continuation of stealing in that area.
Pencurian di daerah itu terus berlangsung.
Stealing in that area continues to go on.

7.   News reports about the coming separation of that province from the Republic of Indonesia are worrying them.
Provinsi itu akan lepas dari Republik Indonesia.
That province will be separate/free from the Republic of Indonesia.

EXERCISE 3

1.   **Lebarnya jalan ini empat meter.**
2.   **Panjangnya papan ini dua setengah meter.**
3.   **Berat saya lima puluh tujuh kilo.**

4.   **Jauhnya rumah saya dari sekolah satu kilometer.**
5.   **Tinggi(nya) Mary berapa?**
6.   **Dalamnya sungai hampir tiga meter di sini.**
7.   **Luas(nya) pertanian Pak Sardi lima hektar.**
8.   **Berapa panjang(nya) tangga ini?**
9.   **Beratnya koper ini kiri-kira sepuluh kilo.**
10.   **Cepatnya mobil itu seratus kilometer sejam.**

EXERCISE 4

1.   **Dia bertanya tentang kedatangan bantuan dari luar negeri.**
      He asked about the coming of help from overseas.
2.   **Dia bertanya tentang kenaikan harga beras.**
      He asked about the rise in the price of rice.
3.   **Dia bertanya tentang pencurian uang itu.**
      He asked about the theft (stealing) of that money.
4.   **Dia bertanya tentang pengumuman keputusan panitia.**
      He asked about the announcement/announcing of the committee's decision.
5.   **Dia bertanya tentang pemeriksaan barang-barang itu.**
      He asked about the inspection of those goods.
6.   **Dia bertanya tentang keberangkatan duta besar.**
      He asked about the departure of the ambassador.
7.   **Dia bertanya tentang kematian perampok itu.**
      He asked about the death of that thief.
8.   **Dia bertanya tentang peningkatan jumlah anak di Indonesia.**
      He asked about the increase in the number of children in Indonesia.
9.   **Dia bertanya tentang pemindahan terminal ke lokasi baru.**
      He asked about the moving of the terminal to a new location.
10.   **Dia bertanya tentang keinginan mereka mendapat kemerdekaan.**
      He asked about their desire to acquire freedom.

30   IDENTIFYING CLAUSES

EXERCISE 1

1.   Mr Bagio was chosen as party leader.
      Pak Bagiolah yang dipilih sebagai pemimpin partai.
      It was Mr Bagio who was chosen as party leader.
2.   My neighbour helped Ali.
      Tetangga sayalah yang membantu Ali.
      It was my neighbour who helped Ali.
3.   That train is very fast.
      Kereta apa itulah yang cepat sekali.
      It is that train which is very fast/That's the train that's very fast.
4.   Mr Siregar lives in this house.
      Pak Siregarlah yang tinggal di rumah ini.
      It is Mr Siregar who lives in this house/Mr Siregar is the one who lives in this house.
5.   My child won.
      Anak sayalah yang menang.
      It was my child who won.

6.   These plates haven't been washed yet.
      Piring-piring inilah yang belum dicuci.
      These are the plates which haven't been washed yet.

7.   The Minister of Education spoke at the meeting.
      Menteri Pendidikanlah yang berbicara dalam rapat itu.
      It was the Minister of Education who spoke at the meeting.

8.   I will sell this painting.
      Lukisan inilah yang akan saya jual.
      This is the painting I will sell.

EXERCISE 2

1.   **Ibu sayalah yang memilih warna ini.**
      My mother is the one who chose this colour.

2.   **Pak Johnsonlah yang mengajar Mary dan Tom.**
      It is Mr Johnson who teaches Mary and Tom.

3.   **Payung merahlah yang dibeli ibu.**
      It was a red umbrella mother bought.

4.   **Adik sayalah yang duduk di bawah pohon.**
      It is my sister who is sitting under the tree.

5.   **Dialah yang tidak saya sukai.**
      He's the one I don't like.

6.   **Majalah olahragalah yang sedang dia baca.**
      It is a sports magazine he is reading.

7.   **Dr Sutomolah yang dipanggil ayah waktu ibu jatuh sakit.**
      Dr Sutomo was the one father called when mother became ill.

8.   **Pintu inilah yang harus dikunci setiap malam.**
      This is the door which has to be locked every night.

9.   **Merekalah yang memilihnya sebagai pemimpin.**
      They are the ones who chose her as leader.

10.   **Hanya Johnlah yang dapat menolong saya.**
      John is the only one who can help me.

EXERCISE 3

1.   **Yang birulah yang paling mahal.**
2.   **Yang besarlah yang sudah saya baca.**
3.   **Yang inilah yang harus kamu pakai.**
4.   **Yang itulah yang membuat saya marah.**
5.   **Yang menunggu di situlah yang mau menemui Anda.**
6.   **Yang paling besarlah yang mau saya makan.**
7.   **Yang inilah yang sedang dicarinya.**
8.   **Yang inilah yang rusak.**

EXERCISE 4

1.   **Bukan saya yang menulis surat itu.**
2.   **John(lah) yang tidak dipilih sebagai pemimpin.**
3.   **Bukan anak saya yang menang.**
4.   **Budi tinggal dekat saya. Pak Siregarlah yang tidak tinggal di jalan saya.**
5.   **Bukan yang ini yang saya pilih.**

6.   **Bukan yang ini yang mereka cari.**
7.   **Yang inilah yang tidak rusak.**
8.   **Bukan lukisan ini yang akan saya jual.**

31   ADJECTIVE CLAUSES WITH COMPLEMENTS

EXERCISE 1

1.   **Komputer ini mudah untuk digunakan.**
2.   **Pertanyaan Anda sukar kami jawab.**
3.   **Pencopet itu tidak mudah ditangkap oleh polisi.**
4.   **Rumahnya tidak akan sukar Anda temukan.**
5.   **Kebiasaan ini sulit untuk dimengerti oleh orang asing.**
6.   **Rok itu tidak sesuai untuk dipakai Mary.**
7.   **Sate ini enak dimakan.**
8.   **Buku ini pantas untuk dibaca anak-anak.**

EXERCISE 2

1.   **Kotak ini terlalu berat untuk saya angkat.**
2.   **Mangga ini belum cukup masak untuk dimakan.**
3.   **Musik ini enak didengar.**
4.   **Saya terlalu sibuk untuk pergi ke kuliah hari ini.**
5.   **Buku-buku Pramoedya Ananta Toer menarik untuk dibaca.**
6.   **Sayang, dia tidak cukup sehat untuk pergi ke pesta.**
7.   **Maaf, saya terlalu cape untuk membantumu.**
8.   **Air ini terlalu kotor untuk diminum.**
9.   **Dia cukup kaya untuk membeli mobil Mercedes.**
10.   **Kemeja ini sudah cukup kering untuk dipakai.**

32   *UNTUK, SUPAYA* AND *BAHWA*

EXERCISE 1

1.   **Guru mengusulkan supaya saya pergi ke dokter.**
      The teacher suggested that I go to the doctor.
2.   **Kami berencana untuk berlibur pada akhir tahun.**
      We plan to have a holiday at the end of the year.
3.   **Saya berpesan supaya dia menjaga anak-anak.**
      I instructed that he look after the children.
4.   **Mereka bersedia untuk menurunkan harga.**
      They are prepared to lower the price.
5.   **Dia memutuskan untuk memberitahu saya.**
      He decided to tell me.
6.   **Dia menginstruksikan supaya sopir membawa tamunya ke hotel.**
      He instructed the driver to take his guest to the hotel.
7.   **Polisi mengimbau supaya warga tetap tinggal di dalam rumah.**
      Police appealed for the populace to remain in doors.
8.   **Dia menolak untuk menyebut nama-nama mereka.**
      He refused to mention their names.

9.   **Dia minta supaya kami meminjaminya uang.**
      He requested that we lend him money.
10.   **Dia berniat untuk menemani saya.**
      He intends to accompany me.

EXERCISE 2

1.   **Dia dianjurkan supaya berobat di Australia.**
      He was urged to have treatment in Australia.
2.   **Dianjurkan supaya dia berobat di Australia.**
      It was recommended that he have treatment in Australia.
3.   **Pemerintah didesak untuk memperkuat sensor terhadap film-film kekerasan.**
      The government was urged/pressed to strengthen censorship against violent films.
4.   **Disarankan supaya mereka kawin.**
      It was suggested that they marry.
5.   **Dihimbau supaya Presiden mencabut keputusan menteri itu.**
      An appeal was made that the president retract the minister's decision.
6.   **Saya diperintahkan untuk mengembalikan uang itu.**
      I was ordered to return the money.
7.   **Diusulkan supaya saya belajar di universitas ini.**
      It was suggested that I study at this university.
8.   **Mereka dipanggil untuk mengambil bagian dalam perundingan.**
      They were called to take part in the discussions.

EXERCISE 3

1.   **Saya hampir lupa bahwa saya harus bertemu dengan Tony hari ini.**
2.   **Dia menjawab bahwa saya harus pergi.**
3.   **Pak Trisno bercita-cita supaya anak perempuannya kawin dengan orang kaya.**
4.   **Dia memohon supaya kami menghadiri rapat itu.**
5.   **Kami percaya bahwa kami dapat menang.**
6.   **Saya mengakui bahwa saya memerlukan bantuan.**
7.   **Dosen menyarankan supaya saya pergi ke kuliahnya.**
8.   **Dia menjelaskan bahwa dia terlambat karena mobilnya mogok.**

33 QUESTIONS

EXERCISE 1

1.   (No) What is the colour of that flower?
2.   **Hari ini panas?**
      Is it hot today? (literally: Is today hot?)
3.   (No) What is the difference between those two stories?
4.   **Dia pandai?**
      Is she clever?
5.   **Kamu sudah makan?**
      Have you eaten?
6.   (No) What is the name of that town?

7. **Itu binatang?**
    Is that an animal?
8. **Kedua cerita itu berbeda?**
    Are those two stories different?
9. **Itu bunga?**
    Is that a flower?
10. **Itu nama kota?**
    Is that the name of a town?

EXERCISE 2

1. **Saya mau minum teh; Anda mau minum apa?**
2. **Anda menelepon siapa?**
3. **Siapa (yang) menulis surat ini?**
4. **Anda menolong siapa?**
5. **Anda bertemu dengan siapa di pasar tadi pagi?**
6. **Ibu membeli apa untuk saya?**
7. **Apa yang menakutkan mereka?**
8. **Kita makan apa di restoran nanti malam?**
9. **Siapa (yang) menolong Anda?**
10. **Anda membuat apa dengan kayu itu?**

EXERCISE 3

1. Whose younger brother/sister are you?
2. Who are you?
3. Who is your younger brother/sister?
4. What shoes are these?
5. What shoes are these?
6. Whose shoes are these?
7. Who is your younger brother/sister?
8. Whose younger brother/sister are you?
9. Whose shoes are these?
10. Are these shoes?

EXERCISE 4

1. **Narti pergi dengan siapa?** *or* **Dengan siapa Narti pergi?**
2. **Untuk siapa kopi ini?** *or* **Kopi ini untuk siapa?**
3. **Guru memberi buku itu kepada siapa?**
4. **Dia pergi ke mana?** *or* **Ke mana dia pergi?**
5. **Untuk apa dia menangis?**
6. **Ayah menggali lubang dengan apa?**
7. **Dia membawa buku itu dari mana?**
8. **Surat ini dari siapa?** *or* **Dari siapa surat ini?**
9. **Untuk apa dia bekerja begitu keras?**
10. **Anda bekerja dengan siapa?**

EXERCISE 5

1. **Apa yang sedang dibaca Umar?**
   What is Umar reading?
2. **Apa yang dicuci ibu?**
   What is mother washing?
3. **Siapa yang saudara cari?**
   Who are you looking for?
4. **Warna apa yang paling kamu sukai?**
   What colour do you most like?
5. **Buku siapa yang kamu pinjam tadi?**
   Whose book did you just borrow?
6. **Buku apa yang kamu beli?**
   What book did you buy?
7. **Film apa yang akan kita tonton?**
   What movie are we going to see?
8. **Siapa yang dipanggil oleh Pak Hadi?**
   Who did Mr Hadi call?
9. **Siapa yang ditunggu mereka?**
   Who are they waiting for?
10. **Apa yang dipesan oleh orang itu?**
    What did that person order?
11. **Rumah siapa yang mereka sewa?**
    Whose house are they renting?
12. **Apa yang kamu pikirkan?**
    What are you thinking about?

EXERCISE 6

1. **Siapa yang mereka percayai?** *or* **Siapa yang dipercayai mereka?**
   Who do they believe?
2. **Apa yang kamu sukai?**
   What do you like?
3. **Siapa yang dikenalnya di sini?**
   Who does she know here?
4. **Apa yang kamu harapkan?**
   What do you hope for?
5. **Apa yang diketahui oleh mereka?**
   What do they know?
6. **Siapa yang dia nikahi?**
   Who did he marry?

EXERCISE 7

Where **yang** occurs twice in parentheses either instance, but not both, can be omitted.
1. **Mereka datang dari kota yang mana?**
2. **Tomo yang mana?** *or* **Yang mana Tomo?**
3. **Guru (yang) mana (yang) menulis buku sejarah ini?**
4. **Jas (yang) mana yang kamu pilih?**
5. **Anda meminjam yang mana?**
6. **(Yang) mana yang kamu lihat?**

7. Toko (yang) mana (yang) menjual payung?
8. Yang mana rumah Tomo? *or* Rumah Tomo'yang mana?
9. Wartawan (yang) mana (yang) menulis artikel ini?
10. (Yang) mana (yang) paling baik?
11. Dia duduk di kursi yang mana?
12. Sepatu (yang) mana yang akan Anda pakai?
13. Majalah (yang) mana yang dibeli Dewi?
14. (Yang) mana (yang) menolong kamu?

EXERCISE 8

1. Saudara bekerja berapa jam sehari?
2. Saudara menonton film apa?
3. Saudara membaca halaman berapa?
4. Kantornya di tingkat/lantai berapa?
5. Saudara membaca berapa halaman?
6. Bulan apa saudara lahir?
7. Berapa hari seminggu saudara pergi ke kantor?
8. Kamu (di) kelas berapa tahun ini?
9. Warna apa bunga itu?
10. Bapak/Ibu mengajar berapa kelas?
11. Berapa bulan saudara tinggal di Jakarta?
12. Nomor berapa telepon saudara?
13. Rumah saudara di jalan apa?
14. Numor berapa rumah saudara?
15. Jam berapa saudara biasanya bangun?

EXERCISE 9

1. Panas hari ini, bukan?   -   Tidak.
2. Dia pandai, bukan?   -   Tidak.
3. Budi adikmu, bukan?   -   Bukan.
4. Anda tiba kemarin, bukan?   -   Tidak.
5. Anda sudah membaca buku ini, bukan?   -   Belum.
6. Hari ini hari Senin, bukan?   -   Bukan.
7. Ini rumah John, bukan?   -   Bukan.
8. Mereka akan berangkat besok pagi, bukan?   -   Tidak.
9. Mereka sudah berangkat, bukan?   -   Belum.
10. Namamu Anthony, bukan?   -   Bukan.

EXERCISE 10

1. Saya tidak tahu siapa orang itu.
    Siapa orang itu?
    Who is that person?
2. Saya tidak tahu apa(kah) dia bisa datang besok.
    (Apakah) dia bisa datang besok?
    Can he come tomorrow?
3. Saya tidak tahu apa yang dibaca John.
    Apa yang dibaca John? *or* John membaca apa?
    What is John reading?

4. **Saya tidak tahu siapa yang ditemui Alice tadi pagi.**
   Siapa yang ditemui Alice tadi pagi? *or* **Alice bertemu dengan siapa tadi pagi?**
   Who did Alice meet this morning?

5. **Saya tidak tahu bagaimana dia bisa berhasil.**
   Bagaimana dia bisa berhasil?
   How could he succeed?

6. **Saya tidak tahu dari mana dia datang.**
   Dari mana dia datang? *or* **Dia datang dari mana?**
   Where did he come from?

7. **Saya tidak tahu apa dia tinggal di sini atau tidak.**
   Apa did tinggal di sini, atau tidak?
   Does she live here, or not?

8. **Saya tidak tahu kapan dia datang ke sini.**
   Kapan dia datang ke sini?
   When did she come here?

9. **Saya tidak tahu apa yang dibeli oleh ibu.**
   Apa yang dibeli oleh ibu? *or* **Ibu membeli apa?**
   What did mother buy?

10. **Saya tidak tahu ke mana kita akan pergi besok.**
    Kita akan pergi ke mana besok?
    Where will we go tomorrow?

11. **Saya tidak tahu jam berapa kantor ini buka.**
    Jam berapa kantor ini buka?
    What time does this office open?

12. **Saya tidak tahu siapa yang datang dengan Alice.**
    Siapa yang datang dengan Alice?
    Who came with Alice?

13. **Saya tidak tahu dengan siapa Alice datang.**
    Dengan siapa Alice datang?
    Who did Alice come with?

14. **Saya tidak tahu yang mana rumah mereka.**
    Yang mana rumah mereka?
    Which is their house?

EXERCISE 11

1. **Sudah pergikah dia?**
   Apakah dia sudah pergi?
2. **Sudahkah dia pergi?**
   Apakah dia sudah pergi?
3. **Ke manakah anak itu pergi?**
4. **Haruskah saya belajar hari ini?**
   Apakah saya harus belajar hari ini?
5. **Jam berapakah pesawat berangkat?**
6. **Sakitkah kamu?**
   Apakah kamu sakit?
7. **Siapakah yang Anda temui?**
8. **Buku siapakah yang Anda pinjam?**
9. **Setujuhkah Anda?**
   Apakah Anda setuju?

10. **Bolehkah saya masuk?**
    Apakah saya boleh masuk?
11. **Apakah yang dia baca?**
12. **Tahukah Anda nama orang itu?**
    Apakah Anda tahu nama orang itu?

34 INDEFINITE PRONOUNS

EXERCISE 1

1. **Saya bisa bekerja dengan siapa saja.**
2. **Pinjam buku mana saja!**
3. **Anda boleh meminjam buku kapan saja.**
4. **Ke mana saja dia pergi anjingnya ikut.**
5. **Anda boleh minum apa saja.**
6. **Barang ini dapat dibeli di pasar mana saja.**
7. **Barang itu bisa dibeli di mana saja.**
8. **Apa saja yang dipakainya indah.**
9. **Siapa saja yang ditemuinya selalu sopan kepadanya.**
10. **Apa saja yang dikatakannya selalu benar.**
11. **Jangan lupa membawa uang ke mana saja kamu pergi.**
12. **Siapa saja yang diundang ke pesta Tomo pergi dengan senang.**

EXERCISE 2

1. **Kamu boleh datang dengan siapa saja.**
   You may come with anyone.
2. **Kamu boleh membaca apa saja.**
   You may read anything.
3. **Kamu boleh membaca majalah mana saja.**
   You may read any magazine at all.
4. **Kamu boleh pergi ke mana saja.**
   You may go anywhere.
5. **Kamu boleh bermain dengan apa saja.**
   You may play with anything.
6. **Kamu boleh duduk di mana saja.**
   You may sit anywhere.
7. **Kamu boleh bertanya kepada siapa saja.**
   You may ask anyone at all.
8. **Kamu boleh pergi ke bioskop kapan saja.**
   You can go to the pictures any time.

EXERCISE 3

1. **Saudara harus menjemput siapa saja?**
   Who/Which people do you have to meet?
2. **Mereka tinggal di pulau mana saja?**
   Which islands to they live on?
3. **Apa saja yang kita perlukan** *or* **Kita memerlukan apa saja?**
   What (things) do we need?

4. **Mahasiswa itu berasal dari mana saja?** *or* **...dari negeri mana saja.**
   Where do those students come from. *or* Which countries do those students come from?

5. **Kapan saja warta berita disiarkan?** *or* **Kapan saja ada siaran warta berita?**
   At what times is the news broadcast? *or* When/What times are the news broadcasts?

6. **Bus ini berhenti di mana saja?**
   Where/At what places does this bus stop?

7. **Siapa saja nama anak Pak Rudi?**
   What are the names of Mr Rudi's children?

8. **Apa saja yang mereka bicarakan tadi malam?** *or* **Mereka membicarakan apa saja tadi malam?**
   What (things) did they discuss last night?

EXERCISE 4

1. **Dengan siapa saudara pergi ke kota kemarin?**
   Saya tidak pergi dengan siapa-siapa.
2. **Saudara pergi ke mana?**
   Saya tidak pergi ke mana-mana.
3. **Dia tahu apa?**
   Dia tidak tahu apa-apa.
4. **Saudara mau menjual mobil itu kepada siapa?**
   Saya tidak mau menjualnya kepada siapa-siapa.
5. **Johnny memukul siapa?**
   Dia tidak memukul siapa-siapa.
6. **Wanita itu pernah menyanyi di mana?**
   Dia belum pernah menyanyi di-mana-mana.
7. **Saudara baru datang dari mana?**
   Saya tidak datang dari mana-mana.
8. **Dia menulis surat dengan apa?**
   Dia tidak menulis dengan apa-apa.
9. **Saudara melihat siapa?**
   Saya tidak melihat siapa-siapa.
10. **Saudara sudah ke mana?**
    Saya tidak ke mana-mana.

EXERCISE 5

1. **Dia tidak mau menolong siapa-siapa.**
2. **Tidak satupun (yang) menarik dia.**
3. **Dia tidak makan apa-apa.**
4. **Kami tidak makan di mana-mana.**
5. **Kami tidak makan di restoran mana saja.**
6. **Kami tidak pergi ke mana-mana.**
7. **Kami tidak pergi ke pantai mana saja.**
8. **Tidak seorangpun yang terlihat di sana.**
9. **Tidak satupun yang dicuri.**
10. **Polisi tidak menangkap siapa-siapa di disko tadi malam.**
11. **Saya tidak membeli apa-apa di toko.**
12. **Saya tidak membeli pakaian apa saja di toko.**

13. **Tidak seorangpun (yang) mau menolong dia.**
14. **Tidak seorangpun bisa lari secepat Soeprapto.**

35 IMPERATIVES

EXERCISE 1

1. **Tulis surat kepada ibu!**
2. **Beli roti dan gula!**
3. **Singgah di rumah saya besok!**
4. **Berbicara pelan-pelan!**
5. **Berangkat besok!**
6. **menyeberang di sini!**
7. **Berikan surat ini kepada Tom!**
8. **Berenang dekat pantai!**
9. **Duduk di kursi ini!**
10. **Menginap di rumah saya nanti malam!**
11. **Bersihkan kamar ini dengan segera!**
12. **Kirimi saya surat setiap minggu!**

EXERCISE 2

1. **Jangan merokok dalam kamar ini!**
2. **Jangan pakai/memakai kemeja itu!**
3. **Jangan tidur di kelas!**
4. **Jangan menari di sini!**
5. **Jangan bermain di jalan!**
6. **Jangan cuci/mencuci pakaian ini!**
7. **Jangan berbelanja di pasar itu!**
8. **Jangan masuk!**
9. **Jangan ambil/mengambil koran itu!**
10. **Jangan tulis/menulis namamu di buku ini!**

EXERCISE 3

1. **Buku ini dibawa ke perpustakaan!**
   Take this book to the library.
2. **Kemeja itu jangan dipakai di kebun!**
   Don't wear that shirt in the garden!
3. **Kamar ini dibersihkan sebelum ibu pulang!**
   Clean this room before mother gets home!
4. **Lampunya dimatikan sebelum tidur!**
   Turn off the light before you go to bed!
5. **Tamu jangan diganggu kalau ia mau tidur!**
   The guest isn't to be disturbed if he wants to sleep!
6. **Jangan saya diserahi tugas yang berat!**
   Don't give me heavy duties!
7. **Jangan diposkan surat itu!**
   That letter isn't to be posted.
8. **Pakaian ini disimpan di lemari!**
   Put those clothes in the cupboard!

9. **Pintu ini jangan ditutup!**
   Don't close this door!

10. **Jangan anak ini dibelikan pakaian mahal!**
    Don't buy this child expensive clothes!

EXERCISE 4

1. **Silakan duduk.**
2. **Silakan minum kopi.**
3. **Tolong jaga koper-koper ini.**
4. **Tolong ambilkan saya kemeja yang bersih.**
5. **Tolong perbaiki sepeda ini.**
6. **Silakan masuk.**
7. **Tolong setrika kemejai ini.**
8. **Silakan berenang kalau panas.**
9. **Silakan istirahat kalau cape.**
10. **Tolong masukkan mobil ke garasi.**

36   EXCLAMATIONS

EXERCISE 1

1. **Bukan main sibuknya pegawai itu!**
   How busy that clerk is!
2. **Bukan main gemuknya kucing itu!**
   Gosh, that cat's fat!
3. **Bukan main sombongnya politisi itu!**
   How arrogant that politician is!
4. **Bukan main kacaunya kantor itu!**
   Gee, that office is chaotic!
5. **Bukan main pedasnya sambal ini!**
   Wow, this *sambal* (chilli sauce) is hot!
6. **Bukan main panasnya hawa hari ini!**
   How hot it is today!

EXERCISE 2

1. How startled those people were when we entered!
2. How disappointed Dewi was to see the behaviour of her child!
3. How fluently that child reads!
4. How nice it would be if the holiday was extended!
5. How expensive those goods are!
6. How beautiful was the park we visited yesterday!

37   ELLIPSIS

EXERCISE 1

1. **Saya membeli pisang itu kemarin tetapi sudah dimakan anak-anak.**
2. **Teh ini terlalu manis. Saya tidak suka.**
3. **Saya pergi ke rumah John tetapi dia sudah berangkat.**
4. **Kita perlu kesabaran kalau kita mau berhasil.**

5.   Saya tidak bisa memakai jas ini karena terlalu kecil.
6.   Saya akan mencuci pakaian ini supaya bersih untuk pesta besok.
7.   Mobil itu baik tapi pintunya rusak.
8.   Saya membelinya kemarin.

EXERCISE 2

1.   Ketika Pak Idrus tiba di rumah dia langsung makan siang.
2.   Kalau terlambat kamu harus tunggu di luar.
3.   Minum air kalau haus.
4.   Mau menjual mobil?
5.   Kita perlu kesabaran kalau mau berhasil.
6.   Maaf, saya terlambat karena ketinggalan bus.
7.   Boleh minum air?
8.   Silakan berenang kalau panas.
9.   Waktu tiba di Jakarta kami naik taksi ke hotel.
10.   Waktu Jack tiba di Jakarta dia naik taksi ke hotel.
11.   Meskipun sudah tua, dia masih sehat.
12.   Kami cape. Kapan boleh pulang?
13.   Saya akan membantu mereka seandainya/kalau kaya.
14.   Ketika pulang Pak Idrus langsung makan siang.
15.   Kapan tiba?
16.   Kami kedinginan tadi malam karena lupa membawa pakaian tebal.
17.   Saya tidak bekerja hari ini karena sakit.
18.   Saya tidak bekerja hari ini karena dia sakit.
19.   Anak-anak menggosok gigi sebelum tidur.
20.   Kembalikan buku itu sesudah selesai membacanya.

INDONESIAN REFERENCE GRAMMAR
James Neil Sneddon

Do you need an accessible and in-depth guide to the grammatical structures presented in the *Understanding Indonesian Grammar* workbook? This reference provides a comprehensive description of the structure of the Indonesian language written in a clear, non-technical manner.

- To aid clarity and usefulness, all word groups and structures discussed are illustrated by examples.

- All the major structures of Indonesian, from words to complex sentences, are described in detail.

- Each level of the language is dealt with in a separate chapter, from words through phrases and clauses to sentences.

- Extensive cross-referencing and a comprehensive index enable readers to locate desired topics without unnecessary searching.

By providing detailed information in a format meaningful to both teachers and students, *Indonesian Reference Grammar* fills a serious gap in the available resources.

ISBN 1 86448 029 7

Enquiries: academic@allen-unwin.com.au

THE LEARNER'S DICTIONARY OF TODAY'S INDONESIAN
George Quinn

When it is time to put your understanding of the Indonesian language into real world situations, *The Learner's Dictionary of Today's Indonesian* will be indispensable. Rich in information on the cultural context in which words are used, it includes notes on the difficulties which learners experience as a result of cultural differences between English-speakers and Indonesians. The dictionary consists of three sections:

- the *introduction* explains the principles on which the dictionary is constructed, its structure, and a succinct account of Bahasa Indonesia's history and contemporary characteristics;

- the *main entries* consist of more than 4000 Indonesian-to-English entries and 1500 English-to-Indonesian entries. They provide detailed information on various possible translations of each word, copious examples and advice on current usage in conversation and writing;

- *topic lists* group the dictionary's words according to 42 semantic areas, among them time, colours, daily activities, the home, sport, occupations, mass media, religion and business.

With its emphasis on contemporary everyday usage, *The Learner's Dictionary of Today's Indonesian* is an ideal, 'user-friendly' aid to the learning of a dynamic language.

George Quinn is one of Australia's most innovative teachers of Indonesian, with 25 years practical experience teaching the language. He holds a Bachelor's degree in Indonesian from Gadjah Mada University (Yogyakarta) and a PhD from the University of Sydney. He is currently senior lecturer in Indonesian and Head of the Southeast Asia Centre at the Australian National University.

ISBN 1 86448 534 4

Enquiries: academic@allen-unwin.com.au